To Veronica,

Happy reading
from Sue and

Dave D

Dedication

I am dedicating our book to the wonderful human parents and carers of all rescue dogs throughout the world, for giving these dogs the chance of new lives, happiness and the security of a loving home; to our friends who have encouraged myself and Dave D as he learned and gained confidence; also to my grandma, May, who loved dogs too and who helped me to become the positive, caring, determined person that I try to be; and, of course, to my amazing and inspirational mum, Barbara, who has always shown me such unconditional love, support, and encouragement.

Sue Morgan

DAVE D'S DIARY

AUSTIN MACAULEY
PUBLISHERS LTD.

A CIP catalogue record for this title is available from the British Library.

ISBN 9781784557898 (Paperback)
ISBN 9781784557904 (Hardback)

www.austinmacauley.com

First Published (2015)
Austin Macauley Publishers Ltd.
25 Canada Square
Canary Wharf
London
E14 5LQ

Printed and bound in Great Britain

Acknowledgements

What can I say? There are so many of you to thank for your support, kindness and encouragement over the past few years since I started considering the idea for producing a manuscript. For your continued and genuine interest as I have been planning, drafting, writing and developing Dave D's Diary in order to produce my first book, thank you.

I want to thank those who have gone through so much of Dave D's journey with me emotionally, for your advice, sharing of your own experiences and offering of so many invaluable strategies to help my nervous collie to make the progress which he has.

Of course I also need to thank those of you who have been through some of Dave D's adventures with us physically, too, and for allowing me to mention you and your collies and families in our book, also for sharing funny and heart-warming memories and tales of your own dogs and other animals. Thank you to those who have joined us on collie walks organised throughout the British Isles, for your understanding and for the wonderful support you have given me and Dave D as we have worked towards building up his trust and confidence.

I want to thank all of my family and friends for their invaluable and unfailing belief in me as I set out to begin, and continued with the challenge of, writing this book. In addition, thanks to my brother Michael, for assisting me with building mine and Dave D's Diary website to keep you all up-to-date with our book developments.

A massive thanks to our main illustrator, Chris Golightly, who, totally free of charge, has worked so hard to produce nearly forty fantastic pencil illustrations which have been included in this book; these drawings are from a combination of photographs, the chapter extracts, and Chris's own imagination, and have captured Dave D and his personality so accurately and wonderfully. I am making an extra donation for her work to my local collie charity, as Chris has requested, and so much appreciate her artistic talent, her genuine kindness and her love of Dave D and all animals.

Of course, very importantly, I want to thank this same charity where we will be donating a percentage from the sale of every book, our fantastic Border Collie Trust GB rescue centre in Staffordshire, where I first met my Dave D. (www.bordercollietrustgb.org.uk). A huge thanks to Ben and every single member of staff there for all their continued dedication to rescuing and re-homing collies throughout Great Britain. Thank you for their constant hard work, for their expert advice, for first allowing me to work for them as a volunteer walking the collies, for their support, friendship and encouragement leading to me giving my wonderful collie, Dave, his new home with me, back in April 2012.

Thank you most sincerely to all those humans owning, and working in, the many dog-friendly places which we visited on our awesome adventures throughout the British Isles, where Dave D and I have always been accommodated and welcomed so warmly.

A big thank you to Nicki Teager, who also loves dogs, for voluntarily assisting with the initial proof-reading of our manuscript and whose advice, professional stance, experience, insight and friendship have been so much valued and appreciated.

Thank you to all who have helped with advice on producing and printing of initial and further manuscripts in the earlier and later stages as I proof-read and developed our book chapters. I have appreciated your interest in our book and your much-valued advice, especially my colleagues Janet, Pat and Sally; also technical advisor, graphic and web designer and printer Martin Roberts of Pwllheli, for his patience, support and invaluable help. Due to the fact that all of the photographs used in this book are actually real ones with no photo-shopping, we needed to ensure that there were no background faces or car number plate details visible.

In addition, a big thanks to illustrator, Helen Turnbull (helen.turnbull@hotmail.com) for her detailed ink drawings of Dave D proudly waiting at his favourite bus stop, on the beach showing confidence with his fellow collies, of baby Jacob, and also so accurately depicting our collie-club walk members on their expedition!

A grateful thanks to all humans working so hard for that marvellous registered charity The Yellow Dog Project, (www.yellowdoguk.co.uk) who seek to raise awareness that some dogs like Dave D may need space for a variety of reasons when out in public. This support is shown in the form of sharing information, leaflets, posters, and press releases; indications are through such as actual markers like the yellow ribbons on the nervous dog's lead or collar, and wording on their lead cover - or printed on the lead itself. An effective alternative option is a yellow 'I need space' vest or bandana worn by the dogs themselves.

A huge thank you to all volunteers that we have mentioned in our book chapters, who undertake such dangerous work on a completely voluntary basis - including the R.N.L.I. lifeboat volunteers (www.rnlishop.org.uk/) who so selflessly save so many lives at sea every day throughout the British Isles. Another massive thanks go to the Wasdale Mountain Rescue Team for their rescue work of lost and injured individuals, both human and four-legged, in the Lake District National Park and more recently for bringing Jasper collie safely down from a mountain in the Scafell Chain, despite the horrific weather conditions. We wish them well as they work towards their worthwhile target of funding to build their new base and for the future.

I most definitely also need to thank Dave D himself, my adorable, but nervous collie with his funny, yet so loveable ways, for the total dedication he has shown to me, and true trust he has placed in me, despite the challenges he faced and continues to experience. He has been a wonderful companion and friend to have by my side on all of our adventures and never failed to make me smile with his entertaining ways, humorous antics, and total enthusiasm for life - also bringing such genuine love, happiness, laughter and friendship to my own life these past few years.

The fact that our entire book of nearly three years of his life has been written from Dave D's perspective is a reflection of the influence that this boy has had, and continues to have, on my own life. Me being able to see so many true adventures through this collie's eyes and understanding him so well has enabled me to write this amusing, yet factual book and shows the unmistakable bond which we share and which has developed over the past years through so many real adventures.

Most importantly of all, I would like to say my heartfelt thanks to my mum and best friend, Barbara Stoker, who has helped me to proof-read, Dave D's Diary, thoroughly, several times, and who has also enjoyed sharing, and learning from, so many of mine and Dave D's amazing experiences and adventures which you will read about. I am also eternally grateful to my mum for her never-ending patience, her genuinely kind nature, her determination, her willingness to assist and non-judgementally advise me in every way, her consistently positive outlook in every situation and circumstance, for helping me to see solutions when there had not seemed to be any, and her overall belief in, and unfailing love for, me as her daughter.

I have grown up recognising and admiring my mum's genuine interest in, love of and enthusiasm for, literacy, travel, adventure, swimming, the outdoors and animals, all of which have inspired and influenced me immensely, not just in the past years and recent months as I planned and wrote this book, but throughout my life.

Contents

The British Isles

Dundee

Isle of Barra

Seaham

Manchester

Staffordshire

Criccieth

Newport

Reading

Chapter One

From homeless to true love

Hello, my name is Dave, Dave-Dog, the border collie. I am just over twelve years old and I was taken to the wonderful Border Collie G.B. re-homing and rescue centre in March 2012, because my old master became poorly and went into a home for old people. He was not allowed to keep me, so I was mixed up. I missed my master, I felt sad in the big house for dogs in my little kennel room and the dogs upset me with their barking. It made me nervous and anxious, as I had not been socialised with other dogs much. However, I was told that the lovely volunteers would help to find me a new home and a new human person to love me. I had to trust them, despite my fear of other dogs. (Even now I frequently worry when I see a dog, either nearby or in the distance, so I often crouch down, watching them closely.)

One day a new lady volunteer called Sue came to take me for a walk. She worked out how to put my soft green harness on me, before attaching a blue lead which she had chosen from a selection on the hooks - and which matched my collar, then taking me walking on a quiet lane away from the rescue centre field where many other dogs were being walked. We went on a long walk in a large, green field and we ran in the grass together which was fun. I had to crouch down very low to squeeze under some wooden gates, but it was an adventure. I felt free and happy, but best of all no longer nervous because there were no other dogs around.

Sue seemed a sad lady, so I would jump up to sit on the small seat next to her by the pretty village pond and let her stroke my soft fur. She took me back each time and left me in the dog house kennel. Every day new dogs would come into the home whose master or mistress didn't want them anymore. I hoped with all my heart that the kind lady would return to walk me. She did come back to walk me, again and again. I always gave her my cutest Dave D smile and often my white paw, too. I truly treasured those precious happy moments by her side.

Another day she took me for a drive in her red car. Before this, Sue had seemed extra happy as she read the special instructions on my kennel door card - which is for staff and volunteers - saying that I was a 'good traveller'. (Many of the other collies weren't.) I felt so happy myself, too, as she took me to see a peaceful, new building without lots of noisy dogs. She explained that it was her own home and allowed me off my lead. I ran in the long garden amongst the grass and in and out of the trees, I saw pigeons peeping at me from the rooftop, and felt the warm sun shining on me as I lay down on her patio. I was so relaxed and wished that I could stay there for ever and ever. Unfortunately, Sue still took me back to the big dogs' home, unclipped my harness and lead, and put me back in my kennel. As she shut that metal door I looked out at her with pleading eyes, willing Sue not to leave me there. After that, I didn't see her for a long time. I missed her very much and felt so sad.

However, her friend Margaret came to see me at the rescue centre and played ball with me in a quiet, enclosed area at one side of the field. Sue had asked her to. I had been sitting waiting for Sue for days, looking through my kennel door bars, barking and hoping that she would hear me. Margaret gently told me that Sue's mum had been in an accident and was in hospital, so Sue had gone to see her in

Manchester. I still missed Sue, but Margaret was kind to me and quite fun. I enjoyed playing with the toys together and appreciated how caringly she spoke to me.

A few days later Sue came to see me but I hadn't known that she was coming and I had been for a walk with another lady and gentleman... off the site. The volunteers had seen Sue arrive and that she was looking for me, but they had told her they weren't sure where I was. As I arrived back, I saw Sue, standing near to my kennel, looking sad. She had seen my empty kennel, my familiar harness gone and had thought that she would never see me again.

Sue ran to me and gave me big loves. My heart was filled with happiness. She walked me down the lanes, before sitting on that seat by the pond, next to the black and white signpost. I jumped up next to her, as I knew how much she liked it when I did this... though little narrow benches with planks on can be hard for collie dogs to balance on! Next, she wiped her happy tears on my soft ears, but I didn't mind. Afterwards, Sue took me back to my kennel and walked eight other dogs but then she came back and walked me again. She had never walked me twice on the same day, or the other dogs more than once the time before. I gave her my most loving look beneath my distinctive pale eyebrows. I knew she was still missing her old dog, but I also knew that I could love her and help her. I just needed her to give me, old Dave Dog, a chance. The man asked her if she wanted to give me a home, but Sue was mixed up and said she wasn't sure.

Sue still walked the other dogs after that but I didn't see her much. I did notice her briefly as I was walked past her in the rescue centre field. I would look over at her and she would glance at me, before looking away. This made me puzzled and confused. The staff told Sue that they could see the special bond between me and her. Sue had been trying to hide that she liked me. She was still finding it hard after unexpectedly losing her other dog just eight weeks previously. I did understand, even though I am just Dave Dog. I knew I could give her my paw, sit up and let her see my cuteness, walk by her side, make her smile again, and I would still lend her my furry ears to wipe any more of those salty tears on.

One day, I was in my kennel and the tall man came to put my lead on, next taking me a different way from usual. Wow... I was at the big office, where they take dogs who leave and don't have to stay in the kennels any more, and... my Sue was there, she was there to take me to the new little home I had once visited. She wanted me. She was my new mum. I was so happy.

So now, I no longer sit in my noisy kennel home, I have my own cushion and a real forever home and that big garden to play in. We go to the forest and to the seaside, we also go to dog-friendly hotels, we meet lovely new friends on walks and go on big buses, boats, trains and in dog-friendly cafes, too. I love my new life.

I hope that you enjoy reading all about my adventures.

Love from Dave Dog xxxxxx

Chapter Two

Then and Now

I am sharing with you how I feel, in my own words, about how my life has been since I left that rescue centre and my Sue welcomed me into her home and life. I came with just my collar and harness, not a single toy to my name, and only knew my local area, but had rarely been walked there. We have now shared so many adventures across the British Isles, travelling thousands of miles together, and have many more times to look forward to.

Sue says that I entered her life at a particular point and changed it, but she has done the same for me. She had been sad, lonely and puzzled after the sudden loss of her old dog, and I had been frightened, alone and confused when I was abandoned in the rescue centre and knew nobody. My Sue felt lost and found it difficult without her old dog to walk and cuddle with, in the now quiet, empty evenings. I found it difficult when the blinds were drawn each evening and I also felt lost behind the bars in my kennel with the sounds of other collies echoing in my sensitive ears, throughout the night. I felt isolated seeing them leave for new homes and finding myself still there, week after week, because nobody seemed to want an old dog, especially not one labelled and colour-coded, to show my fear of other dogs. Understandably, for a human, agreeing to give a new home to a nervous boy like me is also more difficult than homing a dog with no difficulties.

I had barked a lot, I admit - until I had no bark left, in fact, as it made me hoarse - but that was only because I was scared and confused, so almost begging for attention. I am surprised that the staff did not re-name me 'Husky'-dog as that is how my voice came out … but I was just calling out for a human to love me. Some dogs can bark and catch their breath ninety times a minute, for hours on end, but it felt like more than this, and my Sue had not known if my bark would ever return. It would be many weeks before she discovered that it would. She had been happy just having me in her life, anyway, even if I could not bark.

That special, sunny Wednesday afternoon when my Sue came to the rescue centre, chatted to the caring staff who had looked after me and signed some papers, before taking me out and encouraging me to jump into her red car, was my happiest time. As a warm glow filled my Dave D heart, little had I realised that this was to have been the starting journey of those thousands of miles of adventures together in that same car. She carefully fastened a new car safety seatbelt clip to my harness. As we moved forward I focused straight ahead, knowing that we would move through life together and that Sue would love me and keep me safe in every way for ever. We would accompany each other through the next stages of our lives and the whole world seemed to make more sense.

I reflected fondly on my new start and how I suddenly felt a real sense of life and purpose. I wear my harness proudly, preferring this to just my red collar, as it assists Sue in leading me from my chest instead of my neck, so discouraging me from pulling on my strong legs. I receive praise and positive reinforcement consistently for walking without straining on my lead and I now know that even sitting on my bed, listening to commands, and eating all my dinner is good. As a result, I feel proud and at ease when Sue praises me and tells me so. I wag my tail so much these days, with pure happiness, and frequently catch my Sue watching for this sign. I often see her smile then hear her sigh of relief that I am happy when she does. Prior to meeting Sue, I had felt such a failure, so my confidence had been eroded and easily damaged, my once strong collie spirit, like my abandoned heart, all but broken.

When I first moved to my new home I had not experienced the world as a welcoming place, but all that changed along with my micro-chip address and owner details which now have my Sue's name and my new home address on. I was still wearing that blue collar which had been placed on me seven weeks previously when I was left at the rescue centre for re-homing. The impact on my life has been immeasurable and a dream which has come true. My new mum is so gentle and the look of love and warmth in her eyes is like when she used to visit me and walk me as a volunteer. We have always had a special bond from the start. Equally, I often put a supportive but gentle paw on Sue's neck or shoulder, from my snug, warm cushion on the seat behind her, as she drives. Likewise, I may paw her arm and give her a look of trust and adoration... before leaving my paw there, then - being a very inquisitive boy - returning to looking out of the window!

Her life and car had felt empty with no loving dog to share adventures with during the past weeks, so life had now changed for the better, for her too. On one of our walks just before Sue gave me a new home, as she wore her warm jacket and I just my fur coat, she took a photograph as I gave her a Dave D paw love. I did not even try to bark. I just felt hope and contentment, acceptance and that I had found a human I could truly trust. Despite my past, even then it felt right with my paw in her hand. Indeed, before Sue gave me a home, I was at a real crossroads in my life emotionally, as well as literally, lying by that special seat next to the crossroads and pond when we went for our much treasured walks. Since then I have been on an amazing journey of self-discovery and real-life adventures.

Likewise, Panda collie had beauty and intelligence that went unnoticed until she met her new human mum. Like me, she had not had a good life, but was also sweet to her own new mum in spite of her previous neglect, where she trusted no-one. She knew that her mum truly loved her - just like Sue loves me, Dave D. As with Panda, who had learned to trust her Doreen, I had found it so hard to trust anyone all my life, yet I knew then that I could trust my Sue.

My life had been made worse before I went to my new home as so many people did not understand my fear and would shout at me and call me 'bad'. Now it does not matter where I go or what happens as I have an inner security that comes with my Sue choosing to share her life with me. She accepts my strengths and weaknesses, helps me through all my behavioural road bumps and helps me find strategies to overcome many of these. She understands that all dogs are individuals with differences, how I must have been emotionally desperate for a human friend, for love and companionship, support and understanding - all of which I have found with my Sue. My physical needs are simple: I need food, clean water - as I cannot reach the tap, a safe place to sleep - comfortably, a good vet - when I am unwell and another vet for a second opinion if the first vet's diagnosis does not seem accurate; also, a clean bowl which is washed daily, as you would not like to eat off a dirty plate either.

As with so many of us rescued collies, laughter, love and acceptance had been missing from my life for so long. I frequently look at my collection of toys in my very own toy box, which have been wrapped and given to me, by my mum and from friends when we have met - or that have arrived through our letter box - from all over the British Isles, and feel so lucky. As you now know, I never had a single toy before Sue gave me that chance of a new home and life. We are blessed to have each other. Our match feels perfect. I hit the doggy jackpot. I feel ten feet tall!

As a collie, I am developed for rigorous and prolonged exercise. However, as a city collie I obviously do not have a flock of sheep. I attended one Agility class and although completing the course several times, I was focusing on the scary dogs and was not happy in the slightest about being in that small room. My Sue was not comfortable either, so instead, she gives me plenty of long runs, with opportunities to leap over fallen tree trunks, to race after and jump up for my toy frisby, to chase my ball, to run with her down the long forest paths, and so much more, all satisfying my collie boy needs.

My experience is that you 'can' teach an old dog new tricks. I am proof of that and am loving learning because of the trust that my Sue puts in me, plus the unconditional love and acceptance which she shows me. I am loving life and knowing that we have lots of true friends - which we have made together. So many other rescued collies and dogs of all breeds across the British Isles, and indeed the world, must love their owners for the same reasons. I love my Sue for giving me, old Dave D, that new chance and a fresh start, for her patience and for believing in me. I love the pride she shows for my achievements, however small and insignificant they may seem to other collies and humans. I am grateful that so many of our friends actually do recognise the progress I have made, and, I truly treasure every day and night of our amazing journey and adventures together so far. It is as if I have waited all my life just to meet my Sue.

The universe gives you humans; humans need dogs, and they need you, like I needed my Sue. We are not perfect, but neither are you humans, and I had not meant to be 'bad' as I had been labelled. I was just different, but different does not mean bad. Dogs like me just need humans prepared not to judge us, but just to accept us and to give us a chance, to have faith in us, to give us love and patience and care, to take advice, give us support and to see our potential. In return we will give you happiness, along with so much love and support in times of sadness and always. My Sue gave me that chance and I gave her my heart.

If I am nervous my temperature will rise automatically, and sometimes, when I am worried, my foot pads will become wet. This is because I do not have sweat glands all over my body to regulate my body temperature, but I do on my little paw pads. Therefore, this means that if you see wet paw prints it is important that you do not presume I have sneaked out and gone paddling! It is also a sign that I am sweating, maybe after a game of football. My air-conditioning system also requires me to open my mouth, so although you will mainly see my doggy smile, at other times I am panting to help myself to cool down.

I do realise that it was not, and still is not, easy for my Sue at times due to my lack of social skills with fellow dogs. Prior to going home with my Sue, I had not been walked much throughout my life or socialised much with other dogs, especially not in those important first three to six months of my life. Any such contact I had been given the opportunity for was not a positive experience. My previous owner was kind but had little understanding of me, and this led to me developing a fear of dogs running up to me or coming into with contact me, even accidentally. I still have a scar on my nose from one such experience.

Behaviour adjustment is hard for an old collie boy like me, although I have made so much progress. I cannot be magically calm and I cannot help my body language when I see another dog approaching, even in the distance. As you now know, such a trigger sets off that almost instant automatic response from me where I frequently start to tremble, my folded, round-tipped ears will go flat against my head - protectively to keep them safe - my eyes will be wide, looking straight ahead, my tail tucked low between my legs, or I may crouch down if they are nearer to me. If my Sue could wave a magic wand to make my fear disappear I know that she would. Sue tries to hide her own worry from me, but what humans do not seem to realise is that their own bodies give off chemicals in their sweat and we dogs can actually smell their fear.

I try hard to talk to my Sue with my entire body, even though I find it hard to convey how I feel when a dog approaches, as I panic and freeze. The part of my Dave D brain which is wired for life preservation feels threatened by other dogs, so my survival instinct kicks in... against what my new learning is trying to tell me. It is hard to break out of my old habits and fears. When my worry is 'over the threshold', so to speak, I am not even able to allow myself to be distracted by a treat of a toy from Sue. Insecurity is common in rescued dogs. Therefore, I have become what they call 'reactive' towards dogs. I did not, and do not, mean to have a fear of other dogs coming near me, but as I mentioned, if I see a dog, my body sometimes tenses involuntarily. I often lick my lips, which signifies my own fear, and I certainly do not want either my nose or rear end to be sniffed by them or I will growl. They do not show dog politeness by coming so close anyway!

As I have also admitted, my reaction used to make Sue become anxious too, and when I felt her grip on my lead tighten with worry, this added more tension, making me feel even more afraid - to realise that my Sue seemed to be frightened too. That new longer lead of six metres also gave me more confidence on walks as I felt there was more room to run if nervous. My short lead was also too tight and restricting for me, so it unnerved me if I saw another dog, so making me more fearful. I am aware that Sue has been recommended to use this longer lead more often, on me, and that she will need to loop it round her arm like a giant lasso in the films that Lassie collie watches. In fact, Sue tried this once and I loved being able to run so far yet still be with her, yet she kept forgetting to loop it properly! Luckily, neither of us tripped over fully! (Though I bet it was still amusing for anyone who saw our Dave D and Sue funny duo action!)

I know it cannot be easy for Sue when I react and I can tell this especially when tears form in the corners of her eyes, which makes me feel guilty. She has never been responsible for such a scared boy as me before. If I see that sadness in my Sue's eyes, I nudge her hand with my nose, showing genuine concern, to remind her that I am there for her and, as it had been from before she was my mum, that my thick Dave D fur is available and good for absorption of tears. Wherever we are, when I need to cheer Sue up, I lie upside down on my back and wriggle and wriggle with all four legs in the air, or kick just my back legs in the air and do lots of body wags at the same time, until she looks up and smiles, even through any tears. I do look strange and this can cause others to stare at me but I am always thankful that my comical back-scratching manoeuvres seem to help Sue.

Sometimes, I sit quietly, paws crossed, watching her closely and moving next to her, hoping for an open hug of acknowledgement. Often, when Sue is busy, she suddenly looks down and notices me watching her adoringly - as I may have been for many minutes. At such times, I lift just one of my front white paws and place it on her hand, before pulling it towards me with my paw. She often resists at first, so I do it again, gently, but this time making my special little Dave D sound. Eventually, I put my collie nose under her hand and push my Sue's hand up, adding a little whine, until she strokes my cute, velvety nose. My true, loving personality is shining through and my eagerness to love and be loved cannot be mistaken. If she rubs behind my ears I gently nudge her wrist up and press my nose into her hand, lying on her feet like a big collie-shaped slipper!

Other times, I lie next to Sue and just rest my gentle paw comfortably on her hand gazing at her, lovingly, as she writes her lesson plans. I do not expect a fuss, but just let her know that I am there, that I care and I understand that she needs to write. I always know in my heart, that Sue will walk me when she has finished, even if she is tired and the first birds are starting to sing because a brand new day is dawning.

When Sue first met me as a volunteer dog walker, she had read the facts about me on my kennel door data board, so had seen where 'No' had been written in the box saying if I was 'Good with other dogs'. As I have already declared, she had also read with delight that 'Yes' in the box 'Good at travel' (Just as well really!). So right from the start, my Sue had ensured that the rescue centre staff knew that she was aware of my fear of other dogs and would support me, but also that she did a great deal of travelling, so any collie that she rescued would have to be a good traveller too. I was glad that my kennel notes had given me a big tick for that. I had been abandoned more locally, but many of the other collies had come over from Ireland, for their own new start, so staff knew if they were good travellers, too. My Sue and I go almost everywhere together, which enriches my life and sharpens my mind. I love sharing those totally new experiences. I even go back to the Border Collie Trust G.B. rescue centre to reflect and see the staff who still fondly remember me living there all that time ago.

My Sue was already aware that I was not young and that I had anxieties and issues, but she still wanted me and I loved her even more for that. I truly do not ever mean to be a fearful boy, but felt that I could trust her and that she would not give up on me like the others had. My clue to my fear is always my body language, but Sue has developed increased owner awareness and if she sees me acting worried she looks round quickly to find the 'trigger' for my sudden unease - this being what has set me off worrying - then acts accordingly.

If I am playing with a toy and we have seen a dog nearby, Sue keeps outwardly calm as she now realises that we dogs feed off our owner's stress too. I did not used to feel able to carry on playing, at such times, but as the years have passed and my Sue has kept me safe and reassured me - often moving to make more distance between me and the other dog - I am now much more able to focus on the toy and not on the other dog or my fear - or to at least allow myself to be redirected. Yapping barks particularly unnerve me, even when the barking dogs are secured inside a car which we are passing. Consequently, I still feel better when my Sue creates a distance between me and them. She directs me to her and tries to distract me whilst I am still sub-threshold, or praises me for walking the way she has led me and for not looking back, then presents me with my ball as a happy association, (after what, to me, was a scary situation).

I find it especially difficult when walking on narrow paths such as by canals or through thick forests, or on a narrow pavement, because when a strange dog comes towards me, whether on or off lead, I panic as I feel as if I have nowhere to escape to. Collies are not meant to walk in straight, narrow lines anyway! We prefer to zig-zag through the hillsides herding our sheep, not being herded by another dog! After a scare I soon feel better when my Sue takes me for a good run, as it calms me down by releasing endorphins - feel good chemicals - in both her human brain and my Dave D brain alike. Despite my somewhat cute, appearance, my friends including Naomi, Paul, Barbara, Rebecca, Sarah, Maxine and Yvonne understand my inner need for space. They look out for me on walks and warn Sue if they see a dog approaching, so acting to keep me safe.

In addition to this, my friend Jodie takes me to the lake in Burntwood and throws a ball for me, then I give her my paw so she throws my ball again and again. At such times, Sue looks out for other dogs in case they run up to me off their lead and frighten me - but thankfully, we do not usually see any there, so continue to have so much fun. I am glad that they understand me with my funny Dave D ways! People are showing me such wonderful kindness.

We collies can be slower to mature and may have a longer adolescence, even reaching three years, but I am over twelve years old now. A new idea and strategy to help me with my anxiety is 'smelly treats' which I find interesting. When we have been walking and I have spotted a dog, my Sue has recently tried to tempt me away with strong scents that seek to jolt me from my distracted state and to make me focus on her and the treat, away from another dog. We dogs have a larger brain area than humans for categorising smells. It is a worthwhile strategy as much of my brain is involved in processing scent. I have at least forty more scent cells than a human, and smells go straight down my nasal passage through the tunnels to my muzzle nerve, then my brain. When something triggers my fear - even something as small as a sound similar to the rattle of another dog's lead or collar - the thinking part of my brain is often held shut, so a smelly 'reinforcer' aims to open the door to my Dave D thinking brain, albeit slightly, in order to make me think of the smell. This is instead of freezing and searching for the noise source, or glaring at the offending dog. We are still working on this, but I like the idea and I have managed to focus on the cheese or sausage treat and not keep staring back at the dog too much. Sue can read my body language and still does her best to keep me below my threshold level, distracting me calmly or putting a distance between us, redirecting me. As with humans and goose-bumps, I do not like feeling scared and the fur on my back sticking up, so everyone knows I have a problem, but it is something I feel unable to prevent.

In the past, I wanted to go on - and looked forward to - walks with Sue, but unfortunately, at the back of both our minds was still fear and the expectation of trouble. My Sue tried her best to make walks a hide and seek game, as we have reassuringly discovered that many other humans with similarly nervous dogs do. If I saw another dog off its lead and stiffened, then crouched down, my Sue was alert and knew to move me as far as possible away from it. I did not lunge - though dogs lunged at me - and we would about turn, then go and hide in the bushes - or anywhere - until I felt safer and could no longer see the other dog, and it was not likely to see and approach me. Sue sometimes laughed as we calmed down, peering out from our hiding place, as she said we had raised strange looks from other dog owners when we suddenly took off into the bushes. However, it was necessary as I may have snapped with fear if another dog had run up to me and bumped into me, especially my back and rear legs, which are the most sensitive. Sometimes, Sue's own legs were scratched with brambles and she was shaken and tearful, but overall, she was determined to keep me safe. As a result, I often forgot my fear, as she made escaping into an adventure, and praised me for being a good boy as we ran, giving me long, reassuring, calming strokes on my sternum, when we stopped. I once stood on a thorn and held my paw high off the ground, bravely running on three legs, until my Sue realised and took it out so we could carry on making our getaway! True teamwork.

Moving on, such is my progress that I have learnt to lie and relax, with a slightly curved mid-section, my happy face and open-mouthed smile, complete with wagging tail, looking at my mum adoringly. My growing confidence also allowed me to lie down on an outdoor adventure - as on the rocks off Berneray, in the Sound of Harris, North Uist - with my mum, so letting her give me big hugs and still feeling relaxed.

Although my previous impulse always to stop what I was doing immediately and turn my full attention to a nearby dog is still strong, this happens much less frequently. I am a lot better now, as I can even sometimes avert my eyes when I see a dog coming towards me and I do not tremble each time, for which I receive a quiet, "Good boy Dave D", form of praise from Sue.

In comparison, I can watch, tall, strong and bold on my hind legs with white front paws on the window-sill, from our hotel window, without trembling at all, like in our hotel room close to the Lake District and West Yorkshire border. Despite this, although Sue and I peep out, we still stay inside until the dogs have passed. I admit to giving the four-legged fellow dogs some strange looks from my safe look-out spots and many a strange look has been given back to me!

When out walking, I either cross the road with my Sue to keep a distance or peep round corners to watch such dogs until they pass, although I am more relaxed about seeing them and do not feel as much of the old worry as I did two years ago. We both pick up tips to help us and I feel more confident because I know my Sue loves me and is able to give me comfort and guidance. As long as Sue is beside me, I know that I can get through anything. She no longer feels a failure having a nervous collie. I no longer feel such a failure as that collie. As a result, I now understand much better that, as a pup, when I was growing up, I really should have been introduced to new environments and exposed to a variety of stimuli through the socialisation window and beyond.

My fears and emotions are complicated. We no longer only walk alone in the early morning or late at night, when no other dogs and humans are out for a walk. I feel more relaxed and less threatened if I have seen the same dog and owner several times when we have been on our travels. If I do not recognise a dog, I often keep well back, out of sight almost, again just peering at them round corners. I feel safer with most of my body hidden as they often do not see me, so do not approach. Before we enter the ice-cream shop, I always look for fellow dogs tied up outside - waiting for their owners or on a lead with their owner holding this. When they have gone, we enter the shop together and sit down, as it is after all a dog-friendly shop, and dogs are allowed to sit under any of the three tables nearest to the door. Before we knew this, my Sue would go to the counter, but still keep hold of my lead and I would sit and wait at the door entrance, still attached to the end!

As can be recognised, I have been successful in parallel-walking on my lead next to Elwood spaniel, Buster and Red collies, and also little Lily terrier on our Northampton walk. I have been near them on a long lead and displayed calm body language. Lots of positive reinforcement makes me feel good, despite any reservations. A doggy back rub in circles from my neck ruff to the base of my back afterwards works wonders, reducing any anxiety I still feel, with my

Sue pressing through my thick fur so massaging my muscles, this fur also helping protect my collie breed in blustery weather.

On my Criccieth holiday, if we go for a walk to the dog-friendly beach next to the jetty, Sue always checks that no other dogs are there before we walk onto it ready to play. Tia collie's safe place is always the nearest bench to whatever has triggered her to be nervous, such as a child or a scooter. There is no bench here, so if a dog does arrive whilst I am on this beach, I instantly pick up my toy and walk directly to my safe place, which is a sandy hollow next to a large rock in the corner of that beach. Sometimes, when I have needed to do this, there have been strangers without a dog sitting there on beach towels. They have been somewhat puzzled by my sudden appearance so my Sue has needed to explain why I have arrived and am sitting next to them. They always seem to understand about my 'safe place' and allow me to rest there until I feel less worried. Whatever I do, as I have said, I never mean to be what some have labelled naughty as there is always a reason, and my Sue still tries to work this out by scanning the area and reading my body language. I also am the way I am partly due to the chemical in my brain, the emotional portion of the human brain being almost identical to our doggy brain, meaning that we also feel happiness, sadness, wariness, excitement and fear. Despite this, I am continuing to learn to adapt and cope with my inner anxieties, gaining confidence, standing upright, being alert and moving forward positively every paw step of the way.

As is shown in many of my photographs, my new body language oozes confidence and new-found inner strength. Another kind of body language I have started to show is called play-bow, when my front elbows are almost touching the ground and my furry rump is stuck up in the air. Some dogs love to play with other dogs and play-bow to indicate this, so they can then race and chase - although I just play-bow with my Sue. I do not respond positively to dogs who want to play, but still run near other dogs, if I am focused on the ball. Some collies are scared of thunder, but I am just scared of other dogs, who I fear will run up to me quickly and bump into me. My friend, Foster, was scared by a car seat which had been left on the driveway of a house he passed on his walk. His mum Michelle was concerned and actually took him up the stranger's pathway to enable him to sniff that seat and to reassure him that he had no need to be worried by it. Our human mums - and dads - love us and try to help us in all kinds of tactical and impulsive ways.

Most importantly, I feel better on collie walks now as I have learned to run with the others and they do not seem to knock into me as much as I had anticipated. My particularly caring friend, James, reassures me and plays games with me on each Sunderland area walk, away from the other collies, to help me to feel more confident. He protected me when a huge black dog approached me and quickly moved it away – and another time when two Great Danes bounded over towards me! I still need to wear my face-art, in the form of a smart black muzzle when in big groups of dogs, or if another dog nearby is off its lead. Another collie's human mum gave us a fact sheet on how to introduce a dog to one of these objects which they called muzzles, therefore making it fun, by putting treats into the end whilst it is on the floor. This meant that I had to put my nose inside to collect my treat! Eventually, when my Sue actually fastened the muzzle contraption onto my nose I did not mind - nor did it feel too strange, as I had willingly poked my nose inside it so many times anyway!

I do not wear my muzzle all the time and we usually keep it fastened to the end of my lead handle or in my travel bag on every walk, so that if we see a dog approaching Sue puts it on me quickly and we carry on walking. I feel more protected somehow, because, as with the reflex action if a human is knocked into, if the other dog does make contact with me and I panic, then even if I jump or snap in fear, no harm can be caused by me.

Similarly, Sue became calmer from the moment that we learnt how muzzles could be positive and could help me. It opened up our world to more relaxed adventures. When it was just the two of us, she also felt more able to pluck up the courage to ask other dog owners to please put their dog on a lead, explaining that I was nervous of other dogs.

Our walks became more relaxed and we no longer had to hide as much. We now change direction if we see another dog approaching and make a calm, orderly retreat, no longer frantically running through any nearby hedgerow! I sometimes just carry my essential muzzle round my neck in case it needs to be placed on quickly … but I am then permitted to remove it myself, with my front paw, after the dog has walked past and into the distance. However, on collie walks I wear a head strap from my muzzle and this muzzle is attached to my collar too, so that I cannot usually remove it without help from Sue, although I do try!

Furthermore, we often have cafe break stops and I can now sit quietly and calmly close to dogs that I am now familiar with, like Ollie the collie on our last Lake District walk. Therefore, our humans can chat and enjoy a snack together whilst we wait quietly after our own water refreshment. As is regular practice, my Sue will remove my muzzle fully, later on when there are no other dogs around me off their leads.

This means that such types of collie meet-up walks help us both. My Sue and I have formed a close partnership. Despite the fact that Sue had no experience of a collie with such an extreme fear of other dogs until she met me, we are a good and strong team now. I know it was hard for her at first, though, as I do realise that I am a somewhat complicated and challenging boy due to my difficulties. She had agreed to care for me and wanted to do right by me but was not sure how. I am happy that we now have this true companionship and understanding and that we have also made many new friends through my new life. I am glad that she now feels less alone since meeting other humans with anxious collies like me, and that they share strategies, and suggest ideas to help make walks with us more enjoyable. If I wear a muzzle it also helps me, as other owners see me, then call their dogs away, so my worry that dogs will run up to me and make contact is less likely to physically happen. Dogs and some humans seem to have good face-reading skills. My Sue has indeed mastered the art of reading my own facial expressions, like that time she stopped me playing with my new orange squeaky toy present which I loved so much, because I was making too much noise with it and most probably waking up other hotel guests just after six am! I did stop as I am an obedient boy, but the look which I gave her showed that I was not in the slightest impressed!

On another journey, upon seeing her spaniel's reaction to me as I passed by wearing my Mr. Muzzle, a lady commented on how she had never seen her own dog give another dog such a look before! It was rather intense, but unfortunately, I do often receive strange looks from some people and dogs, including Alfie the Bassett hound, who do not yet understand my anxieties. Sue and I have learnt to try and ignore such odd stares as we know that me wearing my muzzle is necessary in order to give me the opportunities to get out and about and to enjoy adventures, which I would otherwise not be able to. My Sue explains this to people who see my muzzle and voice their opinion or show genuine interest and make a fuss of me regardless of my appearance.

When a dog comes too near to me, they are protected by my muzzle, as I tend to curl my lip back and show my teeth behind its rubber. My canines are the long visible ones that warn them not to come too close. I have sharp teeth which my vet was impressed with, as they have not been worn down too much for an old collie dog. We are fortunate that cavities are rare in our dog teeth, because of our low-sugar intake, our different mouth bacteria to your human ones, plus our different shaped teeth. I have low-fat teeth-cleaning chews twice a week to help remove plaque and tartar from my teeth up to my gum line, as I am not keen on having a toothbrush in my mouth like you humans do. We are meant to have them cleaned and Sue does try - using a special white, meat flavoured toothpaste, but I don't keep still for very long - although I am improving! It is a fact that four out of five dogs over the age of three have gum disease caused by the build-up of plaque and tartar which makes doggy gums sore. Raw bones from the butcher also help to clean our teeth as we enjoy them. My Sue gave me one of these for the first time recently and supervised me as I tackled it. My gums are no longer red and sore above my back teeth. However, our humans must not roast these bones for us as they can splinter and hurt our insides if cooked.

I lost my puppy teeth at about twelve weeks old and a healthy dog should have forty-two adult teeth, the same as a wolf, which makes sense as we dogs do descend from wolves, so they are like our cousins! This is more than humans who only have thirty-two, without counting any wisdom teeth. Neither mine nor your teeth can re-grow if broken - which means that they are lost forever. As a result, I have one tooth less than other adult dogs, making just forty-one and this is because I lost a full lower front tooth in my previous home, but I do not dwell on that, as I still have a sweet Dave D smile that humans adore and find so amusing.

As can be seen when I look up at the squirrels, I do have a gap where that lost tooth used to be. Some people find this cute. In contrast, when they notice that I am muzzled, children frequently ask their parents or carers why I have a 'basket' on my nose. In my defence, Sue sometimes explains to them that I wear it because I was a rescue centre collie boy and nervous around other dogs in case they bang into me, but that I am wonderful with humans. My Sue reassures me that it is not my fault and she loves me despite everything. I have not experienced such true and genuine unconditional acknowledgement and acceptance from a human before, so it means a lot. Many people see my muzzle and yellow ribbon and understand my need for space. Recently, in Seaham, a small child ignored all the collies without muzzles, came up to me as I wore my black muzzle, and gave me big loves. He and his mum accepted me in spite of my muzzle and this made my Sue happy. I have learnt to focus even more on a ball or toy and this object distracts me from other dogs around us. It allows me to avert my learned gaze and takes my mind off my anxieties somewhat, meaning that I can even play close to others with my head and tail still held high. Low stress levels have facilitated my learning so I am now able to sometimes look at Sue and ask to go off my lead, actually joining in, only when I feel ready. I have learnt to nudge the ball with my nose when wearing my muzzle whether on land or in the water.

As I mentioned, after a collie walk, as the other collies and their humans have started their journeys home, Sue always removes my familiar muzzle. Seeing my opportunity, I then rub my nose on a rug or the carpet - or grass - for ages, enjoying the free feeling, before being given time to play with a ball without wearing my Mr. Muzzle! I always look forward to this 'us' time. As in human friendships and relationships, too, making quality time for just the two of us is both important and necessary.

Even when it is just my Sue and me, and my worrying does not allow me to ignore four-legged distractions and keep focused on an object - so needing my muzzle on for a short time - she still loves me and understands. She reassures me that she accepts me regardless and will take my muzzle off as soon as they have gone - so that I can catch the ball again, like I used to love doing with my Sue's nephew, Joshua, and Michael - who is my human uncle.

With Mr Muzzle in my red travel bag, we travel all over the British Isles to collie meet-up walks and events. As you have read, the reason that I have a yellow ribbon on my lead is because this is a recognised sign to others and indicates a nervous dog. The Yellow Dog Project scheme is aimed at increasing awareness of dogs with difficulties such as mine and asking other dog owners or minders to respectfully bear this in mind if their dog is off its lead. I sometimes even wear my smart yellow 'I need space' vest which gives off an even clearer message to humans.

At collie group events, the dogs are often off lead, so I still tend to stay at the back to start with, still on my long lead, often crouching to watch the other more confident collies playing and having fun. I start to control my nerves better and now feel more relaxed. I am therefore able to run and join them, often at the front, totally focused on the ball and feeling barely any of my previous fear.

I am clearly am learning to be a braver collie boy in my old age! I hope that you will continue to enjoy reading about all my adventures.

Dave D.

Chapter Three

Toys galore

As I mentioned briefly, when I moved to my new home with Sue I did not own a single toy in the whole world and even my harness was on loan from my rescue centre. I had never had a doggy toy box like other dogs do. As a result, every toy is so precious to me, every walk I treasure, every play time means the world to me, old Dave D. On one occasion, as we set out on a holiday walk in Criccieth, North Wales, I enthusiastically stood up and looked over an old stone wall.

Wow… as you can see from my face, I was so excited to see the beach and glistening, bright, blue sea. We came to a steep hill, which started near the castle and went past that dog-friendly ice-cream shop, right the way down to the old harbour jetty and long golden sands. I wagged my Dave D tail to show my Sue how happy I was, and my heart was full of joy as she smiled in recognition.

I tried not to pull Sue down the hill, although my eagerness to reach what lay at the foot of that hill made this difficult. We played on the sand together. I was glad that Sue had remembered to bring me a toy - as it saved me the usual job as I reached a walk destination of darting here and there, searching for a plastic bottle. For some reason, humans often leave such empty bottles on the ground - even though there are waste bins nearby! This bottle search is particularly difficult when Sue takes me to the field in the dark, as it is even harder for me to spy a potential discarded toy! (Although I usually do… eventually!) After playing with it, I always carry it home and up the path, then drop it next to our blue re-cycling bin for mum to open, and drop the bottle in. (Unlike Raasay collie's twin, Rona collie, who often deliberately ran off with her ball, ignoring her mum's recall, heading across muddy fields with her Pamela following in close pursuit! I bet they looked funny; I love a collie with a sense of humour like me.)

This particular day, upon reaching the beach, as Sue opened my red travel bag, I waited with eager anticipation, wondering which toy she had brought for me this time. She reached in and suddenly threw my tuggy-ball on its rope - high up into the air. I was delighted to realise that it was my favourite, particularly strong and heavy, tuggy, which our friend had posted to me, addressed to 'Mr Dave Dog'! (As always, it had made our postman chuckle!) Well… my tuggy went higher and higher, with the force of mum's unskilled throw and I looked in dismay… watching... following it up, up, up… but unfortunately, it did not land on the sandy beach….

Instead, my treasured toy headed towards the cluster of large rocks and came to a halt somewhere amidst these. "Oh Sue!"- I thought as I bounded towards them, trying to work out exactly which part my tuggy was now hidden in. Which rocks had it landed between? Sighing as I pondered, I was thinking, "Yes my Sue, I do love you, but you are such a bad thrower sometimes!"

I could not see my toy near to the beach side of those rocks, so stood up on my back legs, front paws firmly gripping two cold, grey rocks next to the beach, and prepared to leap up and start tackling the higher rocks. I was anticipating picking my way along the tops of those rocks in search of my tuggy when I heard a sudden shout…

"Stop! Dave D Stop! Leave it alone!"

It was my Sue, by now running quickly towards where I stood staring into those huge rocks on the other side of the jetty, near the towering castle - from where I could hear its two flags flapping in the breeze. I froze on that sandy spot, because I always listen to Sue's commands and could hear panic in her voice. Sue usually tries hard not to raise her voice, or to let me see when she is anxious, by not shouting, and, as you already know, making a conscious effort not to grip my lead too tightly.

I looked at her with my deep, magnetising Dave D eyes which she so loves, my furry brow frowning a little and one of my puzzled facial expressions evident. I so wanted my tuggy ball and rope back, but my mum explained apologetically,

"Dave D, I am sorry but it is much too dangerous for you to climb up those rocks. You could break your long legs".

She smiled as I jumped down, back onto my four legs and off the rocks. I did understand. My Sue had, unexpectedly, broken her own leg on holiday here five years earlier and she had needed to hop to the bus stop, before catching a bus to the big human hospital in Bangor. I was glad I could stay on holiday and would not need to go to the animal hospital or to have to try hopping onto a bus with a broken leg like Sue had!

I loved the feeling of the soft sand between my toes. I was such a happy and fortunate David Dog, (as my dear friend, Claire calls me), and loved seeing my human mum so happy too. I was so glad that she chose me and gave me a new home all those months ago and that she had brought me to the seaside and her grandma's old house for my holidays.

Even so, she had lost my favourite yellow tube toy last time, after throwing it up too high, because it had landed in the sea, then sank... so I really did not want to lose my blue and white tuggy. I stood up on my back legs once more, trying to get a better view of the gaps between the rocks, but venturing no further. This made Sue laugh and she said I looked like a baby kangaroo! Even so, I remembered only too well how my other toy had been lost, so hoped that she realised why I looked so sad and confused.

Realising, my Sue was quick to be by my side, holding me close and stroking my fur, soothingly, telling me she loved me. She explained that the last time she really had tried to find my yellow tube and had even gone to the beach at night - looking determinedly by moonlight, with the aim of retrieving it. It had been low tide and she had done her best, searching for my precious lost toy, (that time in rock pools and under seaweed)... but had not found it. However, this time, she told me how she was going to buy me a new tuggy instead, from the little market next day when she met up with her friends Lisa and Nicolle from Manchester. I had accepted this reassurance and gave Sue my paw and loving eyes in acknowledgement, then ventured a little way up the beach - before spying, much to my delight, an abandoned plastic bottle to play with instead; I proceeded to flick the bottle up into the air before dragging it backwards for several metres with my paws, in true amusing Dave D style. This strange manoeuvre never fails to make Sue smile!

Next day, when I realised that it was walk time, I had picked up my familiar red ring - which my friend Ann had given me, hoping that it would return with me after the walk and that Sue would be a little more accurate when she threw this toy! On this occasion, the tide was high on the only little beach where dogs are allowed, so there was not much room on the sand to play, but we still tried, having to paddle at times. My Sue took her shoes off to join me as I paddled on my long legs. The sun was warm on my dark fur, but I felt refreshed, such a lucky Dave D and on top of the world. Not unusually, Sue was taking some photographs of me as I chased my red ring. I felt a spray of water all around me as I raced into the calm sea, tail held high, to retrieve it time and time again. The beach seaweed was soft and slippery under my paws, but thankfully, I managed to avoid falling over.

As we continued to walk further up the beach, Sue threw my plastic ring again. Hearing the unmistakable sound of seagulls, I pointed my nose up and watched the red of my ring glide across the sunlit sands to where it landed, still on the beach. I bounced across to pick it up, my legs moving at top speed to where I had seen my toy fall.....but it was not there! Oh no! It had gone! My little furry face must have looked full of worry and confusion, so once more, Sue ran up to reassure me with the words,

"Oh Dave D, it is not lost, but as you skidded along, the sand was moved and you buried your ring!"

"Phew!" I thought as Sue pointed to a tiny piece of my red ring which was peeping through the deeper, darkened wet sand, not far from where the waves rolled towards that shore. I had been so puzzled and happily, leapt over to it in one bound then lifted the ring out of that sand with my strong teeth.....but it was covered in sand and tickled my black nose, so I almost sneezed. Brushing some of the sand from my eyes gently, my Sue said that I needed to have a rest but that we could return to the beach later. She placed the ring in my red bag and fastened my harness where I lay.

I did not want to leave the beach, so stayed lying on the sand giving mum my most appealing look, as if to say,

"Please let me stay and play just a little longer."

Turning from the ramp and noticing this - plus the fact that my nose was plastered in sand - Sue soon appeared by my side, removing my harness again, and suggesting,

"Drop, Dave D, I will throw your ring into the sea to get the sand off you both."

I had anticipated the 'drop' command and already dropped my precious red ring on the beach, so I was focusing on her raised hand which prepared to throw it... which she did. It glided over the beach and landed in the sea near to the shore. I was determined that this was one toy which would return to my toy-box and would not be buried - or taken away by the sea. I ran into that sea 'pell mell', as Grandma May would have called it - meaning very fast, the water splashing all over as my long legs made contact with it. The soft, but strong pads of my paws felt somewhat sore as I trod on pebbles beneath the surface, but I bravely carried on.

Unknown to me, in this part of the beach there was lots of dark brown and green seaweed actually floating just below the sea's surface. Even so, I could just make out the shadow of my red ring tangled in the seaweed, so I closed my eyes and ducked my head under the cold water... grabbing where I thought my ring was. Thankfully, I was successful in gripping it tightly in my mouth, but in doing so, it flipped and went up and over my nose and round the top of my head... dragging pieces of long seaweed with it! I am sure that the otters in Scotland appreciate being able to hide from whales in the underwater kelp forests but I definitely had no wish to hide under seaweed in North Wales and therefore glanced at Sue with a puzzled look!

"Oh Dave D", my Sue exclaimed, gently lifting my red ring from my mouth in order to remove the seaweed for me... but leaving two pieces still stuck to my wet head. The long, brown streaks of seaweed felt very strange and one piece was even in my mouth at first. Sue saw that I had an unimpressed expression...but then stroked me as she briefly explained that it would not harm me, because in fact, one of the earliest uses of seaweed was as feed for domestic animals! This revelation caused me to pull even more of a disapproving face as I did not want her to feed me that stringy, brown, sea stuff in my dog bowl instead of my familiar dog biscuits!

Still concerned, but trying to reassure me, she continued to explain how sheep on an island called North Ronaldsay - the most northerly of the Orkney Islands, still have a staple diet of seaweed, so actually live almost entirely on seaweed for several months of the year. I would not like to eat seaweed for any part of the year or have to stay behind a wall next to the sea like these sheep. I am happy to visit this island one year with my Sue though - and to share photographs of me near to these sheep with our dearest collie friends.

I imagine that it will be interesting and that I will have a prime-viewing spot if standing up on my back legs on the village-side of the wall, because these seaweed-eating sheep are confined to the shoreline by a six-feet high dry stone wall, called the sheep dyke. Sue told me that this wall is thirteen miles long, so encloses the whole island in order to conserve the limited grazing inland for other animals. Unlike in the Outer Hebrides, I will not see any black wool here, as the sheep's wool is three shades of brown and it is said to be the only place in the world where sheep are sheared to produce this very special wool. It is used for knitting woollen garments such as those jumpers Sue's mum had knitted for her brothers Michael, and David, when they were just little boys. I will not be expecting her to knit me any form of dog clothes for I already have my fur coat and lovely waterproof-jacket! (Although the inside and collar of this garment are somewhat similar to the colour and texture of a white fleece!)

I had frozen at the word "sheep" and given her a curious look. I had not seen any sheep on that Welsh beach last time and the water had been very salty when I tried to drink it, before Sue had appeared with my water bowl and bottle of fresh water from my red bag.

Therefore, I wondered where the sheep on North Ronaldsay would find water to drink which was not salty and how the sheep's stomach could cope with that seaweed food. Casting my collie mind back, I remembered how I had sometimes eaten green grass which is not normal food for a collie either, but I heard a friend explain that, due to their peculiar diet, these sheep's digestive systems have adapted to extract the sugars in seaweeds more efficiently. I had not even known that there was sugar in seaweed! Instead of grazing during the day as other sheep generally do, the North Ronaldsay sheep graze as the tide reveals the shore, twice every twenty-four hours.

I had not really thought much beyond a sheep's outward appearance before, so was puzzled until I learnt that there is a large storage space in each sheep's body for the seaweed food that they have quickly eaten and which is later brought up, re-chewed and re-swallowed in a process called cud-chewing. This usually happens when the sheep is resting and not eating. Unlike when I eat my meal in one go and hardly chew at all, a healthy mature sheep will chew their cud for several hours each day. Drako the labrador puppy does not eat seaweed, but likes to play with empty plastic bottles like I do. He also has a special red food dish with shapes moulded inside which help him to eat his own meals more slowly, so being better for his digestion. This is a very good invention for dogs, as a solution for those who are known to eat their meals too quickly and is recommended by some vets. Drako is also partial to full plastic containers, once finding one on his walk, quickly proceeding to pick it up and run off with it. Consequently, he punctured the sides in many places with his sharp puppy teeth, so causing fresh milk to squirt in all directions including over Tessa spaniel - who comically proceeded to drink this fresh milk each time it reached her as Drako ran alongside her! I do not run off with full milk containers but Sue does fill my water bottles for adventures and home water bowls from taps for me - although she did reveal how the Ronaldsay sheep's source of fresh water is limited to the few freshwater lakes and ponds along the seashore.

I went to sleep dreaming of seaweed-eating sheep! The next day, I had been bathed and was seaweed free, so Sue went to the Wednesday market. It was a stormy afternoon and she was doing human things like meeting her friend, Lisa, for a coffee in the café which was not dog-friendly. Therefore, they left me at the house, on my soft cushion, smiling, to show that I understood, as the raindrops pattered gently down the window panes. I was rather glad to be warm and cosy indoors to be honest, even though in addition to my fur coat, I do love that smart lined jacket which I wear proudly when I go to the beach, or indeed, anywhere, in the heaviest rain.

I waited like a good boy until they had shut the front door, then ran to the window and stood on my lengthy back legs to watch until Sue and her mum had walked out of sight. Whilst they are away, I frequently trot to the large window, waiting for their return, standing on my four legs, looking out. Sue and her mum always smile to see my eyes and two matching pale eyebrow markings just showing over the top of the old stone window-sill from inside as they arrive back!

In this instance, with it being rainy, instead, I had snuggled down to sleep and wait… dreaming of my tuggy which was lost in the steep rocks, but glad that my Sue had stopped me trying to climb them, so keeping my strong legs safe. All of a sudden, I woke to the sound of a key in the door and ran to greet Sue, my tail wagging so fast, it nearly pulled me backwards! My heart leapt with joy as she handed me a new tuggy and told me,

"Here you are Dave D, I am so glad to see you. I have missed you".

Taking my new toy gently in my mouth, I felt so loved and so cherished, so lucky when mum talked to me like this. My previous lonely life, where humans rarely spoke to me, where I had no toys, and where I felt so unloved were becoming an increasingly distant memory.

Of course, we still had lots of near misses with my new tuggy, including when it actually became stuck high up, on the washing line, during the time my friend Lauren came to visit with her mum, Claire. When she threw it for me it became clear that her aim was similar to Sue's - but thankfully, it improved after Sue took it down for her to throw again. Even so, like when I looked for my lost tuggy, I still had to stand on my two back legs again, to retrieve it from a bush and also when it landed in the fork of a tree. It was young Lauren who said that I looked like a human when I stood up on my back legs to reach my ball. As you know, for my antics and attempts to reach my ball in unusual places, I have also been likened to a kangaroo, which I have to agree with. Even so, as I am a collie I do not have a pouch on my chest. Bouncer-dog used to bounce up and down like he was actually on springs or like a little kangaroo as he chased after his own ball in Reading - which is in Berkshire and where I have been several times.

In addition to my red pouch-type travel bag, which Sue carries for me, I do actually have a real Dave D pouch at the side of my mouth, between my molar teeth and my cheeks. Humans find this a good place to put any required medicine for us dogs. However, it is not as big a pouch as a hamster's. I have seen these creatures in our local pet store which is full of unusual animals and smells. Some hamsters can eat greenery and place it in their cheek pouches, which can then expand to reach the size of their body! I most certainly would not like my own cheeks to be as large as my body after I have eaten my meal, as I would look like a very strange collie boy!

The next time we went on our holidays to the seaside, I was so excited to see my friends Adele, Sam, and Isaac. After giving Sue a hug, Isaac knelt down beside me so I gave him my paw love to show him how happy I was to see him again. He made a fuss of me and I loved the attention.

Sue had bought me a new yellow tube toy by this time and we played with it on the beach until it started to go dark. The boys were throwing it up and down the beach for me and I was absolutely loving the fun which we were having. Unfortunately, the ladies were talking a bit too much and did not realise that I had not been able to find my toy after the last throw. After seeing my dark shape on long legs pacing up and down the beach past them frantically, they eventually realised. Sue started saying how the toy had 'sentimental value to Dave D', also calmly explaining how my last toy had never been found because of being taken away with the tide. She was therefore pointing out that we could not let this replacement be lost, too. As a result, each human started to search the length of that beach for my cherished toy, by the light of their mobile phones! They did look funny to other visitors who were watching from the jetty! Therefore, I started to relax for they were on the case and I enjoyed chasing their telephone lights up and down the dark beach! Thankfully, after what seemed like hours, it was found and next day I was happy to pose for a photograph, with my prized toy which I was gripping tightly with my powerful teeth.

I know how much other collies love their toys too, especially balls. Jake in Middleton loves to run after his ball in the park - showing the biggest doggy smiles. Just seeing this makes his own mum, Lesley, smile every day, too. Each day Jake and his mum share is a happy one, as are mine with Sue. He loves to lie on his back with his ball or tuggy in his mouth, then to take it out of his mouth with his paws, balancing it on his legs, before putting it back into his mouth. I have never tried this, but frequently still cause my mum to stop what she is doing and laugh out loud, as I lie with all my elongated legs kicking up in the air, rolling round on the floor carpet, wiggling from side to side on my back!

Topaz collie, from Scarborough, was also an amazing collie to her mum, and she also loved to play football, once running onto the pitch near to the end of an important competition match in Stockport and repeatedly tackling the players! It was all down to the penalty shoot-out and, at the crucial moment, Topaz stole the ball. The players tried tackling her but she was a good player and they could not retrieve the ball in time because she dribbled it with her clever collie nose, and scored a goal....for the opposite team! She was not scared of the big men and she did not allow them to take the ball off her until it was in the goal. The men were not impressed, but her mum was very proud.

Alfie greyhound is very handsome like me, but also clumsy as he has even longer legs than mine. He is just learning to play with toys and loves his precious, fluffy football that his mum, Louise, throws for him. He runs to fetch it - like I do with my own ball - racing up the garden steps with his ball in his mouth, to show his mum. Much to his dismay, Alfie once even slipped flat on his tummy as he ran in, but must have been equally proud of himself for his actual ball skills, as Topaz must have been scoring her goal

Collies love to play. I met Amber the collie when I visited Scotland. Before this Amber had been playing in her garden when she had trotted inside and dropped a stone-like object on the living room floor in front of her dad, near to his feet. Amber was proudly, dancing round it, when the 'stone' suddenly moved - causing Amber to leap up onto the settee in surprise, shock and horror! Her human dad actually ran out of the room! It was not a stone at all, it was a live toad, and it just sat there watching everything that was going on. Her loving mum, Avril, came to the rescue and picked the stone-coloured toad up, before walking outside to place it back in the garden next to the family's pond. Amber jumped down and followed inquisitively, but cautiously. I have never met a toad, but I shall be extra cautious myself when passing stones on my adventures, just in case they move and make me jump too!

My friend, Zak spaniel, liked playing with a lamb hand-puppet and wrestling with it. Being a collie, I think I would do the same if my Sue gave me a toy which looked like a lamb! There was a white feather stuck to my ball today and it tickled my nose, but it did not worry me and Sue soon removed it. However, Zak was once playing in the garden, when he saw a pale-coloured feather. He approached it at first, running up to that feather several times, then racing away from it. His mum, Dee, picked it up to show him that it would be fun to play with, but he would not go near it! Usually, if I see one on the forest floor or in my garden, I like to play grabbing these feather things and patting them into the air with my collie paws! However, I am aware that I am not meant to leave my actual toys in the garden overnight in case slugs or snails move over them and sit on them. This can be fatally dangerous to me because eating one of these slug creatures by mistake, as I pick up my favourite toy or bone, can cause me inner damage; therefore, next day, my Sue will always wash any toys that I have left out in our garden by mistake, before letting me play with them. The monthly medicine from my vet, placed directly onto the skin at the back of my neck, is meant to keep my fur creature free and additionally, to protect me from any damage through such as poisonous slug or snail traces inside me, but of course, my Sue still likes to be on the safe side.

On one of our other holidays, my friends Max, Buddy, Shep, their mum, Amy, and granny Valorie had given me that fantastic orange toy gift with its big grab handles known as antennas. Consequently, early on the Sunday morning, I had been excitedly playing with it, making it squeak verrrrrrry loudly, picking it up, squeezing it with my mouth, throwing it, pawing it and knocking it across the hotel room, (including into mum's blue and silver chair), with my paws ….. then racing after it, at the same time letting out loud woofs of excitement. I had basically been entertaining myself in true energy-filled Dave D style whilst Sue was busy typing my Diary up.

Understandably, I had been so enjoying playing with my loud squeaky toy, until Sue had told me, "Shhhhhhh" and to "stop for now Dave D", as people were sleeping, although I did see her smile, so I knew that she was far from cross with me! I love it when my cuteness makes my mum smile! Being an obedient collie, I had stopped on command and, although giving her the 'look' initially, I solved this problem by literally wedging myself between the hotel room furniture and just tapping the precious new toy with my two front paws instead! This was fun, although I much prefer to make it squeak loudly at the same time! It amused me seeing mum's resigned expression and the toy's smiling face looking back at me though!

As you may have gathered, I was not too impressed, as I am a typical collie and simply do not like staying still. Sometimes, I stare at shadows but Sue uses a treat-dispensing toy like my kong immediately to try and distract me from shadow-watching. She puts peanut butter inside this kong toy, which reminds me of sheep because I know that sheep like to eat peanuts too. (Humans always need to check the full ingredients first though, in order to make sure that only real sugar is inside with the peanuts.) This plan of mum's is successful because it works my mind and gives me mental stimulation, which I definitely need.

Shadow collie plays a different kind of shadow game! She places her front two paws on her mum Tracy's feet as she washes up the dishes or finishes the cooking, keeping her two cute back collie legs firmly on the kitchen floor! I have never tried this, but may do one day. I do like to jump fully onto my orange toy with my own front paws though, to ensure maximum squeaaaaaaaaaks!

I played with this smiling-faced toy on the grass outside our dog-friendly hotel later, where Amy had been chatting to Sue and we had also been playing, the day before. Next, Sue had taken me to a bakery shop where there was a mouth-watering fresh bread aroma and the kind lady assistant let me sit at the entrance on my long lead - with mum still holding it, as she bought delicious breakfast bread cakes to share with me before we boarded the long train. They gave us plenty of much-needed energy ready for our collie walk. As my Sue knows that dogs can be stolen from outside shops, she will not tie me up and leave me when she goes inside. If we are on holiday, alone, she will look for a shop which has a counter near to the door so that she can reach the counter but still see me and keep hold of my lead. I am a good boy and sit or lie quietly in the doorway where she can always see me. In days before it seemed so dangerous to leave dogs alone when shopping, even for a few seconds, Poppy dog's lead became untied from a designated dog hook as her mum, Yvonne, bought their dinner from a nearby shop. She looked everywhere for Poppy, and was so worried, so, upon arriving home, Yvonne was truly thankful to find the little dog sitting on their doorstep wagging her tail happily!

Understandably, Poppy's mum left her at home the next time she went shopping. Meg collie disappeared from her mum, Jan, on one of their Sussex forest walks. Maybe Meg got bored with not finding any squirrels to chase? (As I know from experience, how much more fun this makes our collie walks!). Jan had looked everywhere for her Meg and was very worried as they were a mile down the lane from home when her little collie went missing. However, as she was still calling Meg's name, Jan was relieved, but puzzled, to receive a sudden telephone call saying that Meg had just arrived home and was safe! I once ran up the beach ramp with my toy as I was thirsty and wanted to go back to the house. Sue had been admiring the rough sea, so had been shocked to turn round and discover that I had vanished! She found me, with my toy still in my mouth, being fussed by a middle-aged diver who had just returned from the sea to his car by the steep and slippery ramp!

In Scotland, seeing the sun on the distant horizon, I was running along the sandy beach excitedly, watching in awe as many spectacular waves from the great Atlantic Ocean crashed onto that shore... actually dodging these large waves as they almost reached me, to ensure my Dave D paws did not become wet. Out of the corner of my ever observant brown eyes, I saw a long, brown, twig-like object washed up on the Scottish beach. My collie instinct told me to investigate and maybe even pick it up…but over the past month my mum had trained me to no longer pick up long sticks to carry, (only thicker smooth-type logs), in case I slipped and fell on it as I ran with it in my mouth, or cut my mouth if a sharp bit stuck into my soft gum. I had been disappointed as, having no toys for ten years of my life, playing with a stick had been a natural part of my walks. As a result, ignoring them was difficult, although I did kind of understand. Some sticks are so massive I would not attempt to lift them anyway!

Therefore, to my amazement, Sue inspected the brown, twig-like specimen, then picked it up and let me sniff it. My sensitive nose told me that this was not a wooden stick after all, but a giant soft, bendy type of sea plant, and looking around me I saw that some still had their roots on. She said it was called a 'kelp' type of seaweed, that some can grow up to thirty centimetres in just one day, and how it must have been pulled up from the seabed during the storm. I was impressed and tapped it out of mum's hand, with a mischievous paw, so flicking it up into the air. As it landed with a thud, I picked it up and gripped it soooooo tightly in my teeth - which Sue said looked funny as my four white fangs seemed massive! It felt soft to grip and to my delight, I realised that it was an excellent replacement for a tree stick and that kelps are indeed the giants of the seaweed world.

I could see that they were over a metre long with large feathery leaf-type attachments held on slender, flexible, stick-like stalks. Later, I picked up the top part, which had broken away from the main stick, and shook the seaweed leaves from side-to-side as fast as I could, before flinging it and scrambling after it, like Kai collie does with her sheep toy. My shadow on the sand made me look like a funny Dave D with strange, long seaweed whiskers!

Not being keen on the excessively loud noises which waves make as they crash onto beaches, I felt extra-impressed as mum said that the waves hit that particular beach with less power as wave energy is decreased by the seaweed out in the sea. There was often still a trace of white foam at the water's edge, though - but that did not worry me, even when it stuck to my tennis ball! In fact, I have learnt that, amazingly, seaweed is actually used by fire-fighters as a part of their life-saving foam. A form of the red seaweed helps to thicken that foam which may be used to tackle a fire, and helps it to stick, making it more effective!

To be truthful, the Scottish seaweed sticks were just the right size for me, although I was amazed at the way they had been attached to the bottom of the sea-bed or rocks before the storms lifted them and the sea washed them onto this beach for me to enjoy playing with. These seaweeds have root holdfasts that can be as big as footballs, my Sue explained. Despite this, I would have preferred my real football but was still satisfied with the seaweed stick itself.

Removing my harness again in case I went into the sea, Sue threw one of the bendy kelp sea sticks for me and I ran after it, picking it up and flicking it into the air in sheer doggy delight. The end broke off mid-flight and I saw that the middle was light-brown in colour, like a twig. I had so missed this game of playing with natural objects which I discovered on our walks.

I remembered how I swam far out at sea, previously, with Mopsi the collie, to fetch a stick that was floating in the calmer sea, and how, with her carrying it, we guided it back to shore, swimming, together. It was the first time Sue had seen me swim and she was *so* proud of me. I was also close to another dog but was not showing my usual nerves, as I was so focused on the stick and actually swimming. I had learnt to relax more that day, even close to Mopsi, which was an achievement. Mopsi and her friend, Sian collie had unwittingly helped me towards decreasing my fear of being close to another dog - and I was becoming more socialised. Natalie and Lisa also showed my Sue how to distract me from scary strange dogs on the beach by encouraging me to focus on an object in their hand. This did help me because, although I did see the dogs out of the corner of my eye, I was able to ignore them and continue to focus on the object as I am very toy-orientated. My Sue was amazed, grateful for the revelation, keen to help me achieve and even more proud of me. I love it when she praises me. After Lisa and Natalie had taken their collies home, Sue took my muzzle off and I practised swimming on my own after a toy and bringing it back to shore. Mum said I looked like one of the dog-faced common seals that we see in the next bay and looked for in Scotland - except for my colour, as these slippery seals have dark brown to pale grey coats, mottled with spots and rings, but my own coat colour is black and white, even including a touch of paler brown - but with no spots or rings!

There are in fact, fish in the shallow water of this same Cardigan Bay called 'dogfish'! They are not collies though, they are sharks and actually the most common and well-known British shark. The dogfish is a common name given by fishermen due to these fishes' habits of hunting shoals of fish in packs like dogs used to! They are actually a member of the Catshark family! I am glad that I am not a member of a Cat collie family as I would not like to be related to cats - even though I have been likened to a meerkat during a hotel visit!

On my walks after storms, I often find the dogfish's empty brown beetle-like egg cases lying washed up on the beach or in the wet seaweed! They are sometimes known as the mermaid's purse. If I do not have a dog toy with me, I like to pick a dry egg-case up and run along the beach with it in my mouth - looking as if I have grown a massive, curly, brown moustache - before shaking it wildly, throwing it into the air, then chasing after it with delight, as the sea breeze whips it up and carries it further across the beach! It is certainly a very natural type of toy!

Two eggs are laid by the mother dogfish every five to six days during the breeding season and their egg cases have curly tendrils at each corner which help to secure the cases to seaweed, whilst the baby fish are growing inside for about nine months, before they hatch as baby dogfish - these being are about ten centimetres long. This time is the same amount of months that human babies are inside their mum's tummy, but dogs only take about sixty-three days before being born! The dogfish may be born earlier or later dependent on water temperatures. Some sharks in the sea are called Blackmouth dogfish! Although I have a black mouth, I am glad that I am a collie as I prefer dry land, daytime walks and normal dog food from my bowl, whereas the dogfish live and feed on the seabed and they sleep during the day. The Spurdog fish do not lay egg cases as they give birth to live young, like my collie mum did when I was born many years ago.

Again in Scotland, on the Isle of Barra, two children had run up to me and said they had found me a stick. I hesitated, before accepting, clearly remembering how one of my fellow collies had been mildly hurt leaping up for a stick which had been thrown for him and landing with his tummy on its pointed end. Being aware of the risks, Sue took the 'stick' from me gently and bent it just enough to show its pale inner section and to reassure me that it was a seaweed stick and totally fine for me to play with. I loved chasing it up and down the beach, as the two enthusiastic and energetic children kept throwing it for me. I was glad my Sue had thought to bring my water and bowl in my red bag though, as I was so thirsty afterwards.

I happily recalled the last time I had enjoyed such games with a lively young person, which was on Blackpool promenade one exceptionally rainy day. My Sue often comments on how good I am with children and I can tell that she is exceedingly proud of me for this. Our friend, Lauren, had thrown my tuggy for me and it went higher and higher and higher, so I had stood up on my back legs in my little raincoat catching it again and again, loving the comments from passers-by about how cute I looked! In fact, I was almost as tall as Lauren when I jumped up. It was such fun and I was in my element, despite the rain!

On our holiday I was exploring the old coach stables at our new dog-friendly hotel by a lake, which is known as a Loch in Scotland. I had been hoping not to meet any other dogs and am happy to say that the only creatures I saw signs of were midges and fish, neither of which caused me any great concern! Either side of the hotel's main corridor was lined with lighted candles flickering - like in a magical film - and I felt like some kind of collie film star as I stared down that long corridor in astonishment. I am fortunate in that I am familiar with candles as my Sue often lights them in our own home, always being careful to blow them out afterwards and to have a working fire-alarm in two rooms, too.

This amazing candle-lit corridor was leading to an old room with an open-fire and luxurious tartan chair, which reminded me of a dog's tartan coat. I was clearly not allowed to sit on this to relax and look at the loch view, so I padded gently, but inquisitively, through to the next room with my Sue in tow. Suddenly, I stopped and stared in total amazement... for there in the last room was wonderful bright lighting, a large, green table, and on it two real balls, seemingly waiting for me to play with them. I gave Sue one of my charming Dave D smiles.

That enthusiastic smile said it all, so in my excitement, and without waiting for an instruction, I leapt up on my strong, back legs, putting my two front legs on the polished wooden table, like a little furry meerkat - (but without their long claws) - my wide open mouth reaching towards a ball when I heard a sudden shrill voice which actually made me freeze in action.

"Dave D stop! Those are not yours to play with. Your balls are all packed in your red bag, still in the car."

"Oooops", I thought!

I quickly, but reluctantly, jumped down from the table and looked at my Sue, sadly. As you will realise, I did not like any humans to raise their voice because it made me feel anxious. However, I knew that there must be a reason, and indeed she explained that it was a billiard table, that the balls were for humans to use and were smaller than the softer ones in my bag, so may be dangerous to dogs, who were at risk of choking on them. Now I understood, and although I do know that objects can be removed by a human, if they put their hand into the back of our mouth to pull out any item blocking our throat, it would still be frightening and not worth risking.

To make up for my disappointment, Sue went and collected my red bag and heavy duty football from the car and said that she would let me play with it in the bath water. I stood on the white towel as I climbed in, then sat relaxing, looking at my ball which was by now balancing on one side of the bath, and waiting patiently while the old-fashioned white tub on legs filled up with water. In fact, it reminded me of Lass's swimming pool, but was deeper. When it was full, I cheekily planned to pat the water hard with my paws and splash Sue too... which I did as I played with my ball! After my bath she wrapped me in my soft, white towelling robe. It was soooo luxurious, although I admit that the shadows in the bathroom had, much to Sue's displeasure, distracted me somewhat as she dried me.

Although much too long, even for my legs, Sue rolled the robe up and I melted into its velvety softness. It also made a welcome change from the silly plastic shower cap she had tried on me at a previous hotel and which I had swiftly removed and ripped with one determined swipe of my strong front paw! As dusk approached, I went back to looking at the picturesque loch and mountain views from our room's window seat with a huge smile on my handsome face.

My Sue promised that I would soon have a surprise. As always, she kept to her word. Next morning I was not allowed down for breakfast, so waited patiently in the loch-view chair - where Sue's mum usually sat to read her book. I wondered if she would be reading my book, Dave D's Diary, there on a future visit and if my Sue would save me a tasty sausage from her breakfast! She did and I ate it all up, licking my lips and savouring the delicious taste, but not on this occasion daring to wipe my nose, lips or whiskers on the posh hotel room carpet!

After breakfast, Sue put my lead and harness on me, and we walked back along the corridors, which looked so different in the light of day. The candles were out but still in their places along the main corridor, which we both thought was a lovely touch. It was like a maze of rooms and corridors, but presently, we came to that green table room again. I was somewhat puzzled as I clearly remembered that dogs were most certainly not allowed to play with the balls in there.

All of a sudden, I heard a rustling sound and turned to see that, unknown to me, Sue had brought my red travel bag down. I had been glad of it the night before, as my large football and toys were inside it and the bath time had been so much fun. I had genuinely thought that my Sue had packed everything away ready for the next part of our drive and adventure on the big ferry, so the next event took me completely by surprise! Mum unclipped my lead and motioned for me to enter, so I gently padded into the green table room.

I actually had to sit down because, as I looked up, my mouth fell open in amazement, for, there in front of me, and replacing the two smaller balls, was my very own big, green, black and white football, perched high up on the wooden table! I ignored the long, wooden stick which I know to be called a cue - and which was within paw and mouth-reaching distance - and the small red and yellow balls at my end of the table. Instead, I was just lying down, one leg tucked under me, eyes totally focused, continuing to stare at my treasured football, hardly daring to believe this was happening... and of course, showing my big Dave D grin.

My heart leapt with glee and happiness for my Sue had kept her promise and I could play there after all, but with a safe ball. I was glad of my recently self-manicured nails as I sprang up towards my favourite ball and opened my mouth soooooo wide, then grabbed it in my strong mouth as my white tip and entire tail, wagged from side-to-side, with happiness. I proceeded to run around the room with that familiar ball firmly grasped in my mouth, as Sue chased and praised me, loving every minute of this unusual morning playtime.

Chapter Four

Golden Treasure and the Giant Tuggy!

I had not brought many toys with me to the Outer Hebrides as we always had so much to fit into the car on long journeys such as this. Therefore, on each beach, I was ever alert, scanning the sands and driftwood, looking for prospective toys. On a beach in Vatersay, in the far south, I had skidded to a halt beside what had seemed like a small, yellow ball but it was hard and dented, half-nestled under brown seaweed entangled with old blue and green ropes. Using her familiar teacher voice, Sue had told me, "It is a buoy, not a toy Dave Dog".

Nevertheless, I did not think that it looked anything like the boys that I knew, and I sooooooooooooo needed to play. Decisively, first I barked and did try to play with it, stretching out my long, playful left paw to tap it and trying to fit it into one paw scoop, barking as I did so.

"Come here! Come here now!" I willed it silently inside my head.

It was not easy to move the yellow treasure, but it picked up speed as I tried spinning it towards me with my front paws - as my rear legs moved me backwards along the sand at the same time. I could tell that Sue was trying to muffle her laughter so as not to distract me, and even I admit that I must have looked somewhat obsessed! I then placed a paw either side of it and determinedly dragged it backwards again for a metre or two, making long, straight marks down the beach heading towards the white waves of the mighty Ocean behind me.

It was some time later that I could hear my Sue's wholesome giggles more clearly, and realised that I must have looked very funny indeed, but it cheered her rainy day up and I felt happy inside, so my pleasure had been hers too! I tried for ages to pick my new 'toy' up and throw it into the air, but eventually Sue made me leave it on the beach, because she said that it was damaged. I think the real reason was that we already had so many sandy beach-combed plastic bottles and items on the floor behind her car seat!

Soon, we continued on our journey. As I sat on my cushion in the car, I reflected on how the collies, Felix and Ms Millie, also moved backwards as I just had, when waiting for a ball to be thrown; in the same way, Colin, Denise, and Kelvin's collie called Dino, in Telford, often runs off and looks behind him, yet still reverses into the living room door! I was glad I had not bumped into anything or even ended up in the sea, unlike Felix, who was so focused on his ball which mum, Lorna, was holding, that he walked backwards into his human aunt's horse called Puzzle. I would not have liked to bump into a horse. I just like to stand and stare at them! When my Sue arrives home from work she is frequently told by my dad that "Dave D has been on his high horse again", but of course, he does not mean literally! They are both used to my quirky ways by now and love me regardless, also now realising that telling me off cannot stop my reactions no matter where I am. In spite of this, and all my other 'issues', Sue always loves my company and sharing adventures together.

Leaving Vatersay island and crossing over the causeway, I turned my furry head as my attention was caught by a collection of orange and yellow ball-like objects at the side of the road, to the left of the causeway. I strained to see them better as we drove past, and I immediately felt my strong Dave D heart beat more quickly with excitement, so I gave a bark to attract Sue's attention - my tail thumping, loudly against my travel bag, with anticipation. Of course, she had already seen them and slowed the car, parking it safely on the deserted road, just past the balls. As Sue unclipped my harness I leapt out. Hearing the command, "Wait!" and turning my head to look for mum's approval, then seeing her nod, I bounded excitedly towards the coloured balls I had just seen.

My heart now leapt with delight for there, there right in front of me, was a yellow ball very much like the one I had just left behind, but this time, a real full-size yellow ball, with a tuggy-type rope already attached. I reached up playfully towards the ball, standing tall on my long Dave D legs, then steadying myself with my front paws by placing them carefully on the metal net-type boxes, before proudly stretching up... and kissing it! Much to my dismay, I soon realised that it wasn't a soft, rubber ball at all, because it was all hard and salty, and felt very rough on my cold nose!

"Oh Dave D, that's not a soft ball, it is another buoy! A buoy is a plastic ball that floats on the water and acts as a marker for a lobster pot attached to it, and these lobster pots are owned by local fishermen", my Sue explained, before adding, upon seeing my disillusioned expression,

"Come on, we will go and find you another real yellow ball to play with".

Jumping down, and although still feeling mischievous, I had already decided it was best not to try and pull the yellow 'ball' off. Mum's approving nod told me that I had made the right decision. The fishermen would not appreciate me taking their equipment away into our red car to play with!

Mum's voice seemed to fade as, in my excitement, I had turned to look behind me and spotted some verrrrrry thick ropes which would be perfect for making large tuggy toys. With just one bound, I used my long legs to leap on top of the weathered coils of rope, tail naturally wagging so quickly from side to side with pure happiness... and began tugging so hard - but with no luck. I tried again, really gripping the rope with my teeth, pausing momentarily and seeing mum's look warning me to 'be careful'.

Harder and harder I pulled with my sharp collie teeth, but all too soon, Sue told me that I must 'leave them alone' as they also belonged to the fishermen. I gave her my cutest Dave D pleading look, but to no avail, as she gently comforted me and explained that the thick ropes were not for making into tuggies, but to fasten boats to their moorings so that they did not float away. I did accept this - knowing that there is always a next time - but still thought to myself,

"Ooooo, this has been such fun, as I do love playing tuggies, even if I can't keep these particular ones!"

It is always important for mums and dads or carers to explain reasons for decisions to their sons and daughters. I loved my mum for helping me to understand why she made such decisions and for taking the time to explain why I could not always have or do everything that I wanted.

"Thank you for being so understanding Dave D", praised my Sue. Still touching just one of the lower ropes with a gentle paw, I gave her my best smile in order to reassure her that there were no hard feelings, not ever.

It was time to face facts as I realised that neither the buoy nor the rope were going to be joining me on our journey. I was resigned to the small toys inside my red travel bag, instead of a souvenir from Scotland. Reluctantly, and with one last glance at the yellow ball and thick rope, I returned to the car but my latest facial expression said it all. As she looked back at me, though, realisation dawned on me and I gave another of my biggest Dave D smiles, for I knew for sure that my Sue would manage to find me a big tuggy of my own before the holiday was out. Sure enough she did, on the last day of our holidays after we had driven many miles along the high, winding, mountain roads. In fact, I actually almost felt like a famous King David Dog as that unexpectedly long road took us through a castle grounds and under wonderful stone arches, towards an amazing sandy beach, a beach my Sue had excitedly pointed out on her map. Although Sue was understandably somewhat hesitant, we were not trespassing as, unusually, the road in fact runs right through this grand castle's grounds including past its huge front door! There were even items of fresh-produce on sale to passers-by in a stable on one side! As we passed, I peered into that stable very cautiously from my discreet window, but thankfully, there was no sign of a fellow dog.

There had been exceptionally steep cliffs to our left and then suddenly I saw it, the beach, long and sandy and oh so inviting for a fun-loving collie like me to play on. Despite this, my excitement was instantly changed and I felt myself start to worry as we drove towards the parking places, because I had spotted a large dog and a smaller one with their master by the side of the road having a picnic. I became anxious and my body tensed. Unknown to me, Sue had picked up on this, changed the plan, turned her indicator off, and kept driving past them towards the end of the beach road, where she stopped. I jumped out of the car, peering round the corner, searching, my now fearful eyes seeking out those scary dogs - but, amazingly, I could not see them as they were out of my vision. Thankfully, my Sue knows me well and had considerately driven to park in a place where I could no longer see them.

Despite the picturesque scenery, I did try again, peeping, but half-hidden, behind our car door... but with much relief I realised that I still could not even see their paws under the line of cars. Sue had blocked my view completely with her car and all the other cars, so I was eventually able to have my snack and drink my water without worrying, as we picnicked. Clever 'Mummy Sue'! (Sadly, unlike some collies, I still cannot usually even eat treats when I am too fearful).

I sat uncomfortably and still somewhat warily next to our car, my unusually still tail underneath me, scanning the empty beach, head turning this way and that. My beloved red travel bag was beside me for added comfort and I was grateful to Sue for helping me. At such times I feel growing confidence because I know that although it hurts her to see me so stressed, Sue loves me. She understands me and also gives me space, comfort and guidance. As long as my Sue is beside me I can conquer some of my fear of other dogs.

After our picnic we climbed down the steep, sandy hill to the beach. Here, I played with my red and green tuggy-ball, first leaping up into the air along the beach on my strong legs to catch it, and then even venturing into the sea to retrieve my toy as Sue threw it for me. I even ignored a large spaniel-type dog at the opposite side of the beach as I was so focused on my tuggy-ball. I knew that mum had my muzzle with her and would be anxious about the other dog, too, though she hid it well. In spite of this, I noticed that she kept glancing to make sure that the spaniel was still a good distance away. I just kept on playing so Sue gave me lots of praise; I therefore felt such a proud boy and thought that I had demonstrated a significant achievement. Sue's mum also said that we had both done so well when she realised that we had indeed both known that the other dog was there all the time!

All of a sudden, I thought my eyes were deceiving me… but to my delight, they weren't! My eyes had spotted gold, real doggy gold… the most enormous yellow ball in the world! Dropping my own tiny tuggy-ball and rope, I leapt towards it, sending sand scattering everywhere. I stopped and stood staring in amazement at the sight before me - that huge yellow ball nestled in the brown, beach seaweed.

"Oh Dave D… what have you found?" my Sue said, with laughter and pride in her voice, "What are you like?!"

I touched the yellow treasure delicately, firstly with my wet nose, then with one cheeky - but gentle - paw, but it did not move! I tried again, tapping harder and harder, but to my dismay, it still did not move. Instead, I leapt high, onto it and yes... it rocked but... oh no... it was hard - another of those hard, dry, plastic buoy things that are to mark areas at sea, (the type I was not allowed to keep last time). I waited for my Sue to say "Stop Dave D!" and for the fun to be over... but she didn't, and to my delight her smile indicated that she was actually encouraging me to play with it!

I barked - making the Dave D equivalent of a human "Yipeeeeeeeeeee" sound, then almost doing a strange collie dance in my excitement - and certainly performing a few peculiar moves! I tried to play with the buoy thing, barking once more and glaring at it, then pawing it at the same time. I could detect mum taking photographs but I was having too much fun to bark at the camera this time and had my mouth full anyway! With my bushy collie tail still waving from side to side, paws still determinedly trying to move the huge ball, the sound of my woofs of delight echoed across the beach.

My paws left sandy marks as I tried to play and these filled the area of beach where I had been prancing around strangely in true, excited collie style. This was characteristic of my energetic collie breed that my Sue knew and loved. She adored how I came to life when I played and all signs of fear of other dogs were far from my mind. I had not even inwardly worried very much about the dog which her mum had observed from far above, as I was so engrossed, so full of huge Dave D smiles and contentment.

My Sue smiled too, when she saw me in play-bow position. I wanted this toy and to play with it forever, more than anything I had ever wished regarding toys in my whole life and she knew it! I knew that I could now persuade her to let me keep the damaged ball buoy whose only use was now with me! I carefully leapt up onto it and momentarily clasped the plastic side piece in my teeth wishing I had a biggggggggg long rope to fasten to it. The sand all around me was no longer smooth and had become increasingly full of patterns where I had jumped around trying, rather unsuccessfully, to fully grip my new yellow toy.

Although fully aware that my bottom was sticking high in the air and that, hearing my delighted doggy noises, by now a group of onlookers had started to watch me from the cliff-top, I carried on regardless. Hearing their comments, I knew that I was in with a definite chance of winning Sue over, too because they were on my side, rooting for me!

I continued playing, my mouth slippery on the hard plastic, and wishing that Sue could read my mind and know just how much easier I would find this game if I had a rope attached to make a giant tuggy-type toy!

I looked at my Sue hopefully... thinking I might just be hoping too much, when... suddenly, Sue ran to a place in that slimy seaweed nearby and, with her back to me, started to pull on a green thing that had been showing slightly between the strands. The item seemed to become longer and longer until it suddenly dawned on me that it actually appeared to be a twisted old rope. Sure enough, a long rope was revealed and Sue started to tie it onto the buoy. Wow! I made even more squealing, happy Dave D noises as I recognised that she had made me my very own gigantic tuggy toy!

I leapt towards it with excitement and reached out my long right front paw to touch the precious green rope, also placing my left front paw on it, in order to pull it back and play. I pulled it northwards, southwards, then east and west, the entire beach continuing to echo with my delighted Dave D sounds and the once smooth sand itself now filled with even more of my paw-prints and the buoy's imprints as I played with it.

Taking time out to look around me at the audience - and understandably needing a quick breather, I realised that dusk would soon be falling and therefore knew that it would shortly be time to return to our camp-site - as we had many winding roads to follow before reaching that destination. Suddenly, a familiar, but much-loved voice, echoed down from the top of that nearby sandy cliff...

"Well, that certainly won't fit in the car!"

My Sue and I looked up at the same time, and there watching us, in puzzlement was Sue's mum. Yes, I obviously knew that our car was packed almost reaching bursting point, but I have also learnt that, in many situations, where there is a will there is usually a way! Sue winked at me as I touched the yellow buoy once more with my head, indicating both my desire and stubborn determination, before proceeding in using the rope to pull my treasure towards the sand dune path - Sue also helping me as we both climbed the steeper part of that sandy cliff. I then knew without a shadow of a doubt that our giant tuggy would be going in the car and that I would be taking it over five hundred miles home to Staffordshire! (Where I am proud to say that it remains to this day, over a year later, in the garden next to our pond.)

Chapter Five

Lifeboats, telescopes and tractors

It was the first day of mine and my Sue's summer holiday in Criccieth, North Wales - this being on a peninsula, which is a stretch of land being surrounded on three sides by sea. We were on our way to the beach, taking a last stroll down the now dark hill towards that beach. I appreciatively tasted the sea-salt on my soft Dave D lips and mouth, my heart once again leaping with joy. The gentle sea breeze ruffled my dark fur, even down to the white tip of my tail fur. Suddenly... I could see a significant number of lights in the distance ... not the type that gave me shadows to watch and follow, but interesting anyway! As you are now aware, collies are particularly prone to shadow-chasing, so Sue usually tries to distract me with those 'kongs', which are food-filled toys, instead. (She did not have one with her on this occasion though.)

As you will have become aware of, we often walk later on at night - or very early in the morning, as do many dogs and humans with nervous dogs, because this means we do not meet as many other dogs. Even though she loves me, having restricted times to walk me without fear of trouble and tension, can be a lonely, seemingly isolated, life for my human at times, but such a strategy helps dogs like me to enjoy walks more, without the usual fear which I have at peak times of the day. I therefore spent much of the first few months of my new life with my Sue only being walked in the quieter times. Even then, to decrease my anxieties, as you know, we often had to about-turn and go into the forest to hide until other approaching humans and their off-lead dogs had passed. (I feel a little safer when the other dogs are on leads.)

In our holiday place by the sea, it was usually deserted at this time of nearly midnight, but as we approached the halfway mark of this familiar hill, most peculiarly, people started arriving, various cars kept pulling up at strange angles and men jumping out, without even locking their doors. I was bemused. This was mine and my Sue's quiet time, but it was far from quiet! I stood perfectly still, full of my usual Dave D alertness, curiosity and love of life, my nose pointing forward and ears upright.

Suddenly, I heard a loud noise, which was not at all welcome to my sensitive ears. Like in the rescue centre many months ago, even when my furry triangular-shaped ear flaps are covering my ear-holes, I can still hear every noise and find it very difficult at times. Emerging from its lifeboat station den was the first part, then more, of a large, unfamiliar, object on wheels - the orange colour of some lawnmowers I like to stare at, follow, and chase on the lawns... but much bigger! Marilyn's Jake-dog used to run up and down barking at the man cutting their park's grass - as if he wanted to eat the machine! - and also barked at hot air balloons as they flew over his garden - attempting to follow them from ground level - yet on this occasion, I was determined to be still and not to bark or attempt to chase the wheels of this lifeboat-related machine!

We dogs have been known to be partial to fresh grass, but I would not say that my fellow collies and I are like mini lawnmowers as we have not grown orange fur for a start! However, we are sometimes tempted to seek out and munch the much taller, wider blades of grass that are frequently missed by our human's lawn mowers, especially fresh spring shoots. Eating grass does seem to aid our digestion in small amounts - but as you can imagine, because of their danger to our insides, we always have to be alert and careful in case slugs and snails have been on this grass and we eat them by mistake - as they can pass on dangerous chemicals which they have picked up from those used on plants. We are also at risk directly from plants when products which are harmful to animals have been used on these plants by humans.

As we stood on the steep hill, watching, our dark Sue and Dave D shapes silhouetted, we realised that the whirling noise beyond was coming from a tractor-like vehicle on huge wheels behind the actual lifeboat. This particular tractor with its trailer was not at all quiet like those tractors or lifeboats that had been stationary and silent in Scotland and which I had spent many a happy holiday moment marvelling over.

I was brought back to the here and now, by that sound becoming much louder but I focused on a blue flashing light on top of the lifeboat trailer, giving it a mastered Dave D collie 'eye' glare. This caused Sue to comment on the slight frown which formed on my forehead and to give me a gentle reassuring ruffle of my neck fur. Sometimes she even puts her hands over my ears to protect them when the sounds are too loud. She knew me well, but I plastered on a smile from my look-out point halfway down the hill.

Following the orange boat on its silver and white trailer, and now appearing fully in front of me, was the huge tractor-like vehicle, with a matching blue flashing light, pushing the lifeboat on its trailer towards the sea. Until our Scotland holiday, I had never, ever, been on a tractor, not even in all my years, but I had heard my Sue mention the time she did, wearing a grass cutting helmet, (which must have looked rather strange!), when she lived in Berkshire and helped on the farms. I am glad that I do not have to wear a helmet, but I do eat grass from time to time, though mum does in fact puts lots of steamed greens in my diet so I benefit from that more. (I am so glad that generally, dogs don't usually have to wear hats, although our collie pals, Sky and Bobby, do wear them to pose at their dad's workplace!)

Passing the ramp, we continued watching from our vantage point as more cars passed us, again being abandoned at strange angles, their drivers then running towards the lifeboat station lights. We noticed that each car had a sticker in their window stating 'Lifeboat Crew Member'. We listened to people talking about how coastguards monitor and act on reports of anyone in distress at sea. The crew of the lifeboat are volunteers and wear pager machines which bleep to tell them when they are needed to help. I thought about how I sprang into action when I saw a pigeon fly onto the top of a roof and knew the men must have moved very fast too. My Sue was full of admiration for this brave lifeboat crew. It is said that an average of twenty-six people are saved each day by lifeboat crews throughout the British Isles.

As we waited near to the top of the ramp, a small lady approached us. The well-wrapped up lady did not have a dog - which I was glad about, so I lay down, stayed still and listened with interest. I heard Sue comment that the men seemed to be as fast as the rocket signal which used to be set off and soar up into the sky. Sue explained that in the olden days when she was little, rockets were used to alert the crew that they were needed to launch the lifeboat and help at sea. The rockets made a *whoosh* as they travelled into the air from that special rocket launching metal stand in front of the lifeboat station, followed by a bang louder than a firework. I cringed, knowing that I would have barked or jumped at that sudden noise for sure. Most dogs I know loathe the sound of fireworks, but a special sounds tape played well before times of real fireworks, does help many dogs to cope better. I am not too frightened of fireworks myself but I do find their noises somewhat unappealing.

I was significantly relieved how the crew now used quiet pagers for the purpose of call-out notification. In the day-time, the lifeboat crew may have been at work as butchers or grocers, or even pet shop managers, but they would be allowed to leave work straight away to rush to their voluntary job of saving lives at sea. I understood that the car people were all lifeboat crew who I had seen information about outside the lifeboat station, when Sue had been reading data on rescues and lives saved. This was usually in the daylight and the details were pinned to the lifeboat station door. Sue told me that she used to go and watch the launches and rescues with her Grandma May and her old dog, Lucky, and how crowds used to gather on the jetty. Lucky was a confident girl and had no problem meeting crowds and other dogs so she was indeed a lucky girl not to have my fear. Fortunately for me, old Dave D, there were no crowds tonight, and still no other dogs.

The whirring became louder as the roaring tractor powerfully pushed that huge, orange lifeboat with crew aboard down that long, concrete ramp towards the open sea with its engine ready to take it through that sea. The lifeboat hit the sea-water with a splash as it entered, shooting off into the darkness, going further and further out to sea. In years gone by men in high boots called waders had used to support the lifeboat as it entered the water, but this time it was just a man on the tractor itself. I tapped the concrete ground with my paw slightly impatiently, longing to reach the beach and run on the sand with my Sue. She got the message! We continued on our walk towards the beach, looking back now and again until the lights from the lifeboat were just tiny dots of light far out at sea taking the crew to help the person or people - or animals - in distress.

My Sue had needed wading boots really, but she did not even have wellingtons, so she had needed to roll her dark jeans up and paddle into the sea to help me retrieve my ball. It had gone too far out for me to reach confidently due to the sea being much too cold for me to swim in. Sue was therefore shivering with icy cold feet and in her wet jeans, but was reassured because she knew from my caring expression that I could emphasize as my own paws were wet too - continuing to explain how we would dry off with big, fluffy towels and by the cosy log fire back at our house. She would then be able to put her favourite fluffy warm socks on!

Socks! Hmm! Once, my Sue had made me wear a paw sock on that lifeboat ramp beach after my nail had broken off whilst playing, in order to keep my then sore paw dry and to prevent possible infection. I have to admit that, despite her kindness, it had looked like a mini grey boxing glove laced to the end of my leg so I had felt ridiculous and embarrassed being taken for walks like this! Of course, I wanted to keep my Sue happy and knew that it made sense to keep my raw, tender, nail area dry and to stop it touching the sandy pebbles. Long nails can make it uncomfortable for a dog like me to walk and balance, so I keep my nails nicely manicured, biting them to keep them trim and short, as I know that Sue found it hard to cut Lucky's nails due to the wick connected to the dog's live nerve centre, being near the end of her white nails. There is a special powder that your vet can give to your human in case your nail does bleed, to stem the blood. I believe that normal flour can be used as alternative in an emergency, although Sue usually uses that ordinary flour when baking cakes. I have noticed that some humans put a big collar on their dog, which look like my fellow dog is wearing a giant lampshade, but if it prevents us biting a wound and stops infection it must be worth it. However, us dogs are said to have antiseptic properties in our mouths anyway, and I would like to see humans wearing these lampshades on both their hands for a whole day to see how they feel!

We returned to the beach the next afternoon, to see the lifeboat training exercise, where I learnt that lifeboats really do rescue dogs as well as humans, and that after we had left, a human and dog from a damaged boat had been saved the evening before and brought ashore wrapped in a warm blanket each. I was momentarily distracted by a small dog in the distance, and started to panic. With the usual alertness which she has developed, my Sue quickly swung into action and pulled my yellow rubber toy from my red bag, whilst managing to present a relaxed and confident stance, which I then followed. It helps me to feel so much calmer when my mum is calm. I was therefore able to relax, toy clamped in my mouth, and watch the lifeboat emerge, this time in daylight, with all its crew on board, again wearing yellow suits and white helmets. I heard a lady talking about each lifeboat crew member's helmet costing over one hundred and eighty pounds and I would like to help the Royal National Lifeboat Institution when I become a famous collie author.

Unfortunately, due to the direct fact that I did not receive that vital early socialisation for those first few years of my life, I have not developed those doggy social skills and my fear of victimisation by other dogs was - and is - higher. Many dogs don't like being growled at, but I sometimes growl when I am scared, or crouch down low and stare at an approaching dog. When mum used to tense up as she was worried for me, and the tension passed down the lead straight to me, it confirmed my own stress. Thankfully, now that Sue is conscious of this and I have my much longer lead, this no longer happens.

By the time I turned round the huge, looming, orange monster was once again being pushed by the powerful tractor, on its lit up silver trailer, and propelled down towards the sea. Sue had told me she would take me on a smaller tractor another day. In my doggy mind I thought that it would be a strange place for me to sit, although acknowledging how it would make my mum happy and me, temporarily, much taller - but I will never be as tall as most adult humans, even when I stand on my four long, furry legs.

Recently, we returned to the Criccieth lifeboat station to reveal that we will be donating some copies of my Dave D's Diary book to their gift shop, for them to sell in order to raise more money for that valuable local lifeboat crew's equipment. I had been beach-combing that day and playing with a large, plastic bottle which I had seen, then run at and pounced on near to the beach. I was delighted to find a shiny, silver, metal dog bowl outside the lifeboat station, with clean water in. The lady shop-assistant made a fuss of me and did not mind me dropping my sandy bottle on her clean floor at the entrance to her shop, while I lapped up the cool water, which she had kindly provided for passing dogs to enjoy.

Telescopes

Next day, down by that same lifeboat station, in the shadow of the huge, towering hill and castle, Lauren pointed to a long, blue metal thing. It was rather odd and I had never seen one before. Sue explained that humans look through such structures with one eye to see what is going on at sea or along the coast. I continued to admire the view just using my own two eyes, although I admit that I also kept checking that the blue machine was not pointing in my direction - like I sometimes caught cameras doing, causing me to bark!

At the time, I had been playing with my soft, similar-coloured blue frisby, which Foster and his mum and Jess and Joe gave to me for my birthday on one of our Forest of Dean collie walks, so I had eyed the painted tube suspiciously and cautiously. Due to being wary, I had not put my paws out to touch it, but my friend Lauren had been braver and positioned it with her little hands, then looked through that long, metal cylinder with a glass end. Even though I tried, I could not see what she could see on the opposite beach, as my vision is not that of a telescope - which I heard her mum say magnifies sights. Besides, I was concentrating fully on trying to drag the toy frisby backwards with my front paws either side, propelling myself with my back legs, so that I could flip the toy up into my mouth! As you can imagine, I was giving it my intense collie eye at the same time.

Not being one to give up, I tried so hard, so was delighted to succeed and proudly carried my blue treasure along the lengthy promende, delighting in the attention and positive comments from passers-by. Glancing up briefly I could see the pride in my Sue's eyes too. I love to make her proud of me, her often complicated collie boy.

To be honest, I find my eyesight to be very good for an old collie anyway, and Sue says that I can spot another dog, even far in the distance. Thankfully, she then goes into 'block mode' so I cannot see it, or we about turn, to stop me worrying!

Several weeks later, after an eleven-hour road and sea journey, we were many hundreds of miles away in Castlebay, on the beautiful island of Barra - off the West coast of the Scottish mainland. We explored - with my red travel bag close to hand and paw, and came across another lifeboat, which I looked at in admiration, and later on also another telescope, which I was more dubious of! Again, a wonderful stone castle was close by - which, if it had been human, could have told a thousand tales. However, this lifeboat was bigger and to me seemed even more amazing, floating in the bay next to that magical-looking castle. I scoured the area but there were no other dogs around. My heart was soooooooooo full of happiness as my Sue sat on the stone wall and we relaxed together. I sat up and gave her one of my happy Dave D smiles along with both my paws, which she held gently. She smiled back. Sue adores my paw loves. This is the life that doggy dreams are made of and I felt so lucky that I had such a wonderful life so full of enjoyable adventures.

Days later, as we drove along, on another island heading north, I noticed a tall object which reminded me of the blue telescope. This new telescope was very high up on a Scottish hillside and much bigger than the thin, blue one in Wales, but it still reminded me of the one by the lifeboat station which Lauren had shown me. We had to drive up a long, steep, bumpy road to reach it. It was cold and windy as I jumped out of the car, concentrating on the increasingly familiar machine. This other one seemed taller and was surrounded by a rectangular stone wall, only entered by a strong gate, which my Sue opened, in order to allow me and her mum to go in. I padded gently up to the silver telescope enquiringly, and looked up at it, stretching my long, white-striped neck and willing it to move down to Dave D level.

I continued to eye it so closely and wondered if I would have a chance to see through the long, silver tube, even barking in true Dave D style to signify that I wanted to look at the view this time, but the shape remained still and silent! In a vain attempt to pull it down to my collie height level, I reached out with my long paw and touched the base below that majestic beast to see if it would move just a little, constantly thinking, then as adrenalin rushed through me, almost chanting,

"Oh great mighty silver eye, show me! - oh lofty eye."

However, there was no way I could reach to see through that eye-hole unless Sue picked me up. Although I am not heavy, it is not very comfortable for a collie to be lifted high into the air - like Sue did once, to protect me when a big dog approached and wouldn't leave me alone. Consequently, as my mum's positive dear old boss Mr. Hall, used to say to her and her teaching colleagues, in such situations, "If there is a problem, show me your solution". Indeed it is always best to attempt to find solutions to problems rather than dwelling on them. I pondered and made a decision. With it being misty, even my Sue won't be able to see much through that telescope on a day like this I thought to myself! However, I was determined to see what was over that stone wall and, when Sue wasn't looking, I stood up so tall on my increasingly famous long hind legs and peered over the top of that wall housing the silver telescope. I had caught my Dave D breath as I looked beyond. Wowwwwww what an amazing view! Mum realised what I was up to and, although reminding me to 'be careful', praised me for my logical thinking, which gave me a warm glow from my nose to the tip of my long Dave D tail.

Tractors

Later, we were on another car adventure, driving along a very dusty country lane, with road debris hitting the side of our paintwork and partly covering our windows in dust as I kept trying to peer out. Sue suddenly started to look over her shoulder, beyond where I sat, and began reversing. I looked out anxiously, collie paws clenched, hoping not to hear the whack of an exhaust or bumper being banged again!

Therefore, I felt an element of relief as our car stopped and Sue unclipped my harness and car seatbelt to allow me to alight, also pulling my red bag from my seat. I blinked in the bright sunlight. My Sue smiled as she watched me closely, as she loves my distinctive black upper eye lashes! I followed where her own thrilled eyes were looking and saw it there, right in front of me, a seemingly abandoned old, white tractor. I remembered Sue's earlier promise that I could go on a tractor, but Sue's mum raised her eyes to the car roof, understandably wondering what on earth her daughter had planned for today's photo shoot! We soon found out when Sue called excitedly, "Come on Dave D, your chance to sit on a tractor at last!"

I must admit I did prefer this silent kind of tractor and was glad she had not tried to sit me on the huge, blue lifeboat tractor. Hesitantly, I alighted from my car seat. Looking from side-to-side suspiciously to check that no farmer, farm dog, or farmhouse were in sight, and with adrenalin rushing through our bodies, we craftily raced through the long grass together until we stood directly in front of the old machine. Looking up, I was surprised to see a large up-turned wellington boot, the type usually worn in a pair by humans, stuck on top of the reddish colour tractor funnel.

Reflecting back, I recalled how the lifeboat crew wore waterproof seagoing gloves to protect their hands, so ensuring a sure grip at sea and also wellington-type hardy yellow sea-boots to steady their feet on a ship's deck on the high seas - these costing over forty pounds a pair. However, this one wellington reminded me more of the muddy pair left in my garden by the famous local Strongman Competition Winner, Richard, along with his own big gloves, after he had put our new fence up to keep me safe. Even so, the tractor boot was not as big as these - but still too big for me to put my leg and paw inside comfortably - although I would have been willing to try if Sue had asked me to! I must have looked puzzled, for Sue explained it would be there to prevent water going into the tractor engine and causing damage, before removing it for just a few seconds whilst she took a photograph of the full tractor.

However, as Sue pushed through the grass, holding the potentially prickly brambles back, so that I could reach it safely, (without scratching my delicate black nose), we came to the tractor cab and looked inside expectantly. Unfortunately, there was no seat. It seemed like an empty shell, only fit for birds to shelter or make their nests in. Consequently, it was not safe for me to climb into the cab as the seat had worn away and its floor had rusted. Still keeping a look out for any approaching farmer, I trotted back round to the front of the tractor, to where my red bag already lay. Inquisitively, I stretched my neck and lifted my head, pointing my long nose upwards and peering towards the white machine, in order to secure a better view. As we returned to the one-track road, my Sue reassured me that she would still find me a tractor to sit on, maybe a red one to match my bag, lead and collar - although I knew that she would still make me wear my green harness for safety. I smiled as I jumped back onto my seat in the car and mum fastened my seatbelt....ready to continue with our quest and next adventure.

Sailing northwards from North Uist, towards the Isle of Harris, before then exploring the lanes alongside the dark blue sea, we took in the beauty, before joining more of a main road. My heart leapt with delight as I saw a tractor sign by the side of the road, so we stopped to try and find one such vehicle. I concentrated on listening intently for the sounds of a tractor engine, as Sue had told me to, but then she laughed because, apparently, I looked funny with my 'concentrating' head on! We saw and heard nothing, not even another car.

Back in our own car, it took a while of searching up and down local side-tracks but as usual, my Sue was determined, so when we finally stopped for the second time, my heart-felt full of warmth and pride as I saw what she had found for me... a bright red tractor with a trailer attached, like the one used to collect sacks of seaweed from many local beaches. The tractor seat looked somewhat high up, but I was confident that Sue would help me on safely and that I would have an amazing view.

However, as I stood up tall ready to board and Sue helped lift me the rest of the way on, out of the corner of our ever-scanning eyes we saw a concerned-looking man appearing from a nearby house on our left. I watched him approaching. My Sue looked worried, as this man may not have liked a big collie with eighteen potentially sharp collie nails - including my two front dew claws - sitting on his pride and joy. She knew she should have tried to find the owner and asked permission first. This would have been more sensible and respectful. To diffuse the potential situation, I turned my collie head towards the owner and gave him my sweetest Dave D grin, knowing full well that it would probably win him over. Indeed, he heard mum apologise and saw how proudly and carefully I was sitting on the real tractor, before motioning to us not to worry and to keep taking the photographs of his renovated red tractor. He then proceeded to proudly show us the engine and to explain how he had restored it himself. We explained about our book, and promised to take him a copy of my Dave D's Diary upon our return, which we will honour next year all being well. I am looking forward to seeing the kind man and his red tractor again, plus lots more adventures. Maybe he will even take me for a ride on it, or in the trailer next time?

My Sue smiled as she saw how proud and contented I looked, also remembering - and explaining - how another kind tractor owner had rescued her and her old dog, after the radiator had broken and steam poured out of her previous car. He had come to the rescue on a blue tractor before disappearing and re-appearing with a second hand radiator off a small tractor which he tied on to her car with rope! I was glad that I had not been there as she said there had been many farm dogs in the barn which he used as a workshop - but thankfully, they had been friendly to her and she had got home safely. I still hope to go on a moving tractor in future travels! In fact, I thought the opportunity had arisen recently as we drove through the Shropshire country lanes. We came across several signs advertising a 'Tractor Pull'. These seemed strange things for humans to pull, but I reasoned that it would be safe for me to sit on the tractor as they pulled, because the engine would not be working. However, if they were expecting me to help pull a big tractor they would be disappointed because I would much rather pull my tuggy rope and ball with my Sue.

Dave D's Photo Album!

Wherever I am, I love to make Sue smile by doing my funny body wiggles!

I peep round obstacles carefully, just in case other dogs are around.

I move forwards - now feeling much more positive, every paw step of the way!

I had been totally determined not to lose my precious red toy in the choppy sea.

…I didn't mind the slimy seaweed pieces clinging to my face, because at least I had saved my toy from that sea!

I was surprised to learn about the seaweed-eating sheep… This sounded like such a strange food choice!

Wedging myself between the hotel furniture, I continued tapping my new toy... even when mum had stopped me from actually chasing it around the room!

Tail held high, I excitedly gripped my newly discovered seaweed stick in my sharp white collie fangs.

Looking like a cute seal, but focusing on my Sue, I bravely swam in the sea off Cardigan Bay with the amazingly scenic Snowdonian mountain range behind me.

Without thinking, I leapt up on my strong back legs, front paws resting on the wooden table… like a cute meerkat!

As I looked at the Loch from this window seat, my heart leapt with joy and a contented smile was unmistakable on my Dave D face.

Placing a paw either side of my newly discovered treasure, I dragged it determinedly towards the blue sea!

Despite still touching the thick old rope near the coloured buoys with a gentle paw, I gave Sue my best Dave D smile to say that I did understand that these were not mine to keep.

I felt like the mighty King David Dog as that winding road took us through the grounds of a majestic castle.

Unintentionally sitting on my bushy tail, I warily scanned that empty beach for any sign of a fellow dog.

My furry bottom sticking high in the air, I touched the buoy with my mouth, totally ignoring the gathering crowd.

Having ignored the other dog and the humans behind me, I realised that dusk would still be falling and how it was time to leave that beach… yet I so wanted to take the treasure too!

Although the loud noise was not welcome to my sensitive collie ears, I watched with fascination as the orange lifeboat object emerged from the left.

I was not one to give up and finally managed to pick up my blue toy, proudly displaying it like a trophy as I walked back down the promenade.

Reaching out towards the silver base with my long paw, I barked loudly, willing the telescope eye towards me so that I could see through it.

My heart felt so full of warmth and pride as I sat up high on that bright
red tractor which Sue had found for me.

I often patiently guarded my Sue's mail on remote country lanes,
staring intently at the snaking road as we waited for the post van.

I excitedly ripped the triangular corner off that brown envelope, realising much too late that this particular package had *not* been addressed to Mr. Dave Dog!

Although always careful to keep my nose and tail safe, I am eager to enter these lift machines as they take me to new places on our wonderful adventures.

On one of our holiday adventures, I made my Sue smile by creeping into her wardrobe, taking my paw-print rug and red bag with me. I pulled a funny face when she saw what I had been up to!

Head tilting upwards, my eyes lit up and my mouth started to water when I saw that tasty sausage treat waiting for me… so I opened my mouth slightly, giving an appreciative 'thank you' smile to our waitress.

I dreamt that I was running happily along the magical candle-lit corridor, poking my inquisitive collie nose round the door of any guest whose door was slightly ajar.

'I am looking out towards the horizon, dreaming of future adventures.'

Chapter Six

Postal Dramas

My Sue is always writing letters and I love to go on walks to the postbox with her – albeit at all hours of the day - and night! We send hand-made birthday cards, prizes, or just notes - in order to keep in touch with our much-valued family and friends. We often sign them with Sue's name and my special Dave D. paw-print stamp, the type an already famous author uses in addition to her own signature when signing copies of her own animal-related books. We carry mail to the postbox in my red bag. I eagerly watch for the post van arriving and then know that our mail is safely on its way. Sometimes we wait for a long time, but it is not a problem, especially when we have a good view from the postbox including fields of sheep or the bright, blue sea!

I loved the recent text which Sue received after we had posted one of our lovely human friends a birthday card early, for the following day. It simply said, 'I've received something in the post. It had paw-prints on the back!' This made us smile. I even posted Bosun and Cassie collies some of my own low-fat chews to help them, so that they can be proud of themselves and their humans could be proud of them losing weight, like I did. However, it does not seem entirely fair on us collies when our humans eat all sorts of treats like chocolate fingers and ginger biscuits and we just have low-fat chew treats! Even so, we do realise that it will increase our lifetime if we are an ideal weight.

Back to writing and post... I am usually such a patient boy and I do not frequently tap my Sue with my paw or interrupt as she writes. Occasionally, as you know, I will stretch out my oh so gentle paw, but often just watch her intently and pad over when she calls me as she breaks from her work for time with me. I do admit that very rarely I will stand under the circular pine table and nudge Sue's arm up, up and up again as she tries to type... However, I have come to realise how this means that I then have to wait even longer for my walk, as I cause her fingers to hit the wrong laptop keys, she loses concentration, then has to read her work through again before deleting jumbled parts and re-typing the work! Once, my Dave D paw even tapped her delicate keyboard causing one of those middle buttons to spring off and up into the air, but she has forgiven me, even though the 'k' button still doesn't work very well and keeps falling off or becoming stuck as she types!

I do usually receive lots of welcome attention though, and thrive on this. Sue makes lots of time for play and cuddles in her busy day and I provide a ready supply of paw loves and cold nose nudges. At home we used to have a letter-box mail-catcher, to stop me opening mail that the mail person brought. My friend Albert terrier found the birthday gift which we had sent to him because, although his mum had placed it high up, he had still managed to reach it! When his mum came home he was sitting in his basket in the middle of the wrapping paper with an empty chew packet too. Albert had eaten them all! I am glad that it was not a chocolate gift to his mum from my mum, as it is dangerous for dogs to eat human chocolate, as our bodies cannot break down the ingredients and it can make us unwell.

Unfortunately, our new door has no letter-box and no longer has a large window through which sunlight shines into the hall. Instead, the window is just a small one, as is the rectangle of sunlight for me to lie in. Rona collie's favourite place was also by her home's front door, where she would sit. Nobody could miss her and she would greet visitors as if she were Lady of the Manor. In which case isn't it only right and proper that I now become known as Lord of the Manor when I guard our front door? Even if the postman tiptoes down our path I still hear him, then the rattle as he inserts mail into the wall-box. However, my collie friend Foster, waits for the mail addressed to his Michelle, Jess and Joe, and actually puts his nose under the envelopes as they come through his letter-box in Newport. I went to Foster's house recently and I saw his letter-box, from the outside, where the post person stands. I could just imagine him proudly standing on the other side, nose poised, ready for the eagerly-awaited mail to arrive.

When I hear the mail person's footsteps approaching our door, I bark to let my human mum or dad know. Sometimes, from the kitchen window, we see the postman smiling as he reads the envelopes addressed to 'Mr Dave Dog', and it is these which my Sue allows me to open. I do so excitedly with my paws, like a young puppy, pulling the envelope then biting my way through the paper to find my treasure.

I felt like saying to the postman, "Hello, it is only me, Dave D", after skidding down the hallway in eager collie mode, sliding on the rugs and hitting the door with a thud before I sat down. My Sue has now sensibly, put mat grips under each hall rug to stop me slipping and hurting myself. She has done the same on rugs in our living-room as the laminate floor is much too slippery for me to walk on safely and I could damage my legs if I fall. One day a huge box arrived addressed to my Sue. Much to my dismay, in this instance, as I ripped it open I was far from amused to discover a life-size furry back and white collie toy poking out of this box - seeming to be looking right back at me! It may have only been a toy dog, but it was in my territory. Grrrr!

Sue often looks at beautiful cards with special words inside, which friends have sent to us and which mean so much to my mum, so of course make me happy too. I received my heaviest tuggy for my birthday in the post from our friend in Cornwall, which was so thoughtful. I still love to play with it. She had even ordered it from my old home, the Border Collie Trust G.B. who have a gift shop adjacent to their kennels.

Sometimes we send carefully chosen gifts to our friends. We sent Mum's friend, Jenny, a photograph of me for her birthday and a gift for her baby with my paw prints on. It suited him. They loved it very much. When I met Jacob with his mum and dad, I was a good boy and let him stroke my fur. He held my long lead tightly and seemed to like me.

When we were in Scotland, we looked for collie postcards to send to our treasured friends and we posted them from little postboxes in the country lanes which we found dotted around the islands. I focused intently on the empty lane, and often guarded our mail until the post van arrived, including one of the postcards with a tri-coloured collie on, (even having the same distinctive eyebrows as mine), which we bought in a little gift shop near Dunoon. The rest were written and safely kept in my red travel bag so that they would not blow away.

Additionally, Sue told me that in rural Scotland, sheep usually shelter near the postboxes.... but there did not seem much protection from the wind when I tried sitting next to one! They are not as big as some of the cylindrical postboxes which we have at home, and I almost felt sorry for the Scottish sheep, but not quite... or I would be seen as going soft in my old age!

One particular afternoon whilst on the island of Barra, my Sue took ages wrapping a gift package in our hotel room, and, not unusually, she took a photograph of me next to it. She explained that it was going to be posted in a one of the red mail boxes and would travel across the world to South America, by air-mail on a big aeroplane in the sky. On our travels Sue gave me the package to look after, so that we could post it together, but I could not quite reach the postbox slot, so she put it in my paws ready for another photograph before she actually posted it.

It all happened so quickly... one minute I, Dave D, was there guarding the precious package ready to post and then... I became confused and thought it was like one of those parcels that we receive addressed to Mr. Dave Dog. (Yes, the ones that make our postman back home smile so much!)

Gripping it tightly in my paws, I gleefully prepared my sharp teeth and bit the package hard.

"Stop! Dave D nooooo!"

Mum shouted out as I excitedly ripped the entire corner off her precious envelope in my excitement.

As I dropped the package the brown corner, now separated from its envelope, fell to the ground.

"Oh Dave D!" my mum exclaimed. "That was for the mail-box and not addressed to Mr Dave-Dog this time!"

She ran over to me and we both looked at the torn triangular corner, now lying detached in the long grass. I looked up at her in dismay... but, knowing my worrying temperament, Mum quickly reassured me.

"It's all right Dave D we will ask the lady at the village store for some kind of tape to seal the corner. We can still send the envelope package to Emily and Joshua in Peru today".

This kind lady smiled as Sue explained about me, Dave D, the sometimes cheeky and often hasty collie dog ..... and how I had made a mistake. Thankfully, she gave us lots of sticky tape to repair the envelope and it was soon safely on its way to South America, with a seal of approval from yours truly, Dave Dog! If I ever wanted to travel out of the British Isles, like Millie and Fly collies do with their Kathryn, I would need a special dog passport and lots of extra vaccinations. Assistance dogs are allowed on additional forms of transport with their owner, including in the aircraft cabin on certain approved international routes, whereas non-qualified dogs like me are not.

I listened as the post-office lady told us how in the olden days on a far off, but world-renowned, Scottish island called St. Kilda, they used to light bonfires if there were any emergencies. Passing ships may have seen the smoke and offered assistance. A way to send letters in the days before postal services was by mail-boat. This was not a real boat that sailed to the mainland but it was a floating buoy with a red flag attached. (I was momentarily distracted, thinking about my red travel bag floating ... then, seeing Sue's stern look, dismissed this image and carried on listening!) The 'mail-boat' had a container under it which was often made out of a sheep's stomach for a message to be placed into. I pricked my ears up at the word 'sheep' but had never heard of them being used for this purpose before. It would take about nine days for the mail to reach the Orkney Islands off the far north coast of Scotland. Sometimes it was even carried across the North Sea on the east side to Norway!

I am happy that Sue will be taking me on a ferry from the North Scottish mainland to the Orkney Islands one summer to visit her and Barbara's friend, Pam, who lives there and who also loves animals.....but whom I have not yet met. The ferry journey will only take an hour and a half, which is much more sensible than nine days floating out at sea. Trees did not grow on St. Kilda and very few of the inhabitants could read and write. Actual human visits to the

Scottish mainland from there were not frequent, and the people returned with amazing stories of what they had seen, things which did not exist on their island, such as rabbits, pigs and even bees. I was to experience meeting some of these creatures myself on my own travels. St. Kilda is fifty miles from those main Outer Hebridean islands. In the future, I also hope to visit this famous island on one of those daily boat rides organised from the Isle of Lewis, as we have discovered that there are puffins there which our friend, Jill, adores, these also being the colour of penguins which are my Sue's favourite bird. I will be an ever-so-good boy and not chase the puffins, or even give them my famous collie 'eye'!

In addition to the buoy mail-boat idea, another method of delivering mail from one Scottish island to another was tried over eighty years ago called Rocket Mail. Prior to this experiment, a scientist attempted to convince the general Post Office to try this new method and said that it was viable, by doing a demonstration on the Sussex Downs, near Brighton in the South of England, a place I have still to visit. The mail was fired over a two-mile area successfully with no damage to the letters inside. For the attempt to improve postal communication between the islands of Scarp and Harris, in the Outer Hebrides, a distance of one thousand and six hundred metres, there were one thousand and two hundred envelopes packed in a rocket's fuselage. (My Sue has addressed a lot of envelopes recently, but not so many!) It was meant to deploy an internal parachute with the mail inside. The island of Scarp had sixteen families living there - (and I wondered how many dogs!) - but the bad weather and strong tides often prevented boats landing there with the islanders' mail. At the first attempt the rocket and contents exploded on launch! Some of the envelopes from inside were recovered, packed into a second rocket and enclosed. Three days later a second attempt was made to fire the mail across the sea to Harris. Again the rocket exploded and it is thought that this was due to the wrong type of fuel being used. I bet that any unfortunate sheep who heard it were shocked. I would have barked and chased the rocket to where it landed - but not damaged any remaining mail with my paws or teeth. The envelopes recovered this time were singed and some are now on display in Scarp's museum. At least the corners were not torn off by a confused collie's teeth like the corner of my Sue's envelope to Peru was!

My mum's friend, Sharon, has a collie boy too and his name is Toby. Back in Staffordshire, little did we know that that the very same day that Sue and I had to run after our local postman to give him a ball-shaped parcel for our friend - because it had been much too wide to fit through the postbox slot - Toby had his very own post van and man encounter - three hundred miles north!

We had been somewhat worried that our post van man had not put our big parcel into his postman sack as he just threw it in the back of his van... but then we received a text from Toby's mum which made us laugh, and caused my Sue to say, "Oh! Toby, you are funny!"

Toby often looked out and tried to see the postman. This particular afternoon, as their postman was emptying the red mail box, he had left his van door open. Toby, who had been walking on his long lead just ahead of his mum, suddenly jumped right into the red van, standing in the middle of all the mail sacks! Toby's postman found it very funny and responded,

"I always said I was Postman Pat but I will be different and have a black and white dog instead of a cat."

Blushing slightly, Toby's mum quickly apologised and pulled him out of the van, then continued on their walk. He had often poked his nose into the red mail box as he passed when the post person was collecting letters, but this was the first time he had actually leapt into a van! I have been on many adventures but still never in the back of a mail van, although I bet that Toby has never been on the back of a big red tractor as I now have on my own adventures! This did in fact give me the idea of leaping into an open workman's van myself later in our North Wales adventures, to shelter from the rain and to escape a pesky dog! Likewise, Buddy-collie had jumped into a car through a door which had been left open whilst the driver went to a cash point in the rain! On that occasion, I bet that man had such a shock to find a wet collie sitting, peering at him from the driver's seat when he returned to his car.

In a similar way, it was not only me and Buddy who ventured into the safety of a stranger's vehicle on their walk. When Tilly collie was younger her mum, Anne, took her for a long walk to the local recreation ground and when they got there Tilly was more than a little tired. In the distance was an old house and when she gathered her strength Tilly saw two 'suited and booted' people emerge from the building and go towards their car. The unknown humans stood talking over the roof of the car - which had both of its front doors open. Tilly must have loved travelling in cars like I do because she suddenly made a bolt for it - with her mum chasing after her and calling for her to come back. The lively collie ran straight up to that stranger's car and jumped in - then sat on the back seat as if to say, "Give me a lift home". She wouldn't get out at first, so one of the humans opened the back door and then Tilly promptly got out, but then went straight back in the front way again! This happened a few times until the little collie's mum managed to get her lead on and start walking away - but the collar came off over her head and Tilly's mum soon realised that her mischievous collie had gone back and entered the car again! Fortunately, the well-dressed people were very understanding and didn't mind Tilly's fur on their seats!

Chapter Seven

Collie Therapy

I had not been used to love and affection, so Sue learned not to envelope me in a hug at first, as it made me feel restricted and I would not stay still, due to needing to be free to leap up quickly if a dog approached. Instead, I have now learned to relax enough to roll over and cuddle up to my Sue, her brothers, and her family when they invite me to lie or sit next to them. I have to admit that I feel most comfortable like this with just one human arm round me, as I still feel free. Now I even flop over on my back to have my soft, white tummy fur rubbed, whereas before I would growl if anyone even touched me near my tail or lower back. It took Sue time to recognise my funny ways and to let me show affection in my own time. Now nothing beats a full doggy back rub from my Sue. Remember that it is good for you humans too as it slows your pulse and lowers your own blood pressure.

Now, I also frequently sit up and put my two front paws on my Sue's legs lovingly when I want some cuddles or to make her smile, even if she has just gone into the kitchen to make some human drinks. I also let her burrow her face in my soft fur, and curl up next to her on the settee.

The first time my Sue met me she noticed my fine jaw, my wide set brown eyes and that I also had a very runny nose. Being somewhat concerned, she had asked the rescue centre staff if I was unwell. Sue was very aware that some collies are prone to hip dysplasia, eye problems or skin allergies but they reassured her that I was in good health but maybe had just a slight chill. Years later, Sue often puts her soft hand on my nose to check that it is wet and cold like it should be, as this indicates to her that I am healthy. Sometimes I put a big paw on Sue's own nose, but am not quite as gentle and may take her by surprise, often whacking her unintentionally. My own nose tip is in fact kept wet by glands inside. This fluid catches scent molecules and helps me to detect odours.

Paw loves are what I give to humans who I feel at ease with - or who seem to look sad, and are when I rest one caring paw - or both - on their hand, knee, shoulder, or leg, with a loving expression. The first time that my Sue saw me sit up on my two back legs and put my two paws onto a human's lap, in a Dave D 'paw love', was two weeks after she had made that donation to the Border Collie Trust G.B., signed for me and given me my new home. We were on a steam train adventure together, high up in the Welsh mountains, and an elderly couple had kept looking at me, then made a fuss of me. Sue had watched me with revelation, amazement and also pride for her new collie boy. People are important to me because, although I have a genuine fear of other dogs, I feel close to humans and like to show this. In a funny Dave D thinking-process kind of way, it makes up for my nervous times, as it shows I am friendly for the majority of the time.

On walks and journeys I admit to still frequently looking around for other potential triggers - dogs in close proximity - but now we do not need to change routes as frequently to avoid them. Indeed, in addition, I have gained so much more confidence in myself, no longer constantly either averting my eyes when I see another dog, or staring, nor becoming shaky, but, in contrast, often standing up strong and tall on my four legs, or even up on my back two legs, to gain a better view when I am out and about. I therefore look and feel much more in control. Sue agrees with our dear friend's comment that "Dave Dog looks like a human when he stands up on his two legs" - as when I enthusiastically looked through the hotel room window at our ferry - which had just brought us on that long five-hour voyage from the western Scottish mainland to my dog-friendly hotel bedroom in Castlebay in the Outer Hebrides. The view was totally awesome and I am fast becoming an experienced traveller.

Sue says that I have the power to pick people up when they are down. When she seems sad, I look closely at her with my concerned, loving eyes under my distinctive eyebrows, as I have from the beginning of our lifetime of adventures, willing her to understand and to believe me as I try to tell her that she will be fine.

"It is all right my Sue, I am here, no matter what is wrong, I can make it better, I am your Dave D."

At such times, I gently nudge under her arm again and again with my whole head until she realises I am there and pulls me into a double cuddle, then relaxes. Words are not necessary. Like the companionship between true human friends, it is a quiet, comfortable silence where no words are needed. I look and see her smile, knowing that I have succeeded in what I aimed to accomplish. I so love to see my Sue smile as it makes my Dave D heart so happy. When animal and humans connect, the match feels perfect. We love ceaselessly.

I do have my complete past fixed in my head, which is what still affects me, but I do like the present better. More importantly, I am trying to make quicker progress and to move forward more and more. I am not too clingy and do not follow Sue from room to room, although I do actually go to check where my Sue is if she leaves the room, but also return to my bed once I have checked.

Sue had no experience of a nervous collie until she met me. We are a good team, although understandably, she found it difficult at times because of her responsibility to do right by me when she was not sure how to. I am grateful to those who have shared constructive, non-critical advice to assist Sue, enabling her to help me. Those who have experienced similar collies, or who know me, realise that I am not troubled and stand-offish for most of the time. It is true that not having been socialised has not helped my confidence, but they recognise that, though anxious about strange dogs, I am also full of personality and eager to receive affection. As you know, I love to roll over and for a human to rub my furry belly, or to give my famous heart-melting paw loves, guaranteed to bring a smile to even the saddest face.

I love it when humans look me in the eye and tell me what a handsome boy I am. I was not used to such fine compliments. I now visit pubs, both inside and outside, and I always seem to make new friends. Customers even jump off their bar stool seats to greet me! Sometimes, when they know that we will be in Manchester, our friends, Karen, Andy, Dee and Dave wear hats and gloves to sit outside in the cold with Sue and I enjoying refreshments at designated tables - because some of the cafes are not dog-friendly inside. I love them very much for accepting me as part of Sue's life and making me part of their own lives too.

In addition, I so love the times when my Sue and I meet our friends and go on walks. Isaac and Sam from Lancashire play football with me in places away from other dogs and make a fuss of me. Such times are great fun and, being a polite boy, I always give them my paw to say 'thank you' afterwards - or when we meet again. I often wish I always had that same confidence and relaxed stance with fellow dogs. Sam even gave me a surprise football gift which I carried to Sue's car with immense collie pride. However, she had to help me in, because my usual gap between her driver's seat and my back seat was not wide enough for me to squeeze through with the ball in my mouth! She then clipped me in safely, with the seatbelt attached to my harness as usual. On our journey, I even used my new football toy as a kind of cushion!

My green harness matches my tough football - but I have a new red collar and a lead with a cushioned handle to match, too. I also have a bone-shaped tag which my friend kindly made for me, with my name and number on. I used to wear two tags but the sound of them jangling was not pleasing to my sensitive ears, so I now just have one and the other is in a musical-box for safe keeping. I have my collar on when out walking or travelling, but Sue is cautious and usually removes this when we arrive home, as I feel more comfortable without it and this also prevents it catching on any of the furniture and possibly hurting me.

On my trip to Berkshire, our dear friend Marilyn was once minding me whilst mum was out, but she was not used to dogs wearing harnesses. As she held it up for me I placed my head through obediently, despite it actually being inside out! On her return, my Sue found me looking quite comical - still wearing my inside-out harness - as the neighbours must have too! I liked it when they laughed because it made me happy too.

Nevertheless, I feel such a lucky boy when we pass other humans and they see how proud and handsome I look, walking beside Sue, with my self-manicured nails clicking gently on the paving stones. That day was no different. I give contented sighs as I recognise such a contrast to my previous life where I felt such a plain, unloved, misunderstood and lonely Dave D collie so much of the time.

Upon seeing me in my green harness, people often ask Sue if I am a guide dog or hearing dog or assistance dog. She is sometimes tempted to say 'yes', so that we can obtain entry into establishments that only allow working dogs in, but of course she does not! However, I do guide her when she is holding my lead but not concentrating - and maybe even texting as we walk - so she needs a gentle tug from her Dave D on the other end of the lead to prevent her from walking into a lamppost or signpost!

Although not an official therapy or animal assistance dog, my Sue does have permission to take me to such as certain housing accommodation residences to see friends like my human friend Bobbie, who always makes me so welcome. I have to sit on a seat in the dark-red carpeted corridor near to her flat instead of going inside, so that her Jack-cat cannot see me. I bet that he can hear me and smell me outside his home door though! I am glad that his friendly mum is always so happy to see me and enjoys my paw loves. I bring happiness to others too, visiting care homes where more humans enjoy speaking to me and fussing me. In Manchester, I always look at mum's face for the signal, then make my way along that familiar paved route to the tranquillity of a care-home opposite the park after our walk. I am delighted when Sue rings the bell, and one of their friendly carers or residents opens the door. Even so, I try not to run through the door to see Tommy and his friends, in case I make them jump, although I have won them over and broken through many silent barriers.

These human friends have started to trust, to make eye contact and to say my name, to reach out and stroke my soft fur. Tommy is eighty years old and always asks, '"How is Dave D?" when he telephones us. He used to be nervous of me, my energy, and my tapping collie paws, so I just sit next to him and look up with my big, brown eyes until he feels confident enough to stroke me or to invite me to give him my paw. I may also rest my head on his knee and let him scratch my head or under my chin. I am not so much seeking attention as helping comfort humans, some of whom have no family of their own. This visit helps my socialisation too and lowers dog blood pressures and feelings of calm, as well as human blood pressure, like a Dave D healing power... but really it is a stress-busting enzyme commonly released through stroking an animal like me - or a cat! Last time, their carer smiled acknowledging how I blended so well into their rug as I lay down, it being the same lime-green and black with white, as my harness!

One day I leapt up and unintentionally, did make everyone jump after seeing what I thought was a green toy wedged under their living room door. Due to this, I pawed it out and flicked it into the air before it came to rest on Tommy's dressing-gown covered knee! My Sue came over to see what on earth I had found, before apologising and gently removing the frog-shaped wedge from where it had landed... then returning it to its rightful place under the door, which made everyone laugh! With this exception, it is also good to see my Sue sit still a while and have a rest from driving me round so much of the British Isles on our adventures! In the same way, Sue comforts me and soothes me when she realises that I need human strokes. As you know, I love to feel Sue's calm contact and to see that smile as it makes my Dave D heart truly happy too.

In Criccieth, I recently made a new friend called Mark, who needs a special wheelchair. I sat up on my back legs on the cold pavement, and placed both of my front legs on the left handle of his electric chair to say, "Hi". I was happy when I heard Mark say that he hopes to give a home to a 'rescue dog', because Mark has a kind face like Sue, and I know that any dog will be lucky to go home with him. Some dogs learn the tug command for a reason beyond playing. They help their masters or mistresses to open doors or cupboards and cabinets using special attachments like short ropes fastened to the door handle. They are trained to shut doors too, or even to unload washing-machines and bring items for their owner when asked to. Brushing their dog also aids human arm movement and I love my mum grooming me with even two or three strokes, but these masters may do twenty brush stokes each side of their dog to strengthen their arm muscles. Such are known as Assistance dogs and they are very clever, because they also learn to help their human undress and to tug their socks off. When my friend, Elwood spaniel pulls socks off the clothes line and makes holes in them, before abandoning them under the garden shrubbery, this is not helpful. In contrast, Shadow collie's daughter, Annie collie, is helpful to her Des, as she actually takes both of her dad's socks off his feet before he goes to bed! Eager for his walk, Robbie-collie would stand by the side of his mum's bed in the morning with her bed sheet in his mouth. He would tug at this sheet to make her arise from bed and if she did not, he would actually rip the sheet! I have never ripped a bed sheet and I let my mum's alarm clock wake her up each morning, but, as she puts her feet onto the bedside rug, I happily hear her - and she can then hear my divulging tail thumping loudly - but automatically, as she approaches the other room - where I have been asleep on my own dog-bed and waiting for our usual precious morning cuddles.

In a more cunning way, while his dad was in the other room watching television, the cheeky cat, who is called Beethoven Jones, pulled his master's kitchen cupboard door open by placing his small, furry paw underneath one corner, then knocking his own cat biscuits box out with a bang! Hearing a crash, his caring dad came running in and found the open cupboard, cat biscuits all over the floor, and crafty Beethoven eating them. I would have glared at that mischievous cat if I had seen him behaving in this way! Now his dad has put child locks on three of their kitchen doors! My own biscuits are kept on the kitchen worktop, so I can quite easily reach them if I stand on my back legs, although to be honest there was once a whole tray of cooked sausages left on top of the cooker and I could easily have reached these too - but I had already eaten and, being a considerate collie, I knew that if I did take these my Sue would not have any food for her own tea.

Toby terrier from near Blackburn is also clever because he goes round the house opening every cupboard door and other doors including the washer, dryer and even the freezer with his nose and paws. If there are any clothes in the washing machine he pulls them out and leaves them on the floor in a pile, but he also actually takes food out of the freezer, lines it up in a row on the kitchen floor and lets it defrost, but does not eat any! However, the main problem is that his mum, Jan, does not need them opening, or any items removed, as Toby does this when she leaves the house! I do not open cupboards or any doors, but I do make strange noises, tap the glass, then try my best to nudge the patio door open, in order to go back into our house if Sue has not seen me waiting patiently after I have been out in the garden.

Some assistance dogs are trained as Reading dogs. They actually go into schools regularly to help children by calmly allowing them to stroke them as they sit so patiently, focusing and listening to the children read - like Polo collie, who lived near to Durham did. Her mum's friend brought her grand-daughter, Summer, round to let Polo into the garden, whilst her mum, Sharon, was away for the day. When her friend went outside, the little girl was sitting on a bistro chair with Polo lying on the decking next to her, reading her book to the attentive collie. Polo kept looking at Summer as if she was listening to the story. Such opportunities to read to one of us dogs can give children confidence, help them to relax and increase fluency, by taking the pressure off reading to an adult. This is part of each selected school student's therapy.

Recently, Sue had to reflect on how good I also am on visits to busy places, as it was a hot day, so she would not leave me in the car or hotel but needed to go to a meeting. Upon plucking up courage to ask the lady if I could be taken into the meeting hall as well - (with me by her side, looking up with my cutest Dave D expression!) - Sue was told that she could take her 'collie' in, too, as long as he was 'quiet'. I smiled to myself and caught my Sue smiling too, as we both knew that the most 'disruption' I would cause would be to give half the humans in the room my gentle paw loves!

It was in this same meeting where I had been lying on the floor, and on my best behaviour, that my attention was caught by the male speaker saying that humans had been 'running round chasing their tails'. I had kept quiet, yet was full of amusement, firstly as I seriously did not know at that stage that humans even had tail bones under their skin, and secondly as this conjured up an image of all the humans at that meeting running round the hall with long, bushy tails like mine attached firmly to their rear ends! He was also speaking about heads and tails, lost sheep and other lost items, which reminded me of the sheep outside and how mum had lost more than one of my leads! Interestingly, I have since learnt how my Sue's human ancestors allegedly had tails but that when they started walking upright, their long tails shrank to just the tail bone under their skin! I am very glad and that my fine collie tail does not shrink when I stand upright!

My friend, Sammi-dog, in Salford is also a very good boy at meetings that he goes to with his mum, Margaret, and he sits quietly like I do. He does not like to be separated from his loving mum. However, I doubt that I would be able to sit as silently as he does if I had gone to the same Photography Club meeting, which Stephen organises, the reason being that I now have the tendency to frequently bark each time I see a camera, much to my Sue's dismay - although she always apologises for me politely and people seem to understand! I know that Stephen enjoys seeing the photographs of me on my travels, so I am sure that he would have still thought that I was a good boy... most of the time!

Collie therapy is a well-known medicine. Whisky the collie from Derby looks very much like me in his markings. In fact we could almost be twins! His mum, Julie, loves her collie therapy hugs now, but first met Whisky as she visited that same Staffordshire rescue centre where my Sue found me, in the little village, not far from where she lives. At the rescue centre office, Julie and her friend looked in a regularly updated book at the photographs and information on collies there, before asking to see three of these collies. However, Julie did not feel in her heart that either of the first two were right for her. Whisky was the third collie brought out and although, like me, he looked older than on his photograph they went for a walk round the rescue centre fields together. In fact his human mum remembers him dragging her round! He must have needed a harness like I do. (The rescue centre's harnesses are usually kept hooked on the top of certain dogs' kennel doors, as mine had been.) It was a warm day, so they both sat on a bench like my Sue and I used to. They looked at each other as we had done too. Each time Julie smiled, Whisky wagged his tail. I have always loved to see my Sue smile at me and I wag my tail too. Whisky then went 'belly up' and showed Julie how friendly he was, like I do, to make Sue laugh. Whisky went home with Julie and she became his new mum. Many years on, the way he makes his mum smile keeps her going no matter what each day brings; he is her rock, as my Sue tells me that I am hers. We often pass each other on collie walk meet ups. I look but I control myself, so I do not growl, as he is our friend.

Likewise, Meg collie in Kings Norton is also super-fabulous because no matter how her mum feels, no matter what kind of a day she has had, when Beth-Louise looks at Meg she can't help but smile. Meg is her mum's natural collie therapy and she loves her so much for this as, indeed, so many other collie owner mums and dads love, and are always made to feel better by, their own collie's loving doggy expressions and antics.

Chapter Eight

Hiding, Hotel Fun, Blankets and Dreams.

I am ever such a happy and lucky collie boy whose life has changed so much since I found my Sue. I have loved the dog-friendly hotels which she has taken me to - including one half-way up a real cliff in Saltburn-by-the-Sea - and the cosy rooms within these places, which we have discovered around the British Isles. I had not realised that dogs could go into hotels, and had certainly never been in one or inside any kind of metal box to reach higher floors in a building before. I used to see this thing as a moving box that seemed to travel through the air with a *swoosh* sound, before arriving in a different place. Early on in my Dave D adventures, I worked out that this form of transport was called a 'lift' because as we wandered the many unfamiliar hotel corridors with their numerous doors, my Sue was always saying to me,

"Oh, Dave D where is the lift?!"

I now know that the strange lift doors open when humans press buttons, and creatures like me have to walk in quickly so the door does not shut on our precious tail. I have to admit that I am fascinated by the buttons, always eager to enter and wait patiently for Sue to press one so that I can see the bright lights. During such times, I also notice shadows both on the lift floor and walls on the way in and when inside! They remind me of shadows and torchlight which Sue always tries to distract me from becoming obsessed by! I stand sensibly and in no time at all, the door opens and I am in a new place! I always look forward to the door opening, being constantly alert and eager to begin a new adventure. To be more precise, lifts are like magic boxes without big car wheels and we often find these boxes on adventures where we stay over.

One rainy afternoon, our train broke down near York. I had been ever so comfortable sitting under the carriage table next to my red travel bag, stretched out with my head on Sue's foot. I had just eaten my healthy tea so was letting it go down and digest before I tried my luck jumping off the floor onto one of the patterned train seats! I was none too happy when a strange voice seemed to come through the train ceiling which caused Sue to start packing my food and water bowls away, then explain to me that we were no longer on a 'direct' train to Manchester! I soon replaced my disappointment with a Dave D smile as I watched with great amusement when my Sue quickly tried to tip the remains of my full water bowl back into the narrow topped plastic bottle to save it for the next part of the journey! In addition to going down her best clothes, I was a little concerned that some water had gone on the train carpet, in case the guard thought that I had made the 'mess'... and that it was not just water!

Having packed and left the broken-down train, we, and many other passengers, had to go along a dark passage with a tiny lift at the end to reach a different platform for a replacement train. We were told that there were no stairs - which we found very strange. I am happy in lifts or on stairs but it is easier for Sue in a lift with all our bags. Many people had children and prams and some were scared of lifts. One little girl was crying, so my Sue looked at the child's mum for permission and pointed me out to the little girl, gently reassuring her that Dave D collie was also standing in the lift and safe. Sue told her that I was fine and that she would be too. I gave the tearful girl my most loving, concerned look, followed by a single clumsy paw love; thankfully, despite the fact that she had been so tearful, the small child stopped crying, became calmer and stroked my soft fur until the heavy lift-door opened, announcing our arrival.

However... when we were in Scotland, Sue talked about a time, on a different holiday, many years ago, when she had hidden in the huge wardrobe at a bed and breakfast place - where they had arrived by mistake and the lady had not been very friendly! There had been a very noisy little white dog on a sun lounger in the garden, barking loudly, and no sheets or blankets on the beds! I bet I would have hated it too as the yapping sheep-colour dog would have made me nervous. No wonder that Sue and her mum did not want to stay there for a whole night!

Therefore, they had decided not to check-in, so it had been necessary to secretly ring another hotel-type place nearer to the mountains, from the most sound-proof place she could find... in a walk-in wardrobe! I bet that noisy dog could still be heard faintly even from inside that furniture! After emerging from there, they quietly grabbed their bags to make their escape... not remembering that there was noisy gravel on the driveway! I could have hidden in that big wardrobe too, but truthfully, am so glad that I was not there as I would have been so nervous of that dog, and would possibly have hurt my paw pads running down that potentially sharp gravel path so quickly. Surprisingly, they managed to hail a cab straight away, which may not have been as easy with a Dave D collie as part of the package! As if by magic, half an hour later they were at a new hotel, high up a steep lane, overlooking the high mountains and a midnight blue loch! It was like something out of a dream or fairy tale, my mum explained, as they gazed at this beautiful view from their bedroom window. I visualised it and, from what they described, would have loved to have stood tall on my hind legs, resting my paws on their window ledge, to look out of that window, too - as you will discover that I often do from our hotel rooms during my travels up and down the British Isles!

Once, when we were at home, packing to go to our own next holiday place, I decided to show my Sue how silly she must have looked, sitting in a wardrobe, and crept into her own wardrobe, taking my harness, blanket and lead with me! That made her laugh and I love to see my Sue happy. Interestingly, collies Cassie in Wolverhampton and Mist near Stranraer, both like to actually make their beds in wardrobes, too! Following this, I did once surprise my Sue, causing her to jump, by making loud, unusual scratchy noises with my nails. Upon investigating, she found a big Dave D collie hiding amidst the garments in her new wooden wardrobe, peering up at her from between these clothes! In spite of this, I do prefer my bed on the floor!

Another time I tugged my blanket somewhere was the time that Sue decided to work in our garden all day, then to even continue gardening, late into the night! As dusk fell and darkness covered the garden, she was still planting pretty flowers. It was rather chilly, even with my fur coat on, and I had been such a patient boy, but I decided it was time to go inside. I had deliberately not given her my paw or nudged her while she was so busy. A kind friend had given my mum forget-me-not seeds in memory of her previous dog, Lucky, and she was making a pretty new flower area, so I considerately left my Sue alone with her thoughts and trotted into our home.

Having arrived inside our bungalow, and looking round at the bare wooden floor with its empty space, I remembered that Sue had not brought my basket, blanket and cushion back in from the garden, so I padded quietly back outside to find them. There they were, still on the patio, now in darkness! I did try to drag my entire plastic dog basket in with my strong Dave D teeth, but it was somewhat bulky and I was not able to manage it.

Sue laughed and praised me an hour or so later, when she finally finished gardening near midnight, went back indoors and saw my solution! There I was curled up all snug and warm, just on my paw-print blanket that I had been successful in pulling all the way from the garden to my special place inside. I opened one collie eye in acknowledgement as she praised me,

"Oh, Dave D I am sorry, you must have been a tired boy... and you were very clever to think of that. Well done!"

It had reminded Sue of when she used to walk a friend's little black and white terrier called Tina, who had a clear heart-shaped marking on her right side. Tina had been lying down on the beach, looking after Sue's clothes, towel and flip flops whilst Sue had been swimming at Black Rock Sands. Unknown to Sue, the tide had come in, covering her belongings, so clever Tina had been busy running in and out of the seawater retrieving one item at a time and dragging it up the beach to the safety of the dry sand - before returning into the sea on her little legs to rescue another of Sue's clothes or items. Quite a crowd of onlookers had gathered to admire the little dog's actions and seeing Tina dragging her towel out of the sea, Sue had been so very proud of her.

In my case, I had carried my blanket in from the garden to form a temporary bed and I had felt so proud and clever, as my Sue gave me a treat, before going out into the garden to collect my basket. Back in its rightful place, I watched as she lovingly placed my cushion and blankets inside my basket, before I jumped in... soon closing both my sleepy eyes and wondering what varied adventures the next day would bring.

A further time around midnight, Sue wrapped her tiger-print car blanket round me after our red car broke down on a motorway and a lady on the orange roadside phone had told us not to stay in the car to wait for the qualified mechanic to come and mend it for us, as it was not a safe place. It felt strange, as my mum had taken me from what had actually felt much more safe, familiar, cosy and warm - because I had been lying on my paw-print cushion behind her seat. She unclipped the seat-belt from my harness and led me to the side of the busy road. We had to climb over the metal barrier onto the grassy hill, and it was so noisy as the big lorries and cars thundered past, their engine and turning wheels sounds amplifying in my sensitive collie ears as we sat, huddled under the blanket, keeping warm together - like at home when our heating boiler broke down!

Knowing that I must have looked comical in my rug head-dress, as we waited at the roadside for the mechanic to arrive, I looked at my Sue and noticed she also looked a bit different. I was not quite sure why at first, so, seeing my puzzled expression, she tickled my velvety ear and explained to me that she had tucked her long hair into her collar as she felt that it would be less obvious to drivers passing by that she was a lady alone in the dark. She was not fully alone, as I was with her, but I still understood her concern.

Tiger Vision and Midnight Fiasco

In this next tale it was that very same car blanket that we took to Scotland and mum put round me in our hotel room to warm me after we had been for a walk in the pouring rain. My Sue had then gone down to the hotel reception, leaving me with her own mum, but missing her, I had decided to go in search of Sue, so had made my way towards the closed door... causing her mum to suddenly cry out in surprise! Out of the corner of her eye she had noticed movement, and, on looking up from the book she was reading, she had seen the back of my tiger blanket going round the corner as I slunk off, dragging it behind me, giving the impression, for one second, that a young tiger had suddenly appeared in our room!

That hotel was amazing. Earlier, I had trotted into the bar wide-eyed, bushy-tailed and ever so proudly, being fully aware that many already checked-in residents were noticing my handsome Dave D cuteness and long collie legs as we strolled through. Some had been watching sports on television but I managed to distract most of them! Still in my smart black raincoat, with little fasteners, I then peered round the corner, smiling, to make my Dave D presence known to readers in a well-stocked library there. An old couple, who were sitting together on a velvet couch, acknowledged me, so I sat up in front of them and gave them a quick paw love each. All the time I was hoping, deep down, that one day they may read about themselves in my Dave D's Diary.

Upon arriving at the Ayr hotel's Reception area, I cast my eyes over a high, wooden modern-style desk, and could just see a pretty lady's head peeping over the top to greet us. She came round to the front of her desk and fussed me, while my Sue looked on proudly, and told us about her own much-loved dog. Although having a kind voice, I was glad that her dog was not there with her! I felt relaxed and wanted to stay that way, for my sake and for Sue's.

When the reception lady showed us to our bedroom, it was beyond even my wildest Dave D hopes and expectations! As she opened the door of room twelve, to my utter amazement, directly in front of my nose - and most unusually - were three beds, side-by-side, all smelling of clean, fresh linen! When the lady had left us, Sue and her mum were giggling at the unexpected sight of an extra bed, with Sue then commenting,

"They have even given us a real bed for Dave D!"

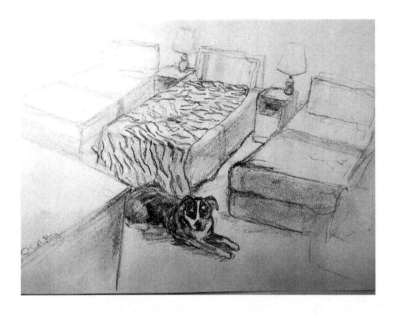

I felt so highly honoured, but, glancing at Sue's mum's expression, I realised that I would never be allowed to sleep *on* this hotel bed! Sue put my red bag next to that 'spare' middle bed and my tiger blanket actually on the bed, in case I jumped on it in my excitement... but I knew better than that. In hotels, I have been trained to sleep in a provided basket or on my fleecy floor cushion next to Sue's bed - and prefer to sleep there anyway, where it is cooler.

Of course, we were delighted to discover tea and shortbread for the humans and water and a dog biscuit for me. I am now aware that human biscuits are not good for me, and the hotel staff must have known this too. As I have learnt from the healthy nutrient e-mails which Sue receives and reads to me, too much cheese is not good for me either, as just two ounces of cheddar cheese are the human calorie equivalent of three hamburgers or three bars of hundred gram chocolate!

With it being a stormy night, when it was walk time again, it felt necessary for Sue to dress me in my black, waterproof coat with fleece hoodie-like collar once more to keep me dry. This coat is our treasured gift from Jack collie's mum, Hazel. He was a very clever and intelligent boy like me and Jack also loved to play on the beach in Criccieth, North Wales, like I do.

Once again, Sue had deliberately walked me through the hotel's bar instead of the main exit, raising yet more smiles from the other residents in there, as I trotted through on my way to the beach! The rain had stopped, but Mum kept my coat on to save her carrying it -

and admittedly because I also looked so cute! The seemingly gigantic moon lit up that exquisite, sandy beach, and my mum told me how she was looking forward to us meeting Charlotte and her collie, Style, next day. Charlotte comes from the Isle of Arran between Ayrshire and the Mull of Kintyre, an island where my adventures have not yet taken me, but one which I very much hope to visit one day. I decided to put on my brave Dave D face and gave Sue a huge grin, eyeing my red bag, where I knew that my muzzle was waiting - although I was aware that Style would be wearing a muzzle too, so I would be safe. Sue unclipped my red lead, being careful to put it into her own raincoat pocket so that she would not lose it! Our footprints and paw prints merged in the sand as we walked together, breathing in the fresh sea air. It was so peaceful with not a human or dog in sight except for my Sue and me.

Returning to our hotel, Sue decided to use the guest computer to post photographs of me on my adventures. However, it was broken and would not let us online. I was not too down-hearted as it can become tedious waiting for ages whilst mum taps away and shares my photographs. I know she is proud of me though, so I am usually a patient boy. Nevertheless, I do sometimes roll my eyes when it reaches midnight at home and I am still waiting for my walk - but she is still marking books for her students! That was why I was so glad it was holiday time and all thoughts of students' books were just in my head and a distant memory.

In this instance, the kindly hotel porter suggested that Sue use the main reception computer while he cleaned the bar. I was worried as I was not sure that this was a good idea, with it surely being against the hotel's company policies. My fears were heightened as the man added that it "would be fine as long as the Manager did not come down", and for my Sue to "just check-in any guests if they arrive" while she was there! My Dave D intuition told me that this may *not* be a good idea, although Sue's instinct seemed to be to 'carry on regardless' and to make the most of the gesture which would still allow us to share our latest adventures with our friends! I was worried that we would get into trouble and knew that Sue would not want to get the kind man into bother either, but she still longed to post my collie photographs! Her determined mind seemed made up.

Gratefully, Sue slid behind the tall reception desk, taking me with her, and onto the pretty lady's empty chair. I lay on the hard floor, peeping round the desk corner, as if on guard, pretending to be a real live collie watch-dog, but looking out for people, not sheep or other dogs, like I did with Alfie on the ferry! My Sue tapped the computer keyboard with her fingers. How I wished I could use my own Dave D paws to do the same and have my very own D.D password which would probably and most appropriately be *DaveDadventurer1*.

As I waited for Sue to finish her posting, my mind recalled many of my collie acquaintances. I remembered how Sky collie, who joins our collie walks on Seaham beach with Bobby collie, and their dad, Gordon, had actually been given permission to be at Gordon's office desk and on the computer - placing an intelligent paw on its controller! Sky's baby son, Hemp collie, is also permitted to sleep in the blue chair which is in his human dad's business reception area.

I have had permission to go for a drive to visit the outside of my Sue's classroom building where she works, but reflected how Jet collie's dad, James, had left his room for just a few minutes and returned to discover Jet sat on the couch with his paw on the laptop mouse-pad staring at the screen, without permission! Lady collie, in Evesham, climbs on her dad, Stephen's hand and taps his fingers with her paw to try to stop him using his telephone keypad.

Just after midnight, with Sue still tapping away at the keyboard, I was brought back to reality, as I heard the distinctive sound of footsteps approaching from outside. As quick as a flash, my ears went up when I suddenly heard the jangle of metal on metal. I feared that it may be a lead with another dog on the end arriving. Heart pounding as that sound echoed across the hotel's courtyard, I strained at my lead, which Sue had looped round her ankle! My body tensed and I prepared to investigate. The heavy front door creaked open, with which I felt a sharp tug on my lead, as Sue pulled me fully behind the reception desk - nearly falling off her four-wheeled chair in the process - and ducked down! She did look funny! We hid and waited silently, her finger gently resting on my wet nose to stop me barking, until the footsteps sounded lighter on the thick carpet and were soon distant. My Sue then logged out of the hotel computer before we both raced along the corridor and up the many stairs to our triple-bed hotel room, Sue giggling and me doing my Dave D grin, to tell her mum all about the drama! What is she like? Never a dull moment on our adventures!

I slept well, but morning came all too soon. After washing my bowl out and giving me a drink of fresh water, I was pleasantly surprised when Sue and her mum prepared to take me downstairs to join them for breakfast! I did recall being privileged enough to be allowed into a breakfast room, once before when we had been staying at our Hartlepool hotel. That time, our friends Stacey and James had kindly given us a lift there after the Seaham walk, but I had been wary of being in the same car as their collie, Rover, although he respectfully stayed away from me, as he must have been able to tell that I was a nervous boy. That time, I felt honoured as we had spent a relaxing night and, instead of leaving me alone with just her jacket for comfort whilst she went for breakfast, my Sue had fastened my lead on and taken me to the dining-room. My nails had clipped on the polished floor and I knew that Sue may worry as she puts those special rug grips on our floor at home so that I cannot slip. I reached our table without mishap and lay down, but looked up alertly and with doggy amazement when the gentleman owner brought a menu and told mum that I, Dave the dog, could order too! Casting my eyes towards that menu, I was impressed! (As was my Sue judging from the look on her own face!)

Back to our Ayr hotel and again I was amused to see that the kind lady had set us up a special table, so that I could sit with my two humans downstairs, for breakfast. (I bet she would have been surprised if she knew that I had been behind her desk in the early hours of that morning!) Other guests in reception said I looked cute as I gave an elderly man my best paw loves. I felt a particularly proud boy, as I would usually have still been waiting quietly in the hotel bedroom for Sue to bring me a tiny piece of sausage that she had sneaked up for me in a serviette!

This time I looked up eagerly at the menu and was surprised when Sue said I was allowed a rest from my diet for my 'wee treat' as the waitress called it. The waitress had sad eyes, as she explained that she was remembering her own dog back in France with her parents. I gave the lady my paw on her apron, hoping that it would make her feel somewhat better, in however small a way. Next, my eyes lit up and my mouth started to water, when I looked up and saw a *whole* sausage treat waiting for me on a separate plate next to my Sue's. I opened my mouth slightly, showing my white teeth as a Dave D sort of 'thank you' smile to our kind waitress.

I remembered my manners and did not jump up at the dining-room table. Acknowledging this, Sue lowered a red serviette with my sausage on it, onto the floor next to me and I ate it all up, savouring the taste. A welcome change from the low-free treats and low-fat biscuit dog food which my vet has put me on!

The day before this adventure started, I had made a new friend when we had just arrived in Penrith, on the fringe of the Lake District. He is a human called Oliver. He also has weigh-ins like I do and was actually on his way there that day, so only had time to make a quick fuss of me. My Sue took our photograph and suggested that he may like to keep-up-to date with my travels on our group collie page, which he has done. This same day, I had special low-fat (but tasty) treats from a pet shop in Oliver's town, before we found a dog-friendly café with a special water bowl outside for dogs. My friends, Chris, Tina and Callum, had said how I looked funny on my photograph there, because it appeared as if I were studying the human menu. In actual fact, it had sounded much tastier than mine!

There is lovely Scottish food like the cottage pie which Sue gave me later in the holiday on the Outer Hebridean Island of Barra. I so enjoyed it, but was not too happy when Honey collie craftily took off with the food tray before I had finished licking all the potato off it! When on walks to the farm with his mum Rachael, Sir Leo collie also liked to run up and pinch breadcrumbs that Stan the goat had left behind after human friends had fed him. They are going to show us this lovely farm in Bury, one day. I may stare at the goats and I expect they will stare back, but I will not pinch their food!

On the next day of our wonderfully relaxing journey up through Scotland towards Oban, we saved several miles of road travel by boarding the ferry north of Ayr across the water to Dunoon. My Sue had briefly left me in the car near there, with her mum, and entered a little gift shop to buy postcards for our collie friends and their humans. She was so excited to see that they had those postcards with a tri-coloured collie, like me, on them, even with the same distinctive eyebrows! Mum enthusiastically rushed to show us one of these cards, before happily returning back inside to purchase lots more. My eyes followed her every move, and glancing back, she saw me watching her lovingly from the back of the car. I felt such love, admiration and also contentment that she knew how very much I loved her and our new life together. I waited and waited for the shop door to re-open and my Sue to return, so we could continue on our exciting adventure.

Eventually, the shop door did open, but Sue was not alone, for behind her walked a tall lady, much older than my Sue, with grey hair framing her older face, but still with a twinkle in her kind eyes. As the stranger, who was to become my friend, spotted me attempting to poke my nose out of the passenger window, she reached out to stroke me with a delicate hand. I was still fastened on my seatbelt clip - and therefore restricted in my movements - as it was meant to have been a brief stop. Knowingly, Sue unclipped my seatbelt and led me to the lady's side, where the caring stranger continued stroking me and told me what a handsome boy I was - before changing to a new language I had not heard previously, and speaking words I was not able to understand. I now know that this was called Scottish Gaelic and is understood by some humans and many dogs, largely in western parts of Scotland.

Sue explained to her own mum how the lady's daughter ran the postcard shop, and that this friendly lady suffered from severe deafness. She had discovered how that lady had lost her own beloved collie some months previously. I saw a tear glisten in the lady's eyes and reached my long paw out to comfort her. As you will realise, through reading my diary, or meeting me, or following my adventures over the years, I love to make new human friends and to give my paw. To be honest, we both love to meet new friends on our adventures. I still firmly believe that paw loves are important to let people know I am a friendly, caring boy, even though my Sue still needs to take my Mr. Muzzle everywhere and to keep it close at hand, as I can also still be so anxious at times and become so frightened when I see another dog - triggering that instantaneous change in my behaviour.

The kindly lady needed to lip-read as Sue told her about me and how I had become her collie a year before - after she met me when helping at her local rescue centre. She explained to the lady how I had helped her so much and eased the pain somewhat, after the loss of her own precious dog. This lady said I had given her hope and that she must find a new collie to rescue, love and give a home to as my Sue had done. I am lucky that I have good hearing and thankful for this. I know that hearing loss in a dog can be inherited, but is most common in dogs with white coats and I am a mostly black-coated dog, with just a tiny part of white. However, I do know that there are canine hearing aids which will help some dogs who have hearing problems with an American therapy dog being the first to actually have a canine hearing aid.

Hearing aids for dogs work the same as hearing aids for humans. Vets need to take a mould of the deaf dog's ear canal and from this a suitable and comfortable device will be built for him or her, this then being fitted in their ear after the necessary tests have been carried out. This type of hearing aid is similar to the 'behind the ear' hearing aids which humans have. If I ever do lose my hearing, I do not think that I would like the sensation of having an object close to my ears, but I would try if my mum asked me to. However, I was fine when Sue put my tiger blanket over me to keep my own ears warm and to turn me into a tiger-faced Dave D!

I know that my friend Toby the collie responds well to sign language, in the form of both finger and hand commands, and I would prefer - and trust - that Sue would use the same strategy if I do become hard of hearing in the future. Dogs are also trained to help their humans with hearing loss and they are called Hearing Dogs. I am happy with the way that Sue already teaches me to respond to some hand signs, as she did with her last dog, Lucky, who had become somewhat deaf. Hand signals are part of a clear training system for us dogs, so can benefit both hearing and non-hearing pets. If I am properly trained, then I will find it easier to adjust to any changes in my hearing as I become older.

Although I do not play with other dogs, dogs who do not know each other often start to play some game where they wiggle, wrestle, chase, and are obviously talking to each other using dog language. I am glad that I know how to respond to my human's facial and hand commands already as it can be difficult to hear Sue speaking if there is a lot of background noise. When playing, if Sue is in the distance and her verbal command is difficult for me to hear or interpret, I understand when she points in a certain area, that I will find my lost ball! To me, this is a positive learning experience and I accept and absorb so much information. I am aware that some dogs would find pointing intimidating though. When I am closer to Sue, a verbal command followed by a hand signal shows visual emphasis and complimenting of the instruction. Being a collie, such keeps me stimulated and focused too.

After an eventful day where I had enjoyed my adventures and meeting new friends, my Sue made my rug into a cosy little Dave D-shaped sleeping bag and I settled down to sleep whilst she carried on writing, then reading her book.

As I slept I had none of the bad dreams which frequently make my whole body twitch, causing Sue to soothe and comfort me. In contrast, this time, I was sleeping so peacefully. The holiday was clearly doing me the world of good. In fact, I dreamt of the old, framed pictures from our previous hotel, and running happily along the enchanting candle-lit corridor with that amazing Loch Awe view. In my wonderful dream I raced up and down that hotel's winding carpeted staircase, skidding round the corners on polished floors, and, as my Sue would certainly not have approved of, poking my inquisitive collie nose round the door of any guest who had left it slightly open!

I imagined a magical world where I felt relaxed and totally at ease with other dogs, even if they banged into me, and knocked my old legs from under me again. I dreamt of a life where I no longer needed to ever wear my muzzle, because I was no longer scared or reactive, and was never again a bystander on my lead missing out on any group collie games. In my dream I felt at ease to run close to and actually play with other dogs, to leap and swim in the waves with them, to catch the ball and fetch another toy that had been thrown, instead of only being able to nose-butt or paw tap it, where my inner fears had vanished and I could be a happy, fearless, relaxed boy like other collies are.

I also dreamt of the other dogs in the many old hotel paintings which I had seen, coming to life and jumping down to join me, with no Mr. Muzzle on my face, (or even in sight) but us all running happily together, hunting, sniffing, eating, swimming, herding, jumping, then all the dogs swapping places and jumping back into the wrong picture frame! I imagined the Spaniel with the shepherd, the Beagle with the Queen, the Chihuahua with the hunter, the Great Dane with the tiny old lady, and the Corgi with the policeman!

I, of course, would return to my Dave D collie sleeping bag in the real world with my Sue and, unlike the dogs in their one painted picture scene, I will have so many real photographs to share as I live through my adventures, recording the many scenes from my own life in my famous Dave D's Diary.

Chapter Nine

A Tale of Tails

In conversation, my Sue was recently asked, "Does he have a tail?" Her friend was referring to me and had not noticed my frowning tail from where he was sitting higher up in his big van by the stone jetty, as the rough sea waves crashed onto that jetty and the beach. I had not been at all amused by the loud noise which the wild sea was making, and even less so by the suggestion that I did not have a tail!

Indeed, of course I do have a very fine tail with a small crook at the end. My tail is thirty-eight centimetres long to be precise, but I was not very keen on having it measured with a classroom ruler which had been one of Sue's latest bizarre ideas! The longest dog tail is actually said to be just over seventy-two centimetres, which is nearly double the length of mine, so I am not exactly close to the record! People say that tails hang like giant pony tails. No matter how you describe my tail, it is all mine and I am very proud of it - nerves, muscle, bone and of course my soft, clean fur, completed by my collie white tip.

When happy, my Dave D tail can be likened to a furry smile or a wave. I do not control this tail because it is like an electric line connected to my brain and shows my emotions, therefore transmitting how I am feeling, like an accurate 'truth-ometer'! In addition to being born deaf and blind, puppies do not begin wagging their tail until they are approximately seven weeks old, so until then, their humans will just have to gauge how they feel through their other kinds of body language - like their barks. Us dogs don't only talk in this way; we actually listen too, and care what our humans have to say.

When I feel sad or worried, my Sue does not usually hear anything but my tail will be hanging down, sometimes between my legs, and it can be likened to a human frown. More positively, much to her delight, Sue often hears the powerful thump, thump of my tail on the floor when I am lying or sitting down, or if I am standing my tail will move in big, wide sweeps, brushing into whoever or whatever is nearby. I recently nearly knocked over a tall standing lamp and its shade but thankfully Sue's mum caught it just in time! Lass's tail does the same and when we visit them, I greatly enjoy watching the free entertainment as Sue, Mary and Jim frequently leap up from the settee, trying to catch various items that Lass's powerful long-haired tail has knocked and sent flying... before these fall off the coffee table and onto the floor!

Whenever I hear it said that humans sometimes feel as if they are chasing their tails, I still smile at the image of my Sue with a tail and chasing it! In fact, I know of a song where the sheep leave their tails behind them and that will now become part of my own tale.

I saw them suddenly and without warning... tails, woolly, black ones. At first I thought my usually reliable Dave D eyes were deceiving me because I had believed that these fluffy creatures, which mum alerted me to each time with the word 'sheep', were always a lighter colour. Yes, there high on the rocky hill in front of me were the strangest creatures, although I am sure a dark, short-haired dog like me, with such light eyebrows looks equally strange to them too!

With puzzlement, I studied them intently through our open car window. They were the same 'sheep' creatures that appeared to be in some kind of disguise and with long black tails. I let out a loud "woof" to tell Sue to stop the car immediately and allow me out to obtain a closer look. My funny expressions rarely fail to make Sue smile and seeing my intensely focused face in her mirror, she stopped the car in a safe place near a gate and unclipped my seatbelt, next putting on my shorter lead. I was pulling in my eagerness to see the creatures close up - as I had firmly decided that I needed to have a much closer look. I was adamant and attempted to race round to the other gate, dragging Sue behind me on the end of the lead. We had been told that white collies were not good as sheepdogs because the white sheep were not scared of them. Consequently, I wondered if black sheep would not be afraid of me because I am mostly a black-haired Dave D?

A short way down this lane, an elderly gentleman standing at his gateway viewed me in my eager state racing in his direction, and commented,

"Oh, I thought you were coming to see me".

Glancing only quickly at the human I was thinking,

"I do not think so, for we are off to see the furry creatures in the next field".

He watched me, at the same time winking and telling Sue and her mum how the sheep who lived there were rare black Hebridean sheep, smaller than other breeds of sheep, and originally from the island of St. Kilda (where that unusual mail method had been used), and that their precious natural wool makes special jumpers and garments. I pawed the road, so Sue took the hint, gave me one of her knowing looks of acknowledgement, thanked the man and we continued down that old Barra lane until we reached the other field. I sniffed. Yes! Definitely a type of sheep had been here. Alas, the field was now completely empty of any of these creatures and indeed, there was not a sheep of any colour in sight.

I pretended to smile, but my smile did not quite reach as far across my collie face as it usually did because, much to my dismay, even when we arrived at the actual original place where I had seen them, by a metal gate, they had gone! The creatures had disappeared and all that remained to give us any clue that they had been there at all was a large piece of their black wool, attached to the wire fence and waving in the breeze!

Was this wool from one of their black, woolly tails, I wondered?

I inspected by sniffing this specimen closely, much to my Sue's amusement as, amidst giggles she said that I looked *so* funny!

I quickly composed myself and gave another big Dave D smile, followed by a further quick sniff at the remaining black wool, which actually tickled my nose... but I cleverly held back my potential sneeze! The strange black sheep must have left their wool behind in their haste to move away when they saw my beady collie eyes watching them from the red car, then leaping out and pulling my human towards their field. Yes, pure sheep wool, but no sheep and certainly not enough wool to make me a jumper! After a warning from my Sue, I had also been very careful not to hurt my nose on the wire.

At that moment, I had been tempted to stamp my paws, as I had been far from happy not to have found the sheep and that they had hidden so quickly when they saw me approaching. However, I had kept my composure, unlike my handsome friend Bailey collie in Leicester. I have met him twice and he is also wary of other dogs, so he has to wear a muzzle near such dogs, like I do. Bailey had been on the field with his mum, Lauren, when he had suddenly seen a cat. Being a collie, he had plans for this creature, so had given chase and tried to herd it. Unfortunately, the clever cat ran away from Bailey and was nowhere to be seen, so this loveable collie rolled around on the field howling and having a tantrum! Howling is in fact natural wolf behaviour which has carried over to us dogs! I was impressed to discover how, later that night, Bailey was looking very studious as his mum showed him some facts linked to cats and dogs. He seemed to be studying it carefully in order to learn more about cats - ready for next time he encountered one!

In our warm hotel later, as I drifted off to sleep, it was sheep that I was half-dreaming about, when I heard what sounded like a herd of these sheep creatures strolling across the floor above us. My Sue was unconcerned, and had just mentioned 'noisy neighbours'! I doubted that I would ever see those black sheep again.

On the contrary, the next day I knew that my stubborn and determined Sue had not given up, when I realised that we were travelling down the same island road where we had left the wool still attached to that long fence. Suddenly, I stood up, straining on my harness and seatbelt, for there, standing on a hill behind the fence were many of those black sheep, now back and grazing peacefully. Sue let me alight from the car and I was able to watch them from a distance, to reassure myself that they had not been figments of my imagination. With it being a warm day, she suggested we walk further alongside the road near their fence to the fresh-water stream, known as a burn, so that I could drink some of the cool liquid falling into the pool under the purple heather. I lowered my head and lapped up the refreshing water. It tasted so wonderful that I pulled a funny, satisfied face, which made my Sue smile!

All of a sudden, I heard a rustle in the coconut-smelling gorse bushes opposite the stream. Straining on my lead, I pulled towards the direction of that sound, thankful that mum allowed me to cross the road sensibly with her. There, in front of me, were two of the famous woolly, black, rare Hebridean sheep, whose wool is sold in its purest form. I know that it can be used to make such as tweed jackets and bow ties, but I already have my own jacket and prefer the normal kind of ties - as bow ties, like collars, would feel too tight around my neck. My Sue had once tried a real tie on me, because she said that she was going to help me to be a famous author and that we would have to look smart and give autographs - and 'pawtographs' too! That time, I made two clear paw-prints in the sand in preparation for giving real my 'pawtographs' at our book signings and gave her my biggest, happiest Dave D smile, too!

I composed myself once again and thought how that very wool which I had sniffed was off a valuable sheep! I had done it! I had found them. Close up, I stared intently and was shocked to recognise that some of them actually had two or four strong curled horns, unlike the sheep which I had seen on the distant hills in North Wales and in other parts of Scotland. Some had brown wool even, where their black wool had faded in the sun. There and then I decided that, despite being a collie, I no longer wanted to be too close to them!

The two nearest sheep pretended not to see me, but I am an intelligent collie and not one to be easily fooled. Besides, I could tell that at least one of them had given me a sideways glance peep - as I do at creatures I do not want to be close to. However, I certainly would not be leaving any trace of my black fur behind for them to prove that I had been there. I wondered if it was one of those two sheep who had left its fur behind on the fence that previous afternoon? Eventually, one of these creatures fully turned to look at me over the top of the long, green grass, so I stared back. Mission accomplished. I could now return to our car and relax.

Dads, Tails and Technology

I wish that my Sue's dad had left the end of my own tail alone, because this time it was my own tail that was the object of some even closer attention! I love to go to visit my human grandparents in Manchester although admittedly, I am a bit wary of the real coal fire there, so prefer to lie quietly, in front of their electric fire in a nearby room. I was lying there relaxing one Sunday evening and, as it was dark outside, they had drawn the green velvet curtain across to separate the room. Therefore, I was alone in the kitchen resting peacefully, head on paw, when suddenly I saw shadows as the curtain moved... I froze and heard heavy human footsteps, then a large human hand reached down and tried to pick up the white tip of my tail! I gritted my old teeth thinking...

"No! Stop! It is me, Dave D resting here by the fire. My tail tip is not the bit of fluff on the carpet that you think it is! Yes, we know how you humans like to tidy up, but trying to put the tip of my tail into the rubbish bin is not funny!"

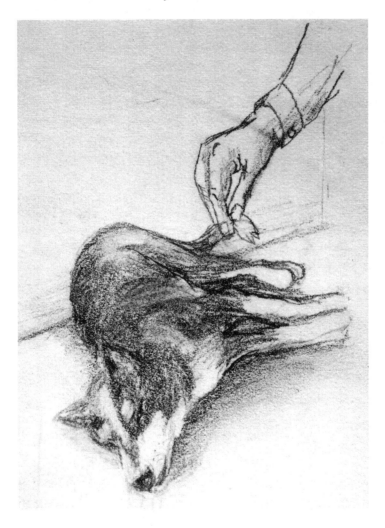

Sue was not amused when her dad went into the dining-room chuckling and told her and her mum what he had tried to do by mistake, because she knows that I don't like my tail to be touched.

Despite this I was a good boy and held my usual growl in, because I have to be on my best Dave D behaviour if I want to go to the Swinton house with Sue.

The following time I went to see my human grandparents in Manchester another mistake was made and this time I was blamed! A strange sound kept transmitting throughout the room in which we were all sitting. I had been lying ever so quietly - also in the well-lit main room this time.

"Listen, what's that?" Sue's dad had asked.

I pricked my ears up. So the humans could hear it too. I had already wondered what it was, but I could barely believe my furry Dave D ears when grandad's voice continued,

"Is it the dog? Is the dog making that strange noise?"

Me?! I was minding my own business and not making a sound, not even snoring, and they thought it was me buzzing!

My Sue obviously leapt to my defence and cleared me of any blame as she explained,

"No, Dad, that is my phone letting me know that it is full of messages!"

"Since when did I, Dave D, make a noise like a mobile phone?!" I wondered to myself. Sue's dad was a beekeeper, so I reasoned that he knew more about other kinds of less technical buzzing. He did not possess a mobile phone, so I presumed that my fellow collie, Blue's dad must have been much more technically minded because I heard that he even had a Bluetooth earpiece for his mobile phone.

I reflected upon those other occasions, when, one time I was mistaken for a kangaroo - after leaping up for my tuggy and standing as that creature does, and a further time, being mistaken for a tiger, when I was just being me, Dave D, walking but unintentionally pulling my warm tiger rug behind me! I was indeed very thankful that I had not been mistaken for a handsome penguin in Dundee town centre, despite the fact that, upon inspecting them closely, the penguins were indeed wearing very similar smart, striped ties to mine.

Chapter Ten

Signposts and Animal Experiences

Back home in England, I am forever coming across those weird orange plastic things which are meant to signify roadworks or that an area needs to be avoided. There is even one that has been standing on the corner, opposite my home for months which the silly workmen must have forgotten to remove when they disappeared in their traffic-cone matching orange jackets with the bright fluorescent stripes!

I see that bright obstacle every time I leave my home and it always makes me wish it would go away! My tail goes between my legs to show that I am not happy and I try to stare it out, but that does not work because the odd cone is still there when I return from my walk. I see it in the distance as I trot back down the road in rain, hail or snow, sun or drizzle. Sometimes, I tap the annoying cone with my paw and try to knock it over, proceeding to watching it wobble. Other times, I just glare at it and carry on. I did once manage to knock the cone over completely and I followed this by biting into the thin, white, plastic strip but, much to my dismay, Sue disapproved, took the cone off me and placed it upright again!

Our friend Giz-dog in Lancashire actually *likes* these cone things! Where he lives, Giz had been eyeing up the cones as workmen put them down and tried to pull his mum, Janet, towards them. It was winter and a little snow had fallen, with some ice on the pavements. In comparison to my black jacket, Giz was wearing a red tartan one and had started to walk down the pavement and across the road, becoming faster as he could see the cones in the distance. He approached and continued forward until he stood by an upright cone, then put his paw up onto this cone. I think he was a little surprised when it moved. His mum tried to give him his favourite plastic toy and to put that into his mouth, but had no luck, as he kept his mouth tightly shut and started moving forward. After several attempts, he positioned the cone in his mouth and toppled it over, dragging it along the road until they got to the end where he put it down. It was several teeth-marks later that Giz found a grip in which he could keep it in his mouth and drag it further. As he was thrilled with his accomplishment and did not want to let go of it, when they arrived home, his mum allowed him to take it up their garden path, but she took it back across the road to join the rest of the cones when Giz was fast asleep!

Our Scottish holiday would lead us past many traffic signposts, but I doubted that I would glare at any like I did that troublesome traffic cone back home! In contrast to unnatural things that need to be avoided, when we arrived on the other side of Barra, I loved to sit in the natural heather and relax with the gentle breeze on my face blowing my long black and white collie whiskers. We had seen a signpost to this beautiful place and had set out in search of it, being told that there was lots of pretty heather along the route. My Mum said I looked happy and relaxed like the tri-coloured collie-dog in the purple-coloured heather on those special postcards which we had sent to our friends, and which I had one of in my paw for a photograph, before we posted it to our dear collie club friend, Clare.

I then looked past the heather, which was tickling my nose, and out over the water between the Isle of Barra, where we were staying, and Vatersay island, where we were heading for. In olden times, heather was picked by the local inhabitants, and used to make beds for humans, although I prefer my soft, fleece, paw-print cushion, as it does not make me sneeze for one thing! The heather was also useful for making brooms, which I could imagine as our very long garden path at home needs a tough brush to sweep it with.

Road signs in Scotland often have two names for each place because, as I have mentioned, the two languages are spoken there and Scottish Gaelic has been the language of the Highlands for hundreds of years, just as my two forms of signing by bark and body language can usually be recognised by humans and fellow dog. As I sniffed the fresh sea air, my happy smile body language told the story of an amazingly happy and fortunate collie. I was looking inquisitively at the road across from me. It was interesting as we were separated from the island by just that long structure called a causeway, with a narrow road down the middle and rocks on each side. If you imagine a capital letter "H" laid on its side, you will have an idea of the shape of this island. I wished it had been in the shape of a D for Dave or even a double D for Dave D!

I heard Sue reading the information booklet to her mum. A quarter of a million tonnes of rocks were used to make this joining causeway. It is useful for people and animals. Although humans used to make the crossing by boat, I felt sorry to learn that cattle such as cows, needing transporting to the mainland, had to swim across this Sound of Vatersay! It is about two hundred and fifty metres! Although now a more confident swimming collie, like Millie and Fly collies are, I was glad that I could go across with mum in the car and that I did not have to swim and wet my fur!

I forced myself out of my heather bed as Sue called me back into the car. She had to ask me twice as my head had been turned the other way. I had sensed the presence of sheep, so had been trying to determine exactly where they were, and if they could see me. We were driving onto the small island for lunch, then to explore. (Unfortunately, although I hoped for peace and quiet once I arrived on the island, this was not to be, as you will read about in the Holes chapter of my Diary).

Frequently, on our travels we refer to signs in the human Highway Code. On the island we looked for otters, seals and herons. My Mum studied the dainty plants as she had been told that a specific flowering one was named Bonnie Prince Charlie - (actually said to originate from French seeds dropped by Bonnie Prince Charlie, in Scotland) - and can be found on Vatersay. We also saw 'dog'-violets with bluish-purple petals, which looked nothing like me! In fact, they did not have any resemblance to any kind of dog, except for the fact that they have those heart-shaped leaves resembling my love for my Sue inside my own heart. These delicate flowers made the island even more beautiful as they were like a soft, purple carpet under my paws. The word dog in the name of this plant means 'lack of scent' as opposed to its cousin, the sweet violet which does have a scent. I am a clean boy and do not smell unless my fur becomes wet and then we have to open the car windows! Overall, Vatersay island is approximately three miles by three in size. I walked right across it with my Sue and her mum, taking care to keep away from the rocky, sloping land leading to the sandy beach.

Later, I was keen to see the sheep and Highland cattle as many road signs indicated that they were likely to appear in the immediate area. Having been told that cars rarely used our road, and after sitting in the back of the car on my own dog-bed straight from that heather bed, mum brought it out to shake and give it an airing. I saw it next to our car and sat on it, which Mum said looked funny as I was in the middle of what seemed like nowhere sitting on my paw-print fleece cushion! I did not think it was that funny as it was a welcome change from sitting in the car's bucket seat! Sue let me keep my red bag and ball with me, as, comfortingly, they are always next to me and my bed on the back seat too. I decided to have a rest and some more of that wonderful fresh air, so I actually lay down while Sue had a break and read her magazine. As my bed was next to a cattle grid I was so hoping to see some sheep or cows and practise my collie herding-by-stare skills. I waited and waited but all in vain! We were now aware that the majority of the sheep in our areas of adventure were called blackface sheep which are horned too! Their wool is short and fine, which is excellent for making carpets and tweed material and the strong and coarse combination means it is also used for making mattresses. I imagined this wool would be softer than a heather mattress. These sheep's faces are either all black or a combination of black and white like my collie face. However, their fleece is completely free of any black, whereas my main fur is mostly black.

As we set off again I searched and searched for a sign of sheep or cows each time I saw a signpost, but they must have been hiding! They had probably heard that Dave D, the city collie, was in the area! I am usually modest, but I knew from Sue's expression that I looked a mighty handsome sight with my cute furry head pointing in the direction I presumed some woolly sheep to be. After a short walk we returned to the car and I thought back to the hour before when I had seen cattle signs and waited at the cattle grid, but had not seen any up there. I decided that I would still give them a firm collie eye when I saw any and poked my nose out of the window in anticipation. My Sue always tells me to "think positive" so I was following her advice! We did in fact see some towards the end of our journey, but we went past them faster than the blink of a human eye - although I still had time to fix them with my beady brown-eyed Dave D stare!

Later I saw another of those road signs warning of cattle on the roads near to a cattle grid. I felt this was a strange idea as even I am not allowed to wander on the roads and always have to wear a lead. I wondered what was so special about these creatures?

Some time later, we were heading to the east coast from Tarbet on the Isle of Harris, when all of a sudden, we saw those previously concealed cattle high up on the cliff top, walking and grazing on plants in the unfenced fields and, surprisingly, also on the rocks near the beach! They were huge creatures with muddy legs from where they sheltered from the strong wind and the rain on those hillside ledges next to the sea and near to where the spectacular rocky sea stacks stood tall with swirling white water surrounding each black stack.

Some of these Highland cattle were even paddling down in the sea, like the black cows which my Sue had seen the year before in the far North of Scotland. I was mighty glad to be sitting in the safety of our car - and thankful that Sue had decided to wait until the next day for us to return to the area for the purpose of taking any photographs, because I had posed quite enough for one day!

We returned the following afternoon and I jumped out, immediately scanning the rocks and surrounding areas. I definitely smelt the cattle but they were no longer there! I must admit they had looked scarier than those black cows lying on the beach, which Sue had been cautious about and shown me a photograph of. I had not been with her then. Some cows are not happy if a dog is near them, so have been known to surround walkers and even to hurt humans who walk near to them with dogs. However, a loud clap from a walker can usually cause the cows to move back. It is always best to turn back and avoid fields with cattle in if you are unsure of your safety and I am sure that Sue will always do so to keep us safe. Feeling relieved, I was even more glad that I had not been there when Sue came across those black beach cows!

Whilst in a local café and like in the western films which Lass collie still watches, we learnt that the Uist cows still swim across stretches of water, but we had not seen this strange sight. With regard to this, we were told that when swimming the cows half float but move their legs like they are running. In olden days a cow was tied to a boat, rowed by its master and when other cows saw that the first one was safe, they followed on across the water. Once again, I felt sorry for the cows as this sounded even more of a strange sight than the time we saw what seemed like hundreds of hens sitting in trees for shelter on our way to Berkshire! However, and also strangely, Rona collie who lived close by, in London, did keep trying to climb the silver birch tree in her own garden, causing her mum to have to place a small fence round it, but this still did not stop that determined and intelligent collie girl! I have never climbed up a tree completely although I did once place my rear legs on a part of a tree bark thirty centimetres up and stretched my whole body as I tried, successfully, to reach a toy which had landed up there.

Whilst on this 'black cow beach', Sue had found what appeared to be a new tennis ball, which she brought back all the hundreds of miles to give to me. She very much wants to show me that long sandy dog-friendly beach at Durness, as long as the cows are no longer there. She is taking me there one year and also hopes to take me to Cape Wrath lighthouse nearby, which is at the furthest northern-westerly point of the Scottish mainland. To reach it we will have to cross a stretch of water on a fifteen-minute journey in a small, wooden boat with a sailor called John. He usually takes his little terrier on board with him if there are not too many passengers. As a precaution, Sue will explain to him that I am not good in small spaces with another dog and hopefully he will leave his dog at the quayside with his other sailor friend for that short time. I am sure that my Sue will have purchased me a dog lifejacket in time for this adventure; we recently saw one in our local pet shop, but I have yet to try it on.

On the other side of this water we will be met by a scheduled mini-bus which will take us on a high winding road to the actual lighthouse. This lighthouse was built in 1828 by Robert Stevenson and it became automated in 1998. I will be able to look for, and most probably be fascinated by, the white light flashing once every thirty seconds. I hope to meet friendly John and Kay who are the sole inhabitants at Cape Wrath. Mum met them last time she and her own mum ventured to this far off place. They have built what is claimed to be Britain's most remote cafe next to the lighthouse. I bet we will be able to buy tasty snacks there to enjoy. A few years ago, Kay travelled from there to Inverness to purchase their Christmas turkey, amongst other items. Due to storms, heavy snow and icy roads she was unable to return home by boat and that steep bending road to Cape Wrath in time for Christmas!

On this particular trip of ours to the western side of Harris, we approached the specific area where we had seen the cattle the previous evening, paddling in the bright blue sea and eating plants from rocks next to the beach. Scanning the area, I kept my red travel bag close and my collie tail lay low, as this was new to me and I half-expected the cattle to emerge and join me on their brown ledge!

I looked all round, turning my collie head this way and that, tail now just half down in anticipation, but all I could find were their hoof prints on that muddy ledge where the cattle must have tried to shelter from the rain. The long, green grass was also soaked with sea mist! No wonder the cows' legs had been so muddy and now mine and Sue's were too!

I was having the time of my life that holiday as I stood where they had stood, feeling invigorated and marvelling at the fantastic views which those cattle saw every day of their own lives. From here, I could see the grass next to those rocks where they can often be seen standing. There were other ledges lower down, where the cattle's hoof prints could be seen clearly, but Sue would not allow me to go right down there as she said that it would be too dangerous. We did see other cattle later in the day, but they were not on a beach or on the mountain road - just resting and lying down in a field of long grass and yellow flowers, and I was safe staring from the car window, although a brown cow gave me a strange look and moooooooed, as if to say,

"Yes, we heard about you, the silly city collie, sitting on its cushion waiting by that cattle grid in the middle of nowhere - at the side of a road that hardly any cars travel down, let alone us cattle! You even had a red travel bag and a football! We were hiding and wondering which team you supported and believe you were hoping to see us? NO chance!"

Even so, I was braver when I saw some cows a few days later as we drove along, and I stared at those cows from a much closer range, but still from the safety of our car - then further on when I saw a Highland calf peering at me inquisitively. The calf was behind a gate in a field with a strong fence all the way around. It even had extra blue rope fastened to the gate to make it more secure. My Sue let me sniff the air near to this calf, but warned me not to go too close. I learnt

166

that these animals are historic because of the fact that they are the oldest pedigree breed of cattle in the world. As there are more than one type and colour of collie, I was also interested to discover that there also used to be two types of Highland cattle. Kyloes were small and black in colour, which reminded me of those disappearing black sheep, and were associated with the West of Scotland and the Islands, whilst the larger red-haired cattle grazed the Highlands. Today they are known collectively as Highland Cattle and the recognised colours are red, black, yellow, dun, white, brindle and silver.

The ones I saw were a red colour, and I felt somewhat worried, but curious, as Sue and I approached the little calf, enquiringly. I wanted to learn more about him and to let him know that I would not harm him, but that I was just an old collie from England on one of my adventures, learning more about signs, other animals and the British Isles. He stared at me and, ignoring Sue's shadow, I stared back. He seemed a young, gentle soul and Sue reassured us both that we had nothing to fear. Nevertheless, I was thankful that there was that a gate and fence between us, for that tied blue rope and that she had kept a caring hand within grabbing distance of my lead!

Later, as we drove along in the late afternoon, we saw signs for deer, and even stopped to look for them, but none crossed the road in front of us, although as darkness fell, my Sue slowed down and pointed out a baby red deer high on the hillside, standing still like statue. Adult red deer can weigh two hundred and forty kilograms, whereas I weigh just twenty-three kilograms. These red deer actually compete to mate and we were told about their loud roar which echoes through the dawn mist of the glens in October. I was very thankful that it was only the month of August as that almighty sound would have been sure to petrify me and therefore make me jump!

I became aware that roe deer have a white flash on their tail, as I have a white tip on my collie tail, and instinctive crouch characteristic of my own breed and inheritance. Red deer can also swim and have therefore arrived on, so now inhabit, various Scottish islands. I enjoy swimming too, although the sea was very cold last time I ran into it chasing my ball. I was so glad we had travelled to the island by boat! I learnt that the red deer can actually bark, as I do, and that stags go to the lowland for food. I was also told that the royal deer have a full rack of antlers with twelve points. I do not have antlers myself but I do have that posh raincoat which makes me look almost royal!

Apparently, deer enjoy eating the hill-slope goodness and go higher up to escape from the biting insects. It would be funny if they all wore midge hoods like I did as you will see in my Insect Experiences Diary entry! As you will recognise, the hoods are green, so they would blend in well with the hillsides where the deer graze. Back home, I am no longer allowed to go off my lead in, or anywhere near to, the local deer area, as they can chase dogs and hurt them, by kicking and trampling us with their hooves when they are protecting their partner or young. I had in fact seen some deer back home in Staffordshire, both crossing some of the many Cannock Chase forest roads, and when two deer ran across a public footpath near us as we walked with our friend, Liz. That time, my Sue had tried to keep calm, but she not been very convincing, as she had suddenly called me to her with a shaky voice before very quickly bundling me safely behind a wooden gate separating the two footpaths.

In Scotland, we did not see signs for strange birds, but we recognised some called grouse which are only found in the British Isles. The male bird had a black ruff of feathers round its neck, as I have mostly black fur round mine, with a line of white. It also had a conspicuous, funny, fleshy red comb growing on its head, just above its eye! Tessa spaniel's fur does actually stick up cutely on top of her head, too. My fur doesn't and although Sue does comb all of my own fur, she has certainly never left my red comb behind on top of my head! Although the shower cap was on my head for a while in the hotel, as Sue tried to help me imitate the grouse's head comb, this was not permanent like the bird's own head attachment, and did not feel exactly right on a collie's fur head. I was not in the least bit amused and do not think that either would be comfortable when I tried to sleep - but I did make the most of being permitted to sit on that luxurious velvety hotel chair!

The black grouse actually eat Scotch pine needles, too, and these then come out as part of their bird dirt, which I am thinking does not sound very pleasant either! I am glad that I am not partial to eating pine needles or else my Sue would need a strong, reinforced poop bag as it would not be possible to use a simple plastic bag successfully, even in an emergency! This grouse bird makes strange sounds, firstly like a car engine trying to start, then like a cork popping from a bottle, followed by the pouring sound as it is poured! I once ran off with the cork from a champagne bottle until my Sue called me to bring it back - twice. I was having fun so had, unusually, pretended not to hear her initial command to return, which was justly given in case I choked on it. Although understandably, I had not been amused by the champagne bottle bang, I had composed myself upon seeing that prospective toy and Sue said it looked funny when they saw me catch the soft cork in my mouth before it landed and how I had then raced off with it at top speed - the paler backs of my back legs and little white bottom showing - as my tail was so high in the air with happiness. I loved it when they all made such a fuss of me. We also heard the grouse making sounds as they flew, which seemed like, "Go back. Go back!" but if he had been there, making that instructive sound to me, I would have ignored him too! I was not ready to go back home yet as I was having far too much fun!

Seeing a signpost for a beach, we went in search of the golden sands and were not disappointed. I was not yet a very experienced swimmer, so I always appreciated Sue rolling her jeans up and wading into the water with me, as I practised gaining confidence with the water on my furry tri-coloured collie legs. I was focusing on a ball she had thrown for me, but my Sue kept saying reassuringly,

"Try to lift your legs up Dave D, you will be fine", when in fact I was actually swimming already! It reminded me of when another black dog, Oliver Labrador, had first experienced water. He had only been a puppy, so much younger than me, and he had been in a park lake, not the Atlantic Ocean where I was. However, this park became Oliver's favourite place in the world and his humans had taken him there to teach him how to swim. As my Sue had, his loving humans also waded into the water knee deep and were trying to get Oliver to swim. They thought that he was walking round them in circles for ages, when in fact he had been swimming round them for about thirty minutes, so he must have wondered what his humans were doing and why they didn't just swim like him! Oliver had his first ice cream that day as a reward. My Sue only gives me the end of her ice cream cone with a tiny piece of ice cream in it. I hope she buys me a whole ice cream next time I swim for her.

Bailey collie puppy is not able to swim yet, so just stands in the shallow part of streams or rivers and flaps one cute paw. He is young so his mum, Jan, is still proud of him as she is sure that he will master the art of swimming one day, like I have - for I was eleven before I first swam in the sea. When Rosie collie went to her new home with her dad, Philip and family, she was not used to water either. The first time she swam was with the ducks and swans for company and the second time she followed two canoeists who were in the river, much to their disbelief! Needless to say she has gained confidence and is now a swimmer like me. Chris and Alan's beautiful golden retriever girls, Valorie and Violet, love to go for long woodland walks with them to the Cannock Chase Forest lakes and each use their tail like a rudder when swimming as it helps them to turn. My own tail just follows the direction I am swimming, but it does help me keep my balance when I run quickly through the forest paths, on the beach, or on our local field after my ball. I instinctively lean into turns, throwing my weight to one side, which stops me from falling over, because I even my weight out by throwing my tail to the opposite side, as I return to my Sue. Bandit collie's first experience of water was a puddle! He stood there staring at the water of that puddle, before tapping it with a solitary paw, then barking at it, making his humans smile. Bandit is now so confident that he races past me into the sea at top speed on our collie walks near Sunderland!

My Sue reminded me how one of the next adventures in our holiday, would be to try and find a collie who had rescued a lost sheep the year before when that sheep had become separated from its flock. The sheep had been scared of the water which it had wandered towards, before becoming disorientated and seemingly trapped. Despite not being a collie, I bet Oliver would have comforted that sheep, too. He was also a very caring boy.

Chapter Eleven

Carry-on-Camping and Seaweed Sticks

This camping lark was a new adventure for me and it was very strange. Since my initial peek at that funny blue thing which humans sleep in, I had been puzzled! In this instance, I travelled with my Sue and my human grandma, many hundreds of miles, first by car, then by ferry, to reach my very first camp-site on South Uist, in the Outer Hebrides off the west coast of the Scottish mainland. Before leaving the ferry, I had been clipped into my doggy seatbelt harness and, anticipating a long drive, I was comfortably curled up in a Dave D sleeping position, with a single paw gently resting over my nose... ready to dream of sheep and squirrels. Therefore, I was not in the slightest bit amused (and more totally bemused) as, in no time at all, the humans seemed to be slowing down my transport. I sat up and started looking out of the window to see what all the human excitement was about. They had only spotted a 'Camp-site' sign!

Soon, we parked up and all jumped out. I looked around for my usual luxurious stop-over point, but no! - Alas, it was not a dog-friendly hotel at all... but a muddy field!

"Oh my goodness, surely we couldn't be sleeping in a field like the sheep I loved to spy on - and often see grazing in such places?" I thought to myself, feeling somewhat puzzled.

To my disbelief, yes, we really seemed to be staying there, in a field with sheep as neighbours! I looked on in amazement as, with enthusiasm and bright eyes, Sue pulled big, blue, bulky bags out of the car's narrow boot and listened as they landed on the floor, *thump, thump, thump*! They were much bigger than my small, red travel bag that comes everywhere with me! My Sue and her mum proceeded to take large material items from inside those blue bags.

Pricking my dark ears up as the cool wind brushed them and their white fur-lining rather harshly, I could hear the sound of waves lapping onto the seashore and longed to go in search of the nearby beach in order to play and explore. Sue looked over and must have read my mind as she told me I would have to 'wait and be a patient boy' whilst they prepared our beds for the night! I was confused as my own bed - the soft and fleecy one with paw-print patterns - was on the back seat of the car and did not need 'preparing', beyond a quick shake. What on earth were they up to? I asked myself, puzzled right down to the tips of my cute Dave D paws and nails! I was far from impressed when they fastened me to the muddy field with my longest lead and a tail-shaped metal object, which they called a tent peg, to secure it, and stop me wandering off! Sensing my discomfort, at being so restricted, Sue had placed just my shorter red lead on me and given me a firm "Stay" instruction!

Although I am an extremely caring boy myself... for most of the time, I was not in the least bit interested in the large, blue object waving in the breeze in front of me as Sue's mum clung on tightly calling for help. I had never seen one opened up before and don't think she was amused as I was ignoring her and straining to see those woolly sheep in the huge field directly behind her. To put it bluntly, she was blocking my view in a big way, plus it looked as if she was wearing a huge, wide skirt like the old-fashioned dolls!

My Sue finally spoke to her own mum, amidst laughter…

"Oops, sorry mum, I know I should have helped you with your tent but I couldn't resist taking a photograph or two of Dave D's reaction……!"

Hmmm… what is my Sue like?! I just wanted to observe those grazing or watching sheep behind Sue's mum, not to have my photograph taken… again! Especially not with sheep watching me as I lay in a blustery field with the wind making my ears flap and my coat look like I had a terribly bad fur day - as had in fact occurred so many times during this windy summer adventure.

I had carried on staring at those nearby sheep and looking cute, when my Sue also had trouble with her blue tent house and it actually blew on its side! Indeed, it was several minutes before I purposefully turned and put just one strong, white paw on one of the long, luminous green cord 'guide ropes' as her tent threatened to blow backwards towards where I sensed potentially pestering dogs may be. I could hear them barking from inside other tents and white caravan things, but I had no wish to encourage them, or for Sue to have to chase her own tent if it blew towards them.

It was cold and not the best weather for a camp-fire, so we all enjoyed our tea in the camp-site kitchen. I did so like that warm communal room near to the tents and the fuss which the other campers gave me. I have to admit that I was a bit worried at one stage as there was most certainly a dog outside the door, seemingly off its lead. I could hear it snuffling its nose on the wooden structure but its owner called it to him when my Sue popped her head round the door and gently explained that I was a nervous collie boy and felt trapped inside the building. Nevertheless, I looked all round apprehensively when we exited the room… searching for this dog whose nails I had definitely heard clipping the path outside - but he had vanished. My Sue said she was glad that the responsible man had understood my genuine fear, instead of saying that his 'dog was friendly' like so many other owners do. To this my mum sometimes chooses to explain that I am still a scared old boy… even of friendly dogs that run up to me, especially of any who are off their lead, and that I don't mean to tremble when I see others - even in the distance - but I do.

After our midnight walk on that little beach opposite our camp-site, we were careful to cross the main road safely, me with a new toy in my mouth, albeit slightly bent. It was actually one of those bottles like those which I retrieve on walks at home when mum will not let me take my real toys to play with on our night walks - as too many have been lost in the dark.

It felt somewhat strange when night time had fallen and we were living in a blue tent thing for the whole evening. I must admit that it took all my willpower not to do a collie prance and dance round inside our tent, chasing the shadows from Sue's lantern and the other lanterns and torches round this camp-site place - which seemed to be shining onto and round our tent too. It was comfy and warm on my fleecy dog bed next to the air-bed where Sue lay all wrapped up inside a human sleeping bag. I did try to join her, nudging her gently with my warm collie body, but she quickly forced me to about-turn and return to my own bed, in case my nails punctured a hole in her airbed and all the air came out making it go flat again. I gave a Dave D smile at that image... for then she would have needed to sleep on the hard ground like me!

Upon waking up inside the tent, on my bed and tiger blanket, I heard the now familiar sound of "baaaaaaaaaaaaaaa". I discreetly lay looking out from the tent flap for a while, admiring a wonderful view, of the large field and rolling hillside beyond, complete with a flock of Scottish sheep, grazing. They had definitely not noticed me, the famous and charismatic collie from Staffordshire!

Presently, my Sue did let me jump out of my cosy tent den but, due to my previous night's sheep fixation, she attached me on my longest black lead, in my smart red collar, to a tent peg again, 'just in case' as Sue said! Just in case indeed! I was hardly going to leap over the fence to reach those sheep as I knew that such would not go down too well and would mean Sue and her mum raising their voices at me! I managed to unintentionally tangle one leg up in my black lead, but I was careful not to be too sheep-obsessed that I sat in my water bowl too - as Sue had once done accidentally - for I did not particularly want a wet fur bottom on an already cold day.

Earlier, I noticed that one of the tent's guide ropes had come undone, but Sue's bottle of water was still there outside our tent, along with my bottle that I had found on that moonlit beach the night before. The red car was still there too and our silver kettle. It is good that people seem trustworthy and nobody moves our belongings in this part of the British Isles. The wind was causing further problems that morning as they prepared a healthy dish of cereal each, the rice cereal being blown from their bowls and across the camp-site before they had even had chance to put milk onto it! It happened so quickly, like popcorn popping, and must have looked very funny to the other campers - yet it left me hungry because in their haste to head to a cafe for breakfast instead, they forgot to give me my own soft, meaty biscuit breakfast! Maybe I should have done what hungry Berkeley the English pointer dog did on his camping trip after smelling freshly-cooked sausages nearby. He ventured out of his mum's tent, daringly entered the next-door strangers' tent, and helped himself to two sausages out of this neighbouring family's frying pan! His humans had been alerted by shouting from that adjacent tent, indicating that their dog had stolen food!

"My breakfast! Bad dog! Get out!"

Sue and her mum chatted to some people from London, who told us about 'wilderness' camping. I had listened as they revealed how there is a rule in Scotland that people can camp anywhere, not only on designated sites like we were. This is not permitted in any other of the British Isles countries which we visited. When camping, I enjoy my walks to, and treats from, the communal camp-site kitchens, also knowing that my humans would not like a place without washing facilities either!

We were carrying a pile of stick-coloured seaweed to our parked car, and the gentleman, Andres, reminded us how seaweed is fine for humans and dogs to eat! (I gave a big silent 'yuk'!). He had cooked some in his aluminium pan on a small camping stove and said that it was like green lettuce. My Sue sometimes gives me salad as part of my evening meal - which she calls my tea - but I always leave the lettuce! However, I am aware that a derivative of red seaweed is indeed used as a thickener in ice-cream and toothpaste but I had not recognised seaweed in either, so thankfully, it must be in an invisible form!

My seaweed stick was brown, which I was glad about, as I had no intention of letting Sue give the man my new seaweed toys to cook and eat! He continued to explain that the green seaweed was a delicacy, but how it did not have an exciting taste. I thought about the sheep which Sue had told me about who live on seaweed and am glad that I am not a sheep. However, she did tell the man about those sheep which eat seaweed for their nutrition. He was interested and continued to share how he had found out that some seaweed was also used as a human medicine. The bladderwrack seaweed, which has jelly-filled floats or bladders, was the original source of iodine, which is still used in their medicine and more possibilities for the use of seaweed as a medicine are being tested. I don't know about human medicine but I don't think much of seaweed face-packs for dogs, as I remember only too well how I had that bubbly seaweed draped over me after I had emerged from the sea-water hundreds of miles away when retrieving my red ring. (That ring toy was extra important to me as it had been one of the gifts I had unwrapped in the bar of that Perth dog-friendly hotel on my twelfth birthday, along with my other presents, before playing with it there, in the lift and in the long corridors, much to the amusement of fellow guests!)

My Sue asked the proprietor at our current hotel more about edible seaweed and was told how carrageenan is the seaweed that humans can eat. He recalled how his own mum used to make tasty milk-pudding from it. She would collect this useful seaweed from the beach and dry it out in their London airing cupboard for several months. It would then be steeped in water, with milk and sugar added. He explained that red seaweed is also used as a thickening agent to improve texture in foods such as cottage cheese, jelly, soy milk, some chocolate, salad-dressing and yoghurt - which Lexi the collie loves to lick out of the seemingly empty pot. Although Sue was fascinated by the uses of seaweed, as it reminded her of her dear Grandma May's resourcefulness, I kept quiet like a faithful Dave D... but was inwardly imagining - and looking out for - a much more tasty menu for my evening meal. I was not disappointed.

The next day, even though it was still windy, we all sat outside our blue tents for breakfast. I was amused to see most of my Sue's rice cereal once again being blown out of her plastic bowl and across the camp-site!! Blushing, she looked round to make sure nobody had seen what happened in case they were laughing at her! Luckily for Sue, no human had, just her Dave D - and I had lots of respect for her, so did not show any kind of doggy grin! However, as I am a firm believer in learning by other's mistakes, I immediately put my protective paw firmly onto my own dog dish, just covering the food inside, to ensure that my morning biscuits were not blown away - or noticed by any dogs on the site. I proceeded to eat them carefully, one at a time. I do not like to rush my dry food, so needing to break it into smaller pieces in my mouth, or else some may become stuck in my tender throat causing me to cough. After breakfast, as my toys were still in the tent inside my red bag, and seeing another plastic bottle being blown across the site, I ran over to catch it. (We still always put these in the re-cycling bin before we leave anywhere.)

Later, I caused some kind of chaos when I joined Sue at the sink, to wash up in the communal area, because, being the oh so inquisitive collie boy that I am, I poked my long nose under the cubicle next to where I was waiting on the end of my lengthy lead. A voice suddenly shrieked, "A dogggggggggg!" from behind the thin wall where a lady was taking a shower. Blushing herself, because of my antics, Sue shortened my lead quickly, but not before I decided to shake off the dirty, soapy water that Sue had clumsily spilt on my fur and nose as she washed up. Understandably, preferring to dry my fur before going into the cold outside, I gave an almighty body shake. Unfortunately, my shaking collie body caused the whole cubicle wall to vibrate with an extremely loud noise, to which the showering lady behind it let out another piercing scream which hurt my delicate ears. Before she could appear, we made a hasty retreat running out of the building and across the camp-site, back to our temporary big, blue, tent home for the night. When we were safely zipped in our tent, with just the top flap open, and lights out, we did glance out, just in time to see a cross and confused-looking woman with dripping wet hair and just wrapped in a towel, marching towards a caravan nearby. Sue and I ducked down quickly! We suspected that this was the unfortunate lady I had frightened with my black nose and collie shake as she had her unforgettable camp-site shower!

This tent was not the style of sleeping place to which I had grown accustomed. At the hotels there had only once been any sounds like a herd of sheep trampling through the corridors, but these noises were frequent here in this field sleeping place! I was again tied to a tent peg by my longest lead, just gazing at the tantalizing sheep only metres away. I felt like I should help my Sue in some way like putting my paws on the cords carefully, or tugging them with my strong teeth, as she attempted to hold her tent in place in the wind. To be honest, I was still much more interested in peering at all the nearby sheep and had a prime-viewing spot.

As we were leaving the following morning, my heart sank, when, hearing a loud clatter, Sue stopped the car just before the camp-site entrance. Peering out from the triangular-shaped car window, I saw a silver item rocking in the road next to our car. Recognition dawned on me. Oh noooooooooo my Sue had nearly run over my lovely metal water bowl with that heavy wide tyre. Having turned to see my expression of dismay, I heard the voice of Sue's mum asking me,

"Oh Dave, did we forget your bowl?"

Oh well, it only had a few dents so I could still use it for my water... in contrast to last year when she ran over the camping stove in its entirety and totally flattened it, so it never cooked again!

At our next rest stop, my newly dented water bowl was positioned next to where we were sitting looking out over the crystal clear sea. This was a cue for a photograph I thought with a sigh. I knew I was doing better by not barking each time that Sue got her camera out, so I was determined to temporarily, be bark-free! It was actually a bearded gentleman on the next seat who beat us to it and asked if we could take a photograph of him and his family. He said that his name was Haydon and I glared at their dog, as mum prepared to take the requested picture. However, I could not help smiling to myself as I heard the man call out to my Sue,

"Watch you don't stand in your dog's water bowl!" - because, by now, I knew that this was very likely!

Later on we journeyed north by ferry. I had fun this time poking my head under the plastic seats from the deck to discreetly peep at Alfie the Bassett hound who was still sitting in his humans' camper-van - which they had parked at the front of those cars that had boarded for the short crossing from North Uist, to the Isle of Harris. As I surveyed the scenic mountain range ahead which we were fast-approaching, I made my Sue smile by acting as look-out dog on the front of the large ferry-boat next to a weathered yellow and black sign which was in both languages.

Leaving the ferry, we waved goodbye to Alfie and his family and headed onwards up the beautiful island. We did stop to admire the views and to let a queue of different types of vehicles past, but presently, we came to Horgabost, where we zealously pitched our tents right next to the sandy beach as waves rolled gently onto this impressive shore.

I was used to these big, blue home things called tents by now and even helped by standing guard over our precious bags whilst my humans worked hard hammering our tent pegs into the ground. I was glad when Sue carefully unzipped our welcoming tent and allowed me to go inside. I tried to relax, lying down low, long white legs on display, and looked out through the open door. Mum had zipped just the thin net door, still enabling me to see out, but to feel safer, as no other dog of any breed could possibly enter our tent.

Shortly afterwards, although I had tried to hide it, I was feeling a little uncomfortable as the camp-site was busy with lots of big tents and so many other dogs and humans arriving. Consequently, Sue thought it would be best to leave the site until later on in the evening, instead of cooking on our small stove, and head to eat elsewhere then explore the new area. As we set off I saw a few sheep but I am not scared of them like I am of other dogs. I am even more confident looking at them closely from my Sue's car window! Of course, as you will have realised, we have learnt to keep to the County Code, including to always close gates when we have passed through.

It was with relief that I heard Sue talking to her mum as she was saying how they had to find other camp-sites in case the number of dogs at our current one became too much for me. Therefore, we explored and searched for another camp-site for the following evening. In doing so, we came across the most amazing place, for there, below us on the steep hillside, were tent pitches and also vehicle things that Sue called *wheelbarrows* to take our tents, my bed, and our cooking pots and pans down in. Each fascinating single tent pitch area was separated from the next by wild grasses and heather, giving everyone their own individual space - perfect for a nervous collie boy like me. The kind man who lived there pointed out that there were several wheelbarrows at the front near to where we had parked the car, to load our camping gear onto, making it easier to transport it down to the tent pitch site. Sue explained to me that a wheelbarrow is a small hand-propelled vehicle, usually with just one wheel, designed to be pushed and guided by a single person using two handles to the rear. I was curious, having already seen the strange objects on the way in and been somewhat puzzled as I had never come across such before. I know that collies are meant to like chasing wheels but I doubted that the pushed wheelbarrow wheel speed would make it worth chasing! (In addition, I certainly would not be able to propel the strange vehicle with my inexperienced collie paws!)

My Sue let me sniff the wheelbarrow as she revealed that in ancient times, some wheelbarrows actually had a sail to push them by the wind's power. The idea of a wheelbarrow with a sail made me grin to myself, but I knew I could trust my Sue to push and guide me safely if I was on board. I could just imagine sitting in that funny one-wheel vehicle with our pots, pans, lanterns and tents. I wondered if there would be room for my dog bed and so wished that we were staying there that evening but, as Sue explained, we had already paid for the other beach camp-site where our tents were currently pitched. If I shut my eyes for long enough I could just imagine myself sitting up tall in that wheelbarrow thing admiring the view and saving my paw pads and Dave D legs as Mum pushed me!

We therefore spent that night at the first camp-site, but I felt very nervous and my little body kept shaking as humans frequently walked near our tent in order to take their dogs on the beach. It was the most enormous camp-site in comparison to our previous sites, with so many big tents and caravans. The manager commented that people would let their dogs off leads, even though the rule board said that they were not allowed to! This sent a shiver down my Dave D spine. It meant I was justified in being worried. I just cannot feel happy with dogs running up to me. Additionally, there was a dog in the tent nearby, whose owner let him run round off-lead. My Sue's mum explained politely to them, that in our tent was me, Dave D, that I was an anxious collie boy and that my Sue could not bring me out until their dog was on a lead, in case he ran up to me, as I would panic. They did not seem to understand, so because of this we waited in our tents and my Sue massaged my back to calm me, until the other campers and dogs had left, and the beach was empty - except for rippling, gentle waves lapping onto it. Keeping my bottom still safely in the tent, I slowly peered out and relaxed, for there were no dogs in sight. A few minutes later, I raced onto the appealing pale golden sands, fear long gone and tail-wagging, my body forming a series of those play-bows as I waited for Sue to throw my ball for me. I raced after it into the glistening, crystal blue sea, feeling more relaxed than I remember and so enjoying that wonderful walk along the beach - and even being on the photographs to show to our friend Peter, also a writer, who lives on this beautiful island, but who was on holiday back in England. I was sad not to have met him as I love to meet new friends and I know how much he also enjoys beach walks. Maybe next time he will have returned and will join us for one of our peaceful beach walks?

Returning next to Lickisto and the chicken and wheelbarrow camp-site - situated just across from the Community Café and off the scenic Golden Road, which is the coastal route around the eastern side of the Isle of Harris, I felt more relaxed. It was quieter; there were no dogs and no more than fifteen tents permitted, but all out of sight of each other. This site is better suited to small or medium-sized tents, so there will be less people in each one. Another good thing was that, although the gentleman said I had to be on my lead, there were no signposts saying dogs were not permitted in the wheelbarrows, so I saw my chance and jumped in the minute I saw my bed cushion nestled at the bottom of the barrow and heard my Sue's instruction to "Lie down Dave D".

"Oh Dave D you do look sooooo funny," she exclaimed as I sat cosily pretending to guard our belongings, but was really waiting to start the ride. Sue explained that she had in fact meant for me to 'lie' on the path and wait while she was loading our camping equipment onto the wheelbarrow - not actually lie down in the barrow itself! However, as I was being good and sitting so comfortably, Sue now indicated for me to lie down inside, as it would be safer and make the wheelbarrow more balanced. I followed her request immediately, in great anticipation, just in case she made me jump out and walk!

My Sue pushed me oh so carefully, saying I was her very precious load! I felt so snug myself, as I sat with my white paws resting perfectly on the front of our barrow and looked out over our camp-site for the night, which was also perched snugly above a Harris sea loch. I imagined I would be given funny looks, if anyone saw me, Dave D collie, sat in the camp-site wheelbarrow, but I was just happy to arrive at our camp-site and having fun in the unusual transport provided to carry equipment downhill to the pitch.

As my Sue and her mum wheeled the two wheelbarrows down that hill, we passed chickens, which Sue said looked as if they were wearing furry trousers. Despite this, I was a good boy and, although giving them the most stern Dave D stare, I did not chase them, for I was much too comfortable in my wheelbarrow cart. (This disapproving stare, with my furrowed forehead, was the one I had used on the clay garden creatures which had been placed in my spot on the red rug in front of the log fire at our holiday house in Wales!) I had never seen such strange-looking chickens before and had thought it rather strange when my dad previously said that he had been 'chicken picking' on his guitar, too, as there had not been a chicken in sight! Apparently, it is to do with the human's style of guitar playing used for country music and using a thicker than normal pick on the strings to play it with! I do like to listen to the guitar being played gently as it is soothing to my collie ears. Some campers play the guitar and sing round their real camp-fire, but we just have a gas camping stove and a whistling kettle!

This heavenly camp-site was still dog-free... except for I, Dave D. It also had two impressive buildings called yurts pitched high up on the site to give splendid sea views. Each came with a wood-burning stove - a warm log fire that humans love to relax near - and running water, a low bed, gas stove, carpets and candles. My Sue told me that we were persevering with the tent for this holiday though, and our small, portable gas stove and barbecue - just for use outside our sleeping area, with it being dangerous to ever take any kind of disposable barbecue into a tent due to their fumes.

Down by the narrow sea loch there is a small landing cove for those who wish to arrive by boat, or if they fancy having a waterside camp-fire, but luckily no humans or dogs came by boat the evening we stayed there. This location is locally known as the little fjords. By this beautiful loch, at sunset, we were delighted to discover that there was a fine seat, made from an old rowing boat, which I sat on with Sue to admire the view. We saw a creature which mum called an otter, carrying a fish supper in its mouth. I remembered the otter signposts from earlier in my journey. I had waited so patiently but had not seen a real one. Now I knew what one looked like. After it had disappeared I moved towards where this sleek-looking otter had been in order to investigate further. I discovered that the otters there had made their den in the lochside, and a tunnel entrance just below the waterline.

There was also a building called a blackhouse with a thatched roof, and local heather almost surrounding it, like the heather I sat in to sniff the Barra air, further south, earlier on in this particular adventure. I was just familiar with normal slates and tiles on roofs, but I was later to see a roof made of grass! I loved to explore this camp-site next morning and to take a close look at the wooden bridges and walkways which dotted the fascinating place. Still no other dogs had arrived there, and I did not see the funny chickens again, whose feathers really did make them appear to be wearing trousers, but this was probably for the best, their tail feathers were safe… as there is only so much temptation a Dave D can take!

Next day we continued our journey north from the Isle of Harris camp-site, towards the Isle of Lewis and we bought a one-piece key-ring for Sue's mum of two islands joined as one to show how the Isles of Lewis and Harris are not in fact separate islands. It was becoming dark when we arrived at our next camp-site and the old car did not appreciate the rocky hill leading to our pitch. We heard a *bang,* but my mum carried on driving, planning to inspect the front of our car next morning! I could not see any dogs here, so felt so much happier and knew that I would have a better night's sleep. Even though it was dark, we were quicker at putting the blue tents up by now as the wind had dropped. As is normal practice wherever I sleep, I settled down, resting my head on one paw, and placing my other paw over my eyes. As I drifted off to sleep I thought how Sue had told me about her friend Jake who had been part collie, too, and his mum, Marilyn. I often visit their home next to a large, green field. It all made sense now! I recalled her pointing out the allotments and laughing as she remembered how her Jake used to run off from his human mum each time he saw a man going past on the way to his vegetable allotments, pushing a wheelbarrow! Jake had been so fast that she could not catch him, so he would then run round and round the man and wheelbarrow barking at the wheel as it went round and round too - with his mum shouting apologies to the gardener! I remembered visiting our lovely friend Camille's allotment in Manchester and the interesting river path walk which we went on together afterwards. She is a kind lady who helped my Sue and I when our car broke with her care, concern, excellent advice and contacts. Camille also has a good sense of humour like me, so I bet that she would have laughed at funny Jake's wheelbarrow antics too.

I awoke to the sound of sheep and pricked up my Dave D ears. This tempted me to go to the door of my tent, which was still zipped up, to see if I could smell them. I had known that we had camped next to a beach the night before, because I had heard the lapping of the waves onto the shore and they had lulled me to sleep. We were not on the Orkney Islands, so I had not imagined that there would actually be sheep on this current beach though. I had also not imagined that there were over sixty islands in Orkney, but now realise that people and animals, including collies like me, only live on seventeen of them. I love 'collecting' islands by visiting as many as I can on my British Isles adventures!

Presently, Sue unzipped the tent door, and, anticipating an amazing view, I stepped out of my warm bed before stretching those well-known long legs and walking onto the grass outside our sun-filled tent, being ever so careful not to knock our kettle over! I was transfixed by the beauty of this scene but also unaware that my Sue was watching with great amusement and smiling at me as I lay on my back rolling and wiggling my whole collie body gleefully, enjoying the warmth of the grass as I kicked my back legs to help me move!

Sometime later, whilst walking to collect fresh water and with Sue firmly holding my lead, I remembered the sheep sounds. Turning my head to the right, I saw them, high on the hillside, what seemed like hundreds of them. However, I behaved very well and chose to resist temptation to drag my Sue up the hill after them. I had been up to enough mischief scaring that innocent lady in her shower at our first camp-site. I am not really a King of Mischief though, and even if I was, I could not beat clever and beautiful Mist collie - who was definitely Queen of Mischief - and her own camp-site antics! Being a clever collie she had learnt how to open the family's caravan door from the inside.... and she did just that - letting all the family's collies out of their holiday caravan! When her human mum returned, she found their other collies wandering around the camp-site and Mist still in the caravan lounging on the settee and looking verrrrrrry smug indeed! Just to be on the safe side, my own mum now places a bin against our back gate so that I cannot open our gate to escape and she will no longer let me sit at the front gate next to the pavement to look out, (which I used to enjoy), as many dogs are unfortunately taken from their own gardens by strangers.

Chapter Twelve

Sheep!

As we drove closer I could see grass, real grass... but it was on the roof of a long croft house on the Isle of Skye, and I couldn't see any sheep of any colour grazing there. My Sue later explained that some houses do still have this type of roof and that others used to have heather roofs, plus that the grass is special grass. Inspecting it closely, it looked like meadow turf and I bet that birds made holes in that roof, which would then leak. I wondered how the humans would use a lawnmower up there to mow this turf roof. It would be tricky, I imagine! Maybe it would be allowed to grow long and mown down just a few times a year? Even so, I was not keen on watching the roof grass grow or, (as the image came into my head), of being anywhere near any pesky orange grass-cutting machine either. I would not be allowed to try and herd it anyway so was more interested in looking for 'sheep' on our travels.

Through listening to my Sue's conversations, I learned how all thatched roofs on that island used to be made of marram grass, like that which I stand on when walking in the sand dunes on the way to some beaches. The tough, shiny, sharp nature of this grass did not appeal to me and hurt my furry legs when the end of a piece stuck into me as I brushed against it. Humans now need special permission to use the marram grass for roofs, as just over three hundred years ago, drifting sand covered several villages - due to the fact that there had not been enough marram grass left to build sand dunes in order to hold the sand better and so protect these villages, which led to its use being banned. Therefore, most marram grass needs to be left alone because it helps to build sand dunes and minimise coastal erosion, stopping the sand dunes from wearing away as quickly. The dunes are also important for a variety of species of butterflies and wild plants.

Common grass is actually the tallest grass to grow in the British Isles. As you know, I am familiar with heather and I also heard that its long stems were additionally used as roofs instead of grass, it being secured in bundles to roof batons, with its roots pointing down. I fondly remembered how I lay in the heather on the Isle of Barra, peeping out, almost camouflaged, and despite an Outer Hebridean breeze, how warm and safe I had felt. Yes, I bet that heather roofs would keep the homes of humans warm and dry on this Inner Hebridean Island of Skye, too. As for another alternative – using oat and barley straw for roofs - I was unsure about the efficiency of that, and whether horses would try to eat them; I definitely would not have agreed with seaweed roofs, as it would be much more useful to fertilise their crops, or for dogs to play with on the beach! However, I still would not like to eat this seaweed, although, as I mentioned, I do realise that I already eat it, in some form, each time I have any ice-cream. I love ice cream and the parts of her cones that Sue shares with me - but not those silly plastic cones that vets make some of us dogs wear! In North Wales, we did see signs for pork and seaweed sausages which - despite my reservations - did actually sound quite tempting to a collie boy like me with a good appetite!

Admittedly, I had not had much experience of being a real working city sheepdog as I had not been allowed off my lead near sheep. However, I had gained a taster of herding sheep on a previous holiday in Wales. I was there with Sue and her family when I spotted some bold sheep actually walking past our red car down a lane in the quiet Snowdonian village of Beddgelert, famous for another breed of dog and his adventure. As Sue unclipped my seatbelt, my collie herding instinct kicked in and I prepared to jump out of the car. I heard the click and felt Sue attach my lead to my harness... then saw my chance! Before Sue had hold of my lead handle, I leapt over the seat and out through the open car door. Sue's brother had already seen the sheep and shouted a warning to Sue, so presumably the nimble sheep must have heard too.

"Hold on to Dave D... there are sheep!" Mike had shouted.

Unfortunately for Sue, it was too late as I had seen the woolly creatures before mum had and although on a lead, I was already half-way towards them by now, bounding down the lane. My Sue was being dragged behind, grasping the middle and just about holding on halfway down my lead, in a vain bid to slow me down and stop me herding the now running sheep. Their woolly bottoms were moving up and down as they ran and it was like something out of a ridiculous movie. We must indeed have looked quite a spectacle, as was evident when I heard strangers gasping and laughing. I was in my element and ran faster and faster after the two woolly sheep, pulling my Sue behind me, her smooth shoes failing to grip the slippery road. The puzzled creatures must have heard and been even more concerned to hear my panting and black paw nails slipping on the stone road as I strained, then crouching almost in a herding position, towards them.

"Baa baaa" they echoed as they ran, next turning right through a gateway.

"Wooooooooooof" I responded, carrying on in strong pursuit, only finally stopping when my Sue grabbed hold of a large tree trunk, jolting my lead, which wrapped itself and her round the thick tree. To my own displeasure, I was stopped in my tracks, much to the relief of Sue and the increasingly uneasy sheep!

Back in Scotland, I gained a further taster of sheep-herding when mum allowed me to look from our car window at various sheep as we travelled down scenic country roads, but she refused to stop or even slow down. Despite this, I did catch the eye of a solitary sheep with huge, curling horns, responding by giving it the collie eye as we passed!

However, later, I was out of the car, on my shortest lead, as four big, even more woolly sheep passed nearby on an isolated road. They saw me, they heard me, but they rudely did not even increase the pace of their walk to a trot. How I would so have loved to herd them, but with mum tightly gripping *all* of my lead, there was no chance of that this time! Therefore, I could but stand and stare as they looked back at me, defiantly and not at all concerned, showing me no respect whatsoever!

Another time, we had been for a walk on the Isle of Skye and returned to the now dirty car when, on the opposite field and hillside, I saw more alluring sheep and wanted so badly to race into that field and round them up. To chase is my normal instinct and a working collie has this moulded to serve by working the sheep. As a city collie I still have my chasing instinct and because it has not been moulded in the same way, some of us are tempted to chase bikes as they pass us with big wheels spinning or such as car and van wheels, instead. Once, I tried to chase a white van which was moving slowly uphill in the cold, slippery snow, its wheels spinning, temptingly - which had given my Sue a shock as I had never done this when walking with her before, no matter what the weather.

Returning to the field of sheep which I had seen, and knowing my instinct to chase, Sue was having none of that, however, and kept me firmly in her sight, with a strict "Stay Dave D" command. Of course, I obeyed and sat next to my red travel bag, focused and fixing a definite border-collie eye stare in their direction - the type which teachers give to their students when they expect an immediate response!

Despite them being in the distance, I stared again and again at those sheep, both collectively and individually. Almost immediately, the sheep, who had been staring nervously in my own direction, started to move together in a v-shape formation up the steep hill. I had done it! I, Dave D, had herded the straggling sheep! A city dog in the countryside working country sheepdog-type magic!

I was not sure if my Sue had been impressed, for the very next day she announced that we were going to see a 'real' working collie at work in the field herding a flock of sheep.

When a puppy, my fellow collie, Amber, had once rounded up two older retriever dogs by lying on her stomach, (like Toby terrier does when he sees children), much to their confusion and greatly surprising their owner - who was wearing a tweed skirt and fancy jacket! Amber would not let them go and the rounded-up dogs could not move! Amber's mum, Avril, had so wished that she had taken her camera with her to capture this priceless scene in order to show a photograph to her wonderful granddaughter, Caitlin, and to Amber's human dad! As you know I am also an amusing and clever collie, so I hope to meet Caitlin next time I am in Scotland and to make her laugh too. She will be able to take her own photographs of me and to tell her favourite teacher and best friends about granny's friend, Dave D, being such a funny collie boy!

Dyson collie in North Wales, had run over to his family's chickens, when they escaped, acting all macho and supposedly to help with rounding them up. However, the chickens chased him and poor Dyson ended up cowering in the family's kitchen. In contrast, Meg, who was then a very young collie puppy, was the opposite. As she trotted along through the local park, off her lead, showing signs of independence - yet turning round every few steps to check that her mum was still there - five tiny ducklings appeared from behind a bush waddling in single file across Meg's path! Instead of giving in to her border collie instinct to chase or herd them, she simply sat, and with a tilt of her little head watched as they crossed from one side to the other, then carried on scampering ahead as if nothing had happened!

As for Mopsi collie in Bangor, she once focused on and circled a whole crowd of tourists, quietly trying to round them up! They had called out in shock! Mopsi's mum, Lisa, (who had been trying not to laugh), had eventually gone to their rescue and called for Mopsi to go to her! Jess collie is a fellow tri-coloured collie who lives in picturesque Peebles, which I have travelled to and admired on my travels. I have met Jess and learnt that she was far from amused when a young lamb, with black legs and a black face - including its ears - tried to round her up, confidently following her up the country lane, close on her collie heels, possibly even copying the herding skills it had learnt from the farm's clever sheepdog collie! Wee Jess turned to her left and gave a surprised look - rather than her usual collie stare, then quickly trotted off after her mum, Caroline, for safety.

It was like role reversal and I was glad that a lamb had not chased me when I was in that area during my travels on our way to Edinburgh. Little did I realise that not one lamb but a whole herd of sheep and eighty hooves would soon be echoing across a field towards me!

The very next day, I knew that I was going to have to face facts that my Sue was going to ask me to be a brave boy and become close to another collie boy, because she was going to return and hopefully find that collie, which they had been visited by high on the mountain road a year before. Indeed, this had actually been the main reason for our return journey to Scotland. My mum had shown me the collie's photograph and I had hidden my concern as I knew that she was determined to meet him again. Previously, an old farmer had told her that he was called Corrie, after the collie had appeared and sheltered from the storm by the side of their parked car. They had watched with interest as he had then run high up onto the heather-covered hills to bring a small, orange-wool coloured stray sheep safely back to the rest of the herd. My Sue had been awestruck as Corrie had darted here and there, herding the disorientated sheep into a safe place nearer to the others.

After a camping breakfast, with that damaged bumper tied as securely as possible, the wheel hub still missing, and almost a whole year on, we retraced their memorable journey and saw the heroic collie almost immediately. Corrie the collie ran towards us as if he remembered the car and two kind humans, also giving them big friendly doggy smiles. He did not see me at first but I saw him, through my triangular window! He reminded me of myself somewhat, but his confident stance suggested that he did not have the same anxiety round other dogs which I unfortunately have. He had the same collar that I recognised from his photograph. I did not feel jealous, but did feel a little worried, although I trusted my Sue to keep me safely in the car. Corrie approached our car as we stopped. He was tall like me and stood on his hind legs, placed his front paws on the car and looked at me through my little car window closely. I stared back with an air of worry. I noticed that he was definitely also a tri-coloured collie like me, whose fur coat was a similar colour and shade to my own, including brown fur on the back of his rear legs and white fur on the tip of his tail.

Instantly, my Sue told me that I was fine, how this was the collie she had told me about - albeit now a year older - and that I must not worry, because the doors were all shut and my window less than half-open. I felt safer on my soft cushion and gave Corrie another one of my famous Dave D stares! Mum chatted to the owners and explained how she had met Corrie by chance the year before. The lady said that he was six years old now and that she had only given him a home two years ago as her pet. He had been walked on leads in his early years and was therefore too house-trained to be taught to work as a sheepdog. His humans were impressed as Sue explained how amazed she and her mum had been with the way Corrie rescued the little lost sheep. They said that he had not been good as a farm sheepdog as he often chased the sheep, scattering them, but did not bring them back. My Sue made it clear how good he had been that the day she and her mum saw him bringing that lost sheep back. His owners continued to explain how Corrie loved to wander around behind the sand dunes over the machair - which is the low-lying open land made of grass, fertile soil and a thin layer of calcium-rich shells blown onto the land from the West Atlantic gales - next to the camp-site and visit the campers there. The machair is where lots of birds, crops and wild flowers also flourish. Sometimes Corrie was still there with the campers after midnight, and Mr. McDonald would go searching for him, on some occasions as late as four o' clock in the morning.

Corrie's owners told us about a female collie dog that really did work the sheep on a farm down the road and my Sue decided she would go in search of this working collie on the other side of the hill, and ask her humans if we could see her at work. She indicated that I would then see what real sheepdog collies do all day - whilst I relax in my big garden, watching pigeons and rolling on my back in the soft grass! Saying goodbye to Corrie's family, we drove along and I looked out in half-hearted anticipation. I would much rather it was just us and no other collies on our holiday, but I realised that I needed to know the working-collie facts for my Diary. I tensed when I thought I saw white sheep, but as we approached, I discovered that they were just white-painted boulders! I sniffed the air with what was to be short-lived relief, but there was definitely no sheep smell reaching my sensitive nose… yet!

We finally arrived at the working farm and Sue boldly went to talk to the tall farmer. He did not have his whistle but kindly said that he would still give us a proper sheep-herding demonstration using his voice, as his collie had learnt to respond to both forms of communication when working the sheep. The collie who lives and sleeps in the outer barn appeared, leaping a fence on command, to join the sheep in their field. Although separated by the fence and a flock of sheep, it was with some trepidation that I agreed to leave the safety of my warm and secure seat in the car to venture out into the farmyard home of Trudy collie. My Sue, ever-thinking ahead, left her car door open and seat leading to my back seat cushion, pulled forward, to reassure me that I could return if I felt too uncomfortable about the other collie coming too close to me. Sitting upright on the grass, ready to leave if I felt unsafe, I watched with interest and fascination as the helpful farmer shouted commands in that different language called Scottish Gaelic, to his collie - Trudy then responding, both with her border-collie crouch and running round the sheep. I heard directional commands such as "Come bye" which I worked out means face the sheep, then circle clockwise round the sheep, keeping her distance but moving them calmly as directed. She scanned the field, approached the sheep, lay down, rounded the sheep from the right, then from the left. Moving under her influence she got them to walk towards her master - which is called the 'lift'. (Much different to the mechanical type of lift which I am familiar with on my adventures!) When the "Away" command was given, I recognised how Trudy took those sheep in an anti-clockwise direction towards her master. "Get back" was instructed when Trudy was working too close to the sheep and likely to cause them stress. This command sent the collie further out in order to give the sheep more room. As can be expected, everyone needs their own space - even woolly sheep! I wish that fellow dogs would understand my Sue when she shouts "Get back!" to them as I nervously see them approach me off their leads!

Keeping my distance and despite my fear of all dogs, I watched with collie pride for a fellow collie, as she also obeyed instructions to round up three sheep which had become separated high up on a nearby hillside. I had thought how calmly Trudy worked the sheep from one place to another, while I, being Dave D, would have been tempted to just chase them and nip them into place.

However, after some time, as I watched that working collie herding the sheep, I was dismayed to hear the thundering sound of many sheep hooves coming towards the gate and fence - which I lay on the other side of. I imagined being head-butted or lunged at by one of those approaching sheep - so I jumped up, my went tail between my legs, I about-turned and started to run towards our car. Almost instantly, Sue called me back saying that she had never heard of a collie who was afraid of sheep and I had to lie down and watch for a few more minutes. (I have since learnt that there *are* large, stubborn, lowland creatures called Heavy sheep which are difficult for a sheepdog to move and that they will sometimes even attack a dog; such would have a disastrous effect on any collie's confidence, as indeed my own slowly re-growing confidence was affected by events in my previous life, so many years ago.)

In this instance, I obediently settled back down to watch them, trying to relax, realising that I was safe behind the field gate, but still being prepared to jump back into our car if the collie leapt that field gate and came too near me. I noted how loyal Trudy collie skilfully controlled those sheep well with her stares and body, not with her teeth, only nudging two with her nose and moving them from one place to another in accordance with her master's voice commands. She would outrun them, before moving around the flock, again bringing them towards her master, rounding them from the right, then the left. Her collie-dog instinct and the farmer's experience had developed into something mutually understood, and there was a close bond, although she only ever spent the night in that outhouse barn or was fastened up in the yard.

It was such a different collie life from my own life, living in a town house with a real log-fire and my dog cushion, my home-stitched raincoat to keep my back dry - and rear legs protected if it rains - and never left chained up alone anywhere, day or night. Trudy was hardy, used to all weathers with the wind blowing in from the sea against her thick coat, which would become heavy with lashing rain in the freezing winter. It would make it harder to run but she would still run with speed. Even in the heat of the summer she would be twisting and turning, driving the flock from valley to hill and hill back to valley, holding a hundred sheep, moving them down the hill like a white waterfall. She had been trained to work the sheep from being a puppy, more usually by the whistle command. In a training pen, dogs work with sheep without being too close, which enable them to practise herding, not chasing. I was glad that her master was not using the whistle communication method today, as my ears were feeling sensitive as usual.

I am thankful that Sue does not use whistles - except in the playground at work when I am not around to hear it - and that she mainly just uses calm voice commands to direct me. In comparison to the working collie, I know different instructions including to stop, wait, give kisses, roll over, give a paw and jump up, up, Dave D! Although full of admiration, I did not wish to meet Trudy collie face to collie face because, as you know, I am not a fan of rubbing noses with other dogs. I was therefore relieved when Sue gave me my own collie-command, to return back into our stationary car. I was giving Trudy her territory respect and also felt safer in my spot just peeping out through the car windows! As I watched intently, the last I saw of Trudy was as she ran past our car, leapt fully over a nearby five bar gate on her long, agile collie legs and zipped off up the heather-filled hillside, pushing the flock of sheep ahead.

My Sue explained to me that in a Sheepdog Trial, it is called a 'Fetch' when Trudy brings those sheep in a controlled manner through a set of gates towards her handler - taking them close to and behind him, also ensuring that they all go through. (Thankfully, the only fetching I do is of my toys when Sue throws them for me!) The next phrase is known as the 'drive', where the sheepdog must take the sheep away from its handler, through two more sets of gates in as straight a line as possible, sometimes with obstacles in the way - as this imitates real working conditions - driving them round the course. As you are fully aware, my Sue and I, her Dave Dog also find many obstacles in our way during our own drives and adventures, which we, too, manage with determination.

I am aware that the final command, "That'll do", is used to indicate to the working collie to stop herding those sheep and return directly to its master. (I usually return directly to my Sue when instructed, although admittedly I only turn my head towards her and then back to the focus of my collie eye stare if another dog is nearby and therefore may need to be called several times before actually going to her.) A good sheepdog needs what is known as 'eye' which is a kind of powerful glare the dog can fix on sheep to make them move in the direction this dog wants. A dog with 'too much eye' can become entranced, and instead stand rooted to the spot glaring at the sheep, ignoring all commands from its master.

I was interested to learn that I am still like a working collie in a small sense, as their handlers sometimes choose to muzzle their young collie and fasten a long lead or washing line to its collar for control when introducing them to sheep. In the same way that Sue is very aware of my own possibly unpredictable behaviour when meeting other dogs, the sheepdog pup's handler does not know what its first reaction will be to sheep and realises that their instinct could be to bring down its prey! I have admitted to sometimes stalking fellow collies like a lion and staring intently at other dogs of all breeds. I bet those collie pups also rub their face on the ground to try and free themselves of that muzzle contraption - like I occasionally do!

Our friend, Milissa, had a working collie called Dew, who responded well to her flanking whistle commands, running as the sound told her to, rounding up the sheep or goats. However, one particular day in the early summer, her mum was surprised when Dew started working the sheep at the far end of the pasture in the opposite ways to those she had commanded on the whistle, so Milissa started giving a second whistle to correct her collie girl. This happened for several days, with her mum blowing the whistle commands and Dew even zig-zagging and going the wrong way. Her mum was quite firm with Dew, but she just looked back as if to say

"I am doing what you told me!"

I felt sorry for Dew collie, as she seemed adamant that she was responding to her mum's whistle. Another day, Dew's response to the whistle was flawless when moving sheep from home to a neighbour's patch to graze. Her mum then decided to fetch some of the goats and go down to the far end of the pasture with Dew, but as soon as Milissa whistled a command, it was strangely followed by another whistle!

It was a few days later that she whistled again, and from the beautiful willow trees by the pond came a mockingbird's reply! Its voice resembled Dew's mum's whistle and was almost an imitation, so the collie was hearing and responding to that in addition to his mistress's whistle. In the end the clever collie learnt to recognise the difference in location and to distinguish between the two, only responding to her mum's cues and ignoring the troublesome bird! Dew's mum was so relieved as she had been very worried in case her collie had a hearing difficulty... but Dew must have been puzzled, too and thought that her mum was mysteriously communicating from two places at once!

Another time I encountered sheep was a few days after our visit to the working farm where I had felt so intimidated by that herd of horned sheep racing towards me, staring at me from behind the gate. This time, we had gone to an extremely long beach with rocks at one end. I was innocently looking some way along this unusual beach, scanning it for the movement of a fellow dog as I walked with my humans, totally minding my own business. I had seen no dogs, not even in the distance. Suddenly, I heard my Sue let out an involuntary gasp, so I looked all round, finally following the direction of her eyes upwards. To my utter astonishment, what seemed like dozens of the sheep creatures were looking down at us from the cliff-top! This time there was no working collie to round them up and no fence separating us! I admit that my tail immediately went between my legs and that I stared up feeling totally taken aback. They kept staring back as if to say,

"Is that Dave D? We think it is... oh Dave D, your fame precedes you... Dave D the nervous, but adorable town collie from England!"

I gave a little run towards them but, being concerned, Sue called me back and warned me that if I did try to chase them I would be back with her on my lead straight away! I sat with a resigned thud, staring up at the sheep. Eighteen beady sheep eyes stared back at me!

I was disappointed but, to be truthful, I had not felt confident of trying to approach or herd them anyway! I had realised that I was not cut out to be a working collie, and Sue knew this, although it would do my confidence good to be at close quarters with the woolly creatures for a while. I moved a little closer, wondering what they were really thinking, before Sue called me towards her to make more distance between me and them.

I lay down again, mouth slightly open, staring upwards and Sue put my red bag beside me for comfort. It was quite full so I hoped they would think that there were two collie dogs, even if one had a red plastic coat on. My Sue was sitting nearby. To be even more honest, I was unnerved and glad when it was time to walk further up the beach and away from these somewhat intimidating and staring sheep!

On the way back from our walk, I strained my eyes looking for those same sheep high up on the cliff-top, but they were not there. To reassure me, Sue suggested that we climb up to the area from where they had been peering. With my little Dave D heart pounding, but Sue encouraging me and by my side, we headed inquisitively upwards before soon arriving at the sandy, green, cliff-top. There was still not a sheep in sight and I intuitively suspected that they would not be far away, but with Sue's arm round me I felt braver so barked loudly, as if to say,

"Here I am!"

Old Hemp

Another famous tri-coloured collie boy lived over a hundred years before me and his name was Old Hemp. Hemp was a male rough-coated collie too, with a mostly black coat like me who also had two white front legs, complimented by some white on his chest, as I do. We were both born with white on the tip of our tail. His dad was a black, white and tan good-natured collie called Roy and his mum was a black sheepdog called Meg. Old Hemp's back legs were black with just white paws.

Old Hemp was used as a working dog to herd sheep, whereas I am a city or town collie and do not work sheep - but as you know, I do help my Mum with her work by keeping her company and giving her my paw. His dad, Adam, understood collie behaviour well, as he had worked as a hired shepherd and later as a farmer. I have been in our car through Northumberland where Old Hemp lived all those years ago. He was a quiet, mild-mannered collie who also physically trembled like I do, but not when he saw other dogs, just when he was herding his sheep, due to working so intensely.

My friend, Gordon, cleverly wrote a poem about border collies like myself and Old Hemp as he recognises how intelligent, outstanding and renowned we are. Old Hemp had an amazing herding ability, unlike me - although you know that I do crouch down, in true sheepdog style, if I see other dogs, rather than sheep! Old Hemp's style was different from that commonly seen during his era, as he worked far more quietly than the other sheepdogs of the time. As a result, this style was adopted and used by breeders and trainers. It actually became the most common style among Border Collies and Old Hemp's descendants became successful international sheepdog champions.

Although I, personally, am short-haired too, I have a ruff of thick fur round my neck and this coat protects me when I am outdoors with Sue in all weathers, as Old Hemp's coat must have protected him all those years ago. Like Old Hemp, I am also athletic, muscular and have a lean back, walking on the tops of my toes, these being well-arched with deep pads, and strong, thick nails.

Chapter Thirteen

Hole Explorations and Revelations

The first time I ever went to the Welsh seaside was with my Sue. We stayed in a big house and I loved having a new place to explore. I was sure that I could smell cats, so, naturally, I went looking for them. As I searched inside the old house, with no luck, I was curious after discovering a heavy, wooden kitchen door with a little rectangular hole cut into it near to collie eye and paw level. Except for a key hole or letter-box, I had never seen a hole cut inside a door before, so did not know what it was for, and therefore went to investigate. I could hear feathered pigeons or seagulls outside - and suspected that prowling cats may also be on the other side of it - so curiously stuck my collie head slightly through to see if I was right. I could not see any. It was a strange type of door and I could hear the wind howling through it each evening, which was somewhat bothersome as I tried to sleep!

On the final day in our holiday home, Sue had gone out shopping and I, despite never having suffered from actual separation anxiety, was worrying and missing her, so when I heard her coming up the side path, I excitedly rammed my full Dave D head through the door hole to greet her.

Suddenly, there was a loud crack as the entire plastic door flap broke off and shot up into the air before landing on the other side next to her feet! It had given me such a shock as it rose into the air and clattered down. Even so, I was not too worried, as I knew that my Sue would understand and forgive me, as she knew that I had missed her. Her dad eventually repaired the door and that entire hole vanished, almost without trace! I discovered that it had been called a cat flap and that he had replaced it with a piece of wood, which means I now have to stand on my back legs to look out of the big windows instead! It is fortunate that Ellie the Labrador puppy found a cat flap in her neighbour's door at four o'clock in the morning, two nights after being lost on a woodland and heathland adventure. Our friend Jan, explained how Ellie had let herself in, to the safety and warmth of that neighbouring home and was there when they woke up, much to her owner's relief.

Rover collie also uses a hole in his Sunderland home, but for a different reason. The hole is in his house wall, where there used to be a large air brick for a back boiler. Rover runs outside into his yard when his human mum or dad prepares to use the vacuum cleaner. He does not like them and waits outside until the room cleaner, (which humans also call a hoover), stops making a noise, then pokes his head through the hole in the wall, to check whether the loud machine has been put away! I have been to Rover's house on my way home from

Dundee and have seen this hole, but was much more interested in staring at their cautious cat, Jess, who was perched high up on a tall wooden cabinet, before strolling along the top of it, all the time watching me intently! Rover's younger brother, Bandit collie, also uses the hole method of entering and leaving the house, but he is not afraid of the vacuum and has in fact actually tried to bite it! Being inquisitive, I do not mind noisy hoovers and bravely watch my mum vacuuming, at close quarters, occasionally putting a white paw on the strange purple electrical creature-type object, only to be stopped in my tracks with a firm look from Sue! Nevertheless, I do think that orange lawnmower machines are rather too noisy, so as I have previously admitted, I am sometimes a little cheeky and do try to chase and herd that big orange machine to stop it when my human grandma tries to cut the lawn. On one particular occasion, Sue had stopped me from snapping at it playfully, to save me from breaking my teeth….. so I just lifted my left front paw and gave it my intense collie stare instead!

It has recently been reported that people have spoken out against the lawnmower's noisy hum in defence of flowers! To a collie with fragile ears like mine, this seems like a good idea as, compared to lawnmowers, flowers are not noisy, unless they have a buzzing bee inside them drinking their sweet nectar. The people say that fellow humans should give up their lawnmowers and let their grass grow in order to make it more bee-friendly, to protect daisies, lavender and primroses from being mowed down - these being plants which provide vital pollen for bees. This is because it is said that the bee population is falling across the British Isles and indeed across the whole world, although we do not want to encourage bees into our own garden, for reasons you will learn. Primroses grow in our Wales house garden and we often admire them when we are there. These same flowers are also always very welcome sights in Scotland as their appearance signals the end of the long winter.

Due to my reaction to lawnmowers, I am often shut in the small kitchen whilst lawn-mowing is taking place but I still used to spy on that orange monster through the cat-flap to check when it had been unplugged and returned to the porch. Some dogs are scared of thunder as well as any vacuum machine noise, and many are helped by wearing a thunder-jacket, which is snug-fitting and puts gentle, constant pressure on our furry body. I have only ever worn my raincoat-type jacket myself but that is also snug-fitting and makes me feel so protected and secure in rainy weather too.

The very next day, upon climbing up a stone pathway leading to Criccieth Castle, I certainly felt even more mischievous when I found another hole not far from that cat-flap door. As we had approached this historic castle, the flags were flying as if they had known that I, the author Dave D, would be arriving and there was even a bowl of clean water at the entrance! The lovely lady in the ticket office made me so welcome and said, upon hearing my tale, how glad she was that Sue had rescued me. With Claire and Sue following behind, I pulled Lauren up to the top of the steep, stone steps, then looked down on the fabulous view with rapture and amazement, before going to explore.

On entering one of the twin inner gatehouse tower rooms, I looked at Sue for permission, then she let go of my red lead as I leapt onto a stone shelf to have a closer look at a long, slit-type hole - which I now know to be called a loop-hole, in the tower wall. Its width was about that of a human's palm width, but just wider than two of my paw widths. In the past, arrows would have been fired from here by archers who were protecting the castle from any enemies. I proceeded to peer through this loop-hole, having a fine view of the back legs of a pale-coloured greyhound with its master beneath me, both oblivious to the fact that I was there, my red lead trailing! Sue had laughed at the funny scene of my back end as I stood with my nose poking out through the ancient castle's arrow hole.

If only those dogs and humans had known that there was a collie watching them intently, and that I, Dave D, was acting like king of that particular castle as they walked below without realising I was there. Initially, I glared at the many dogs, before deciding to sit down to relax and just watch the world, and dogs, go by.

Eventually, Sue left me with Lauren and walked round to the front of the historic castle to take a photograph of my seemingly tiny furry face, looking out of the hole which had been used to fire those arrows through hundreds of years before. I did not bark at the camera on this occasion, as I did not want to give my high up hidey-hole place away. In addition to noticing Sue, I was by now spying on a steady stream of dogs and humans, of various shapes and sizes, from the safety of that Welsh castle tower's loop-hole. I could see them, far below! They were unaware so still could not see me giving them that famous 'collie eye', as I lay comfortably, despite the stone floor, staring out from my cute Dave D face, little pink tongue and two white paws in front of me. I felt inconspicuous, safe and relaxed there, loving the views for miles around.

As evening arrived and darkness fell, my human friends got the giggles, as Claire spent ages trying to open the sturdy door of the cosy house where she was staying with our lovely Thomas family friends. She had spent two days with another welcoming family at a nearby bed and breakfast house the evenings before, so this new door was not as familiar to her. Claire and my Sue had been struggling with a usually simply task, puzzling over why the issued key would not fit in the hole and open the house door. I watched with great amusement, because, being an observant collie, I had known all along that it was the house next door which she and Lauren had been going in and out of all day, and that Claire was actually attempting to put the correct key in the key-hole of the wrong door! They finally realised their mistake when a surprised-looking lady opened her front door and said that she thought we were trying to open the wrong door! To which Claire and my Sue apologised and both must have blushed in the dark night, before erupting in laughter as the wrong door was closed with a bang, proceeding to open the correct door to the house on our right. I was glad that no dogs lived there, only very caring and friendly humans.

Sand holes

The year before, when I was on my holidays in Scotland, my Sue had driven a considerable way to a quiet beach as she said that there was less chance of us meeting any other dogs there. To begin with, I was concerned about the smell of sheep from the moment I jumped out of the car. Secondly, running to a pen-like enclosure and poking my inquisitive Dave D head through the gate bars, I could see plenty of evidence of woolly-coated creatures in the form of lots of wool on the concrete ground, but not an actual sheep... even though I sniffed and checked the entire pen with my sharp collie eyes. I scanned the beach and hillside beyond, but still could not see sheep or creatures of any kind. I breathed a sigh of relief but, alas, as previously, this was to be short-lived - much to my dismay.

"Come on Dave D, it is time for our picnic", Sue called encouragingly, as she held a metal gate open for me, leading down to the long, white-coloured sandy beach. I recognised this gorgeous beach as being the very same one we had seen in the distance, from our dog-friendly hotel across the shimmering bay and had set off on our quest to find. My Sue's map reading skills had been accurate this time! I ran through the open gate and, again remembering the Country Code - one main rule being to always close gates which you go through - Sue shut the gate behind me. Alert as always, we were all scanning the beach for dogs in case I would need my muzzle, which we had already checked was in my red travel bag along with my tray of tasty dinner! All we saw near the beach gate were two old-fashioned bikes, which was supposedly a good sign as it suggested that there would not be a dog with their owners. I could tell that mum was relieved too, though I was worried about hurting my legs if I tried to walk up and over the spaced out wooden steps. However, she lifted me over the construction called a stile, then let me off my lead so I could run down that tempting sandy pathway which opened onto those dream-like sands and the turquoise sea beyond, rippling gently.

This was such a contrast to the huge, noisy waves rolling in from the North Atlantic Ocean on the opposite side of the same island, where we had discovered the brown seaweed that looked like sticks. I still had one of those, now dried, seaweed sticks with me, which I had brought from the other beach, but I kept losing it in the sand as I played! I settled down on the sand waiting for my special treat and water. No sooner had we opened our picnic, when a human walker appeared in the distance, approaching from the opposite side of the beach. I was alarmed to spot that accompanying them was, unmistakably, a dog, still high up on the rocky hillside! My Sue was amazed because she had brought me to the most remote beach that she had ever been to and I was still going to encounter the very thing she had been lovingly trying to protect me from! I could tell that it was a collie before it even reached our picnic spot and it was now zig-zagging down that hill, coming closer and closer to 'our' beach. Sue saw my look of extreme alarm and assured me that I would be safe as the dog must be with an owner. Sue pointed out that small human figure in the distance, to me, and said that she would ask this advancing walker to please put her dog on a lead as they came closer. I did gain comfort from Sue's words of reassurance but I still felt unnerved. My body temperature had risen and I could feel myself shuddering as I do when I am nervous of another dog. The dog was tri-coloured like me, but smaller and younger, its mostly dark fur coat a little longer than mine.

I was not usually free on a beach but we were miles from the nearest house so a lead had not seemed necessary. Seeing the dog now running directly towards us, I had started to worry, as there was not time for mum to put my lead on as well as my muzzle. Leads can make me feel more frightened and restricted at such times, anyway, so my Sue quickly reached for my now familiar muzzle to place on me, in order to keep the other dog safe if it came too close. This was in case I panicked if that fast-approaching collie ran, circled and bumped into me from behind, knocking my legs from under me, which another dog had unintentionally done once before on a beach. That time, soon after Sue had given me a home, my back and legs hurt as I hit the hard sand, so I had turned in shock and almost automatically actually bitten the other collie. I will never forget the look of dismay and disbelief on my Sue's face as she shouted "Stop!" I had felt so genuinely shocked and totally ashamed of myself, but being knocked into at speed had taken me off-guard so I had, thankfully, not been blamed - and no permanent harm had been done either. However, realising that she would now be asking for - and taking - friends' and experts' advice, I had known that from then on, my Sue would always ensure a safety guard in place. (Mr. Muzzle joining us on walks has since become a consistent part of my life.)

On this occasion, I stood trembling on that previously peaceful beach as the Scottish collie approached, almost praying that it would not barge into me as it ran. As a precaution, I felt Sue gently putting my soft, black muzzle - with its strap to match my lead, round my head. She comforted me and reassured me that she would look after me and that I could take my familiar muzzle off as soon as the little dog had gone.

As I looked back, I recalled wearing it once before by the sea on the way to Black Rock sands and caves, when I had walked with my mum's friends' collies Mopsi and Sian. I'd had to keep my muzzle on as we were all racing down the wet beach at low tide and, as I explained, this is necessary because I become scared if another dog bangs into me, and my muzzle keeps the other dogs safe in case my reflex and anxiety makes me react in fear. I try so hard to be a confident boy and my Sue was proud of me for sitting so close to the other collies on the hill above the dark caves and Black Rock Sands.

Being totally truthful, I feel safer with my muzzle on as it warns dogs off and gives humans a signal that it may be wise and fair to responsibly put their own dog on a lead - if it is not already on one. When I saw a dog and felt worried, I crouched down, which is instinctive collie behaviour, when we intend to round something up. As my friend James told me, our collie breed's shoulder bones are different from other dogs and allow this sort of movement more easily. Seventy-five percent of a dog's weight is also carried on our shoulders and front legs. In fact, we do have somewhat similar skeletons to you humans - but about a hundred more bones!

Returning to the beach part of my Diary, as it happens, the lady knew that the collie was called Honey, but said it was not actually her collie and that it had just followed her round the north of the island! It had kept darting on ahead, seeming to keep to well-worn sheep tracks, and stopping to seek out vantage points. It was almost as if it was her land and she was acting as a guide for the route, knowing the territory and keeping the lady holiday-maker safe. It reminded me of our friend Pete's clever dog, Ben, who had proudly and confidently guided his six-year old brother round Banbury town, with help from his human mum. Therefore, as the knowledgeable collie approached, I gave a startled little growl before racing after it up the beach. The run did my legs good as they thrive on the opportunity for speed.

I was surprised that Sue had not called me back as she could only see me in the distance. I realised that my tail was between my legs, but I hoped that my Sue would not be worrying about me. She seemed to be learning not to worry as much and to trust me more. This voluntary closeness to another dog was progress - a new and most unfamiliar part of my new life and adventure.

As our running up and down the beach continued, and Honey kept giving play-bows, her ears up, her front paws extended, but not knocking into me or reacting to my fear, my temperature started to decrease a little... and I felt some of that fear slip away, like it does on collie-club walks. The other collie's tail kept wagging from side-to-side and she was indicating by her body language posture that she was ready to play and have fun with me. I noted how the white fur stripe on her neck was much wider than mine, before turning my head away! Little did she know that I was unusual in that I do not usually play with other dogs! The other collie did not seem a threat to me, so I started to relax somewhat, which thankfully made my Sue calmer too.

I was intrigued and although not exactly 'playing' with her, I still tried to find Honey when she attempted to play hide and seek with me, weaving in and out of the lowest sand dunes, then down by the small rocks. However, I stopped when she ran wide, into the sea, and began swimming. I am not allowed to swim from unfamiliar beaches, and, as you know, I was not used to playing with - or even being so close to, other dogs. I could tell that my Sue was proud of me by the look I saw when I glanced over to her. As a human, my Sue knows that I only move into the play-bow position when I am with her, and that it is for the express purpose of inviting her to play a game with her Dave D. After she returns from her teaching work I greet Sue with my tail wagging and big smiling Dave D face, then we go into the long garden. In this instance, I communicate by means of a stutter bark, which starts off with a low "arrrrrrr", followed by a louder "ruff!" When she accepts my invitation, we begin by running round and chasing each other. Although she looks funny, my mum sometimes even mimics my play-bow as well, which I find exciting, so I then accept her own invitation and the fun begins.

Last time I was on holiday on a beach in North Wales, I had shared my smooth sea-carried stick with Mopsi collie, but today, I was much keener to chase this intruding collie away from our picnic. I decided to attempt conquering my fear and beat that threshold, which I seem to reach upon seeing another dog, by continuing to run and chase the other dog - but Honey still seemed totally oblivious to how much of a nervous boy I am. Once again, she hid in those sand dunes and I kept trying to spot her, though keeping more of a distance by then, but not growling. On organised collie walks, Sue always checks with the other human owners how their collies will be with her nervous Dave D. I hear her tell them how she worries that dogs will understandably react in self-preservation and bite me if I growl at them, so I have been trying not to show any fear and not growling. In the end, Honey ran and played in the crystal clear sea on her own, wagging her tail, seemingly unaware of my own tail being so low.

Coming out of the sea, it appeared that Honey collie had eventually realised I was not the most friendly of collie boys and wanted to chase her but not play, so she decided to go and investigate our personal picnic things, before running off with my nearly empty food tray of Scottish meal - potatoes and minced beef, clumsily scattering thousands of sand grains all over our plates and in my water bowl!

Honey's behaviour around my beach lunch, reminded me somewhat of how little Lily terrier from Northampton had run off from her mum on a beach visit and landed right in the middle of a family's picnic! Consequently, Elaine had to apologise to the astonished family who proceeded to try and shake the sand off their carefully made sandwiches! Likewise, lovely Maisie Labrador had run off from her mum, Bev, whilst walking near a local lake, then decided to pinch the warm sausages which a family had just cooked on a beach barbecue and left in a tray for their own lunch! Understandably, they had not been impressed!

Minutes later, Honey returned, without my now empty food tray! I looked on with amazement as this cheeky collie suddenly did a strange kind of dive and started to pat the dry sand, then putting her two front paws into this sand, scooping it up and aiming it behind her, scattering the sand seemingly everywhere…including all over me! I shook my treasured fur coat in disgust, but curiosity took over my initial cross feeling. I continued to watch, no longer knowing what to make of the situation!

Sue and her mum had now covered up our picnic items and, being aware of the unfolding drama, they started to laugh. I just stared, although it did look odd as deeper and deeper into the sand the unwavering collie was going until her little bottom stuck up in the air, but with sand continuing to fly everywhere. I kept watching with my usual collie fixation and reflected on my life up until this day… including how I had never seen any beach or the sand or felt the sea gently lapping at my Dave D paws until my Sue had rescued me and taken me to her home, then on our adventures round the wonderful British Isles. I love being by the sea, although I admit to having been wary of the larger waves to start with.

Although keeping one protective eye on me, Sue continued to chuckle as the younger collie dug deeper and deeper until half of its furry body was now hidden and just her rump and question mark shaped collie tail sticking up from the hole. I had never tried digging in the sand before but decided that next time I would. Honey collie looked so odd. I then closed my eyes to think and also to stop any sand going in, also visualising my own furry bottom stuck up in the air - if I only I knew how to dig a real hole.

Keeping my Dave D eyes closed, I remembered walking by the Saltburn sea with our dear friend Clare, and how she loves her own dogs so very much, like my Sue loves me. Clare explained to us how dogs have three eye-lids on each eye, the third one being to remove debris such as sand, but it can still be uncomfortable. I felt grateful that they both understood me and my difficulties so well. Clare helps so many dogs like me who have anxieties, so she did not judge me and even made me special biscuits with red ribbons on, in the shape of bones which I ate all up. They were delicious and I felt so loved and fortunate there on my holidays, meeting such a lovely new friend.

Clare's dogs are always there for her and a consistent part of her life as I am of my Sue's and she is of mine. Opening my eyes again, I was also willing my body temperature to go down even more but I was definitely feeling more at ease. The young collie girl was still not interested in worrying me, just in making a verrrrrrrrrrrry deep hole! However, Sue did see the fear in my eyes before I shut them and knows how we dogs produce fewer stress hormones if we are petted. Shep's mum had actually explained to her how this helped Shep collie learn to cope in certain situations too, so Sue started to stroke my back with long, firm strokes, pressing hard through my skin to massage my muscles. I soooooooo loved my doggy back rubs and how she soothed and reassured me in a calm voice that I loved.

It was my turn to look odd later on that day as we returned to the camp-site and I did my usual scan for dogs. To be frank, I can reveal that we dogs do pick up on our human's emotions and anxieties, so I knew that my mum did the same sort of scan - much as she tried to hide the fact! There were signs of dogs the other side of the camp-site so Sue presented me with a toy rabbit to distract me in a caring attempt to try catching me before I went 'over the threshold' as the humans call it - this being when I panic when other dogs appear or are even in sight. In Wales, I frequently run to my safe spot on that little beach we visit, but in this case, the Scottish beach was not familiar to me. This time my 'safe place' was the tent, but mum's plan worked successfully as I was fascinated by the strange toy creature which I had not realised that she had brought in the car with us.

I felt no threat and, wagging my white-tipped tail, I gave the soft brown and white rabbit a good sniff, by now feeling relaxed and confident, patting it with my paws, then around a small part of the beach and through the tough, shiny stems of the now familiar roof-making marram grass in those sand dunes. Much to my Sue's amusement, and as I personally, was not any longer amused by this furry rabbit creature, I gave it a subtle kick with my paws, before standing on it, grinning, and making sure it was half-covered in sand!

"Oh Dave D what are you like?" I heard my Sue ask knowingly, but with an adoring smile!

Later, after being called to come out from the security of my tent to play (following the eventful day with that other collie and her holes), Sue explained that, as well as some dogs, real rabbits dig holes too, leading to passages called burrows - which are like secret underground roads, where they live. My mind recalled how that young collie had done a splendid job of burrowing in the sand earlier that day. I was glad that I did not live in a rabbit hole though!

Even so, I had gained so much confidence through my frequent observations and did try to dig like a rabbit, with mum encouraging me by pointing my paw to a sand dune next to the camp-site. I clearly remembered how the other collie had been digging. Scooping enthusiastically, my nose pointing down, I dug deeper and deeper, scooping pawful after pawful of sand, totally focused, my long white legs turning a sandy colour. It was such fun.

Despite not being a puppy for over twelve years, this was a totally new skill to me and, although not fully successful, I felt proud trying. I had heard of hares, which look a bit like rabbits but live on the ground, not in holes. I had not yet, seen any of these on my travels. I had also heard humans speak of 'hare-brained' ideas which are out of the ordinary ideas, and my Sue has many of those! I would have recognised the hare though as Sue had read and explained that these hares have black tips on their ears, whereas my own ears are all black. I sat in the heather more than once on our Scottish holiday with one ear or both stuck up pretending to be a hare or a rabbit hiding! A young hare is called a leveret, but they are not easily fooled by a half-camouflaged collie boy, so I have not yet seen one of these either! I saw a few domestic cats, but did not see any wildcats on my travels. They are known as hunters of rabbits, although their own kittens can fall prey to the golden eagle. I am glad that the golden eagle has never tried to hunt me during my travels!

Unlike Tess collie in Gloucester - who ran after her ball and returned to her mum, Maddy, with a real rabbit - beyond one quick flash of brown, I did not see a single real rabbit nor the long upright ears of a brown hare at any stage of my holiday. The hares' ears are between six and eight centimetres long. I was not too happy when Sue appeared with her classroom ruler and measured the length of my own ears before declaring that they are nine centimetres long!

Despite it being summer, I did not see a moulted, now white-coated, mountain hare in the heather or gorse either, but I would like to have done, as they are even smaller than the brown hare, yet with feet that are broad like snow shoes - and I do love the snow so much, as I will explain when I am writing my 'At one with nature and myself' diary entries.

I learnt more about the smaller collie that I had chased earlier in the day from a friendly gentleman who was talking to my Sue. He said that the uninvited collie was like an unofficial four-legged tour guide for the island of Vatersay and frequently showed visitors all the way round this island. However, the collie once followed a touring cyclist all the way to Castlebay, where our ferry came, in. Consequently, the landlord of a local bar had to ring her lady owner to come and collect her. This lady had arrived on her farm tractor and given Honey a lift home by the same form of transport. I had still not been on a tractor at this stage, but had already decided that I would be a good boy when I saw one and not chase after the big turning wheels.

Although having that strong instinct to chase pebbles which I see being thrown into the sea by humans, I am not allowed to in case they damage my teeth.. However, some collies are even more fixated on chasing bike wheels, also being determined and cunning, so when we are walking, their humans still have to keep them on short leads and put a hand out between their collie and a cyclist as they pass, to stop their dog still trying to reach the cycle wheels or tug the cyclist's leg, or even give chase as they pass like on the Surrey collie walk deep in a forest! In contrast, in times gone by, black and white Dalmatian dogs were actually coach dogs and both encouraged and trusted to run along the road, clearing the way for horse-drawn carriages.

The next day we returned to the beach and I leapt out of our car eagerly, then became more cautious. I tried very so hard to be a brave little 'tri-collie' as I scanned up and down the beach, praying with all my doggy heart that I would be the only dog on that whole beach. I knew that Sue understood - although so many humans mistakenly think that I will be fine, that I should already have learnt to socialise, that my fear is not real. Unfortunately, it is frighteningly real. After checking there were no sheep in the pen and scouring the beach to check that there were no collies there - or on the distant hillside - and being thankful that none was in sight, I started to run gleefully, with the wind whistling through my half bent ears, which were flapping like birds' wings.

Sue followed at a more leisurely pace with her bag of food and my red travel bag. Having put our bags down, she pointed to the inviting sand and scooped some out with her hand. It reminded me of when she play-bows to me and made her look sooooooo funny. Quickly becoming aware of this, she turned and warned her own mum not to take a photograph of her, although I bet that she would have taken one of me! I got the hint and imagined my furry paws doing the same. I gently padded over that soft sand to where my Sue had started her hole, also beginning to feel braver and more confident inside. I wanted to make her proud, and believed that I could do it, even though it was new to me. I so wanted to please my Sue but knew in my heart that digging a big hole for the first time would also be a personal achievement for me, an old collie boy.

I saw the opportunity to copy yesterday's collie again by digging in that fine sand. Although I had practised briefly on the side of the camp-site's sand dune, that previous evening, it was not the same as in the flat sand. I positioned myself and prepared to scoop with my Dave D paws eagerly. Showing true determination - and much to my Sue's amusement - big paw scoops of sand flew up behind me as I dug and dug. I heard her chuckling, then, words of encouragement in the gentle, positive voice I had grown to know and love with all my heart. "Yes! You *can* do it Dave D!"

I was in full collie digging mode, so poked my head out and grinned as I looked sideways, then gave her my biggest, most genuine, Dave D smile, as if to say:

"Yes, you were right, I can do it! Look at me!"

Deeper and deeper I dug, almost re-enacting that collie girl's actions the day before, until all that my Sue could see was my tail and cute rear end sticking up just like in the image which I had imagined when I had closed my eyes the previous day! I knew it was very likely that Sue would now be taking photographs, which would usually cause me to respond with a glare and series of sharp barks, but I carried on regardless and with absolutely no inclination to bark. I could not see the camera anyway, so just popped my little head up again to give another of those big Dave D grins, my tail wagging and held high, so reflecting my true happiness. To be honest, I was feeling rather pleased with myself and was having such fun as the sand flew backwards, scattering on the beach behind me and almost reaching the sea.

As my legs began to tire and I felt that it was time for a rest and to drink some of the cold water in my bowl, I came across a pale, blue rope, buried deep in the sand. It was almost like the type on my favourite tuggy toy. Closing my eyes temporarily, to keep out the sand, I had imagined a giant tuggy-ball attached to the end to play with, and both pawed and pulled at it determinedly, in a vain attempt to find the end and see if my vision was right.

Even though I had a tight grip with my old but sharp collie teeth, the tough rope was stuck fast in the sand. Sue explained that it looked like the same sort of rope which is attached to the lobster-pot marker buoys, usually floating in the sea. I returned to our picnic area and my much-needed drink, secretly hoping that I would indeed have my dream of a giant tuggy come true later in our fantastic holiday adventure, which as you now know, it did!

Attic Holes

It had been a very relaxing day. I had been in the newly-designed garden and my Sue had been to work teaching Geography and English to children, doing her break duty and then to the hairdresser's. She had groomed my own fur when she returned, and I had delighted in a doggy massage before enjoying a brisk walk in the nearby forest before dark.

Consequently, I was now resting with my one paw under my chin, and had just closed my eyes when I heard a metal sliding sound and footsteps. I therefore guessed that Sue was going up that big ladder into the hole in our kitchen ceiling leading to the attic - probably to find the blue tent thing she told me that we would soon be living in for several nights. It had sounded odd, as I much prefer to live in my bungalow on my cushion; additionally, I did not like my Sue climbing high ladders and disappearing through that hole in the ceiling anyway. I heard a *whoosh* followed by a thud as a blue, circular object appeared above me, then landed in the hall, next to where I lay, opening one eye then sleepily returning to my relaxed Dave D composure - but keeping one ear alert in case Sue needed me.

Suddenly, I was jolted wide awake by a loud bang and clatter of metal followed by my Sue shouting,

"Help!"

Still half asleep, I leapt to my four long legs as fast as they would allow me and set off in search of Sue. I looked all round our home, padding into each room frantically looking for my mum, but to no avail. She was not in the bedroom or kitchen or bathroom or living room... and then I heard it, a frightened sound, almost a whimper.

Racking my brains, I suddenly remembered where I had last seen Sue with her lovely new hair style, and padded into our kitchen, nails clicking on the tile floor. Glancing up at the loft-hatch hole in our kitchen ceiling, I saw a white-faced Sue gripping the sides of the loft hatch tightly! I realised that her long ladder was no longer attached to the metal hooks at the top, but was lying at an angle in the kitchen, with half on the worktop! She was marooned. The ladder had fallen down and Sue had leapt to safety but she was still up in the attic roof hole.

I looked up at her lovingly and hoped she realised just how much I loved her and that I would go to fetch help for her. Quick as a flash, I

ran into the other room to ask for that help from my human dad. I barked loudly but he told me to, "Shhh Dave D", as he was watching a good action film. Little did he realise about the dramatic action in our own home! I barked again and again, and kept running to the kitchen to check that Sue was still safe and awaiting rescue, and to reassure her that I was on the case, then racing back to dad and barking once more. I did not care that he was enjoying watching a western film like some collies also do. Backwards and forwards I went until he followed me and found Sue, still trembling slightly, still perched high up in the ceiling hole! He stood up tall to re-connect the ladder and make it safe, enabling our Sue to come down the ladder warily and join us in the kitchen! I put my paws on the lower rung of the ladder to help her, my tail wagging and lots of paw loves at the ready for Sue. As she lay down on the settee to stop her dizziness, I joined my mum, stretching fully to make my furry body longer, in an attempt to comfort all of her. She says cuddling me always helps her to feel calmer, so I thought that this was a very good plan.

Unexpected encounter and bolt-holes

I hope you are finding my diary to be full of enjoyable tales including what I have achieved in spite of my impeding fears. My experiences can lead to all sorts of unexpected behaviour by me and often takes even my human mum by surprise.

Take the short February walk to the beach from our holiday house in Wales in the bad storm for example! One minute I was walking sensibly and the next... much to my astonishment, a large, black, doggy nose set in white fur, was poking out at me from a hole-type gap beneath a wooden gate... unnerving me to say the least! At first I froze... yes, my whole Dave D furry body seemingly freezing with fear... watching, staring, waiting for the rest of the dog to emerge... but I could see no eyes, just a wet-looking nose and white fur!

Sue was reassuring me that I would be fine and I finally realised that this long nose belonged to a creature much too large to ever emerge from underneath that sturdy gate, so I was safe!

Shuddering, I continued to walk a few more paw steps down to the familiar beach. I still wished that we had been safe in our red car though, as I can always stare much more safely at strange creatures with big, long noses from there! I also longed for my warm coat that mum usually places on me, with its big, white fleecy collar, especially as she had her own warm coat and hood on! I am always comforted when wearing my raincoat and, imagining this comfort, I longed for it to be fastened round my furry body, or for some kind of additional reassurance of safety.

As if by magic, extra reassurance and warmth indeed presented itself to me! Unexpectedly, this opportunity appeared in the form of a large, unattended van, with its side doors open. I had not really stopped to think fully, but I was still a shivery Dave D partly due to my fear of the dog and partly due to the stormy weather. Without thinking for more than a millisecond, I stood up on my strong back legs and leapt into the back of the van, landing amidst fluorescent jackets and tools, plus a range of other mostly strange objects! I was not afraid as it was warmer and I had been careful where I put my paws.

However, my human did not seem to be impressed by my leap and new seat - or my best Dave D grin, as I looked out at her from the warmth of that useful van, which I realised, without a shadow of a doubt, as I felt a tug on the lead attached to my harness and heard Sue say, in a slightly raised voice,

"Dave D get out of there now!"

I was certain that my collie pals' mums had used some similar words to those when they behaved as I did. I imagined Toby's mum as he leapt into that open post van as the mail man had been collecting the mail near to his home, and Buddy collie's mum up in Dundee, when he jumped in and sought shelter from the rain on that stranger's car seat… and Badger's mum, Heather, as he leapt from his walk on the canal path onto a stranger's barge and into the actual cabin, where he had smelt sandwiches and quite fancied sharing them! I was just being a typical mischievous collie, like so many others in our collie group, with a mind of my own!

Still on the subject of holes, our humans have a strange word for the place where they put food, called a cakehole. It means their mouth, so we dogs all have a cake-hole too, which we certainly make the most of! Us collies love food, as clever Badger clearly does as was shown by his cheeky barge food-theft antics! Likewise, Smokey-dog was also crafty about food, as his mum, Claire, had been making a picnic for them all to enjoy, but when she turned around, the whole loaf of bread had disappeared! She was totally astonished and could not understand where it had gone to. After some searching she discovered Smokey with a half-eaten loaf, so she was then obliged to make a smaller picnic! Dolly the collie was also cunning, as she saw her chance when her mum left their fridge door open, pinching the entire piece of stilton cheese that had been bought especially for her humans to enjoy on Christmas Day! Just as Dolly's mum arrived at the fridge shelf and discovered it to be empty, Dolly had cheekily re-appeared to check if there was any more! She had been careful not to touch the grapes though as she knows that these are harmful to us dogs. Rosie collie had gone one step better and was also up to mischief when she ignored her dad and ran off from him on their walk, making her way towards the smell of food. After thirty minutes of searching, her Dad, Phil, heard laughter from inside a local engineering factory where employees were having their lunch-break. Upon investigating the sounds of laughter, Rosie's dad found his collie in their canteen enjoying a corned beef sandwich with two amused workmen who had found her! It reminded me of Cassie collie in Wolverhampton who runs off round her home and steals whole packets of crisps from her mum's cupboard then hides them in the garden or in her mum's bed. Parli collie also used to fetch items for her mum, then hide them! More food-orientated doggy mischief came from Buddy collie who once ran and pinched the fishing bait from the fishermens' containers as they fished in the River Tay in Dundee. I saw where he had taken this bait from on one of my walks with his mum. As for me, I once pinched a very long green-skinned vegetable called a cucumber and bit the end off, much to my Sue's dismay, as she had thought that I was just sniffing it - but at least I had now given her another photographic opportunity!

Young Susie, the collie-cross from Reading, had a feast after her mum, Marylyn, went out leaving a whole plate of freshly-cooked chicken on the kitchen work surface to cool. Her humans had been unaware that Susie could actually reach up on her back legs like I do. (I must have more self-restraint, being an older collie boy.) Upon returning, her mum found the worktop empty and just stopped herself falling on the slippery, greasy floor, where Susie had pulled the warm chicken down and enjoyed her unexpected feast! As for Bobby-dog, whilst his family were out visiting their friends for just a short time, he entered the kitchen pantry and discovered a special giant gateau, which had been carefully placed there to thaw by his mum. Pulling this down, Bobby had such a wonderful feast too and when his humans arrived home, they found that he had eaten half the gateau and that it was all over his long fur coat, the floor and everything that he had walked past! Midnight labrador loved to drink from his master's cup of tea when he was not looking, but Maurice and his family always forgave him, as they loved him so much. I am a good boy when I go on Criccieth beach - and admit to sniffing the air which is often full of picnic food aromas……. but in days gone by, I believe that Grandma May's terrier used to be exceptionally mischievous……cunningly watching families on the beach… then sneaking into people's beach huts to search for food whilst they were enjoying a swim in the sea, next taking it back to his human family proudly! Once Tinker terrier even took a whole chocolate cake and presented it to them!

Natural holes

As with the arrow holes built in huge stone castles, holes are not just built or dug in the sand, and have often actually been formed hundreds of years ago. Some may be found in the form of twisted tree root holes that have appeared above the ground and which I can see through, or hollow tree trunks in which I can sit inside to shelter from the bitter wind and rain - yet can still be seen from the outside of so clearly. There is one such hole near to my home in the Cannock Chase Forest where both Elwood spaniel and I sometimes choose to sit down in the middle of our walk, to hide from dogs, just to rest, or to shelter from the rain. We have usually been running in the narrow stream or chasing rabbits or squirrels so are in need of a break. I keep my muzzle round my neck ready for Sue to put on to me if a dog suddenly appears without a lead - which I am constantly on the look-out for.

I was very brave recently, when exploring the Derbyshire countryside with Dolly the collie and other friends at a collie meet-up walk. There had been three of us wearing muzzles that day, so I did not feel like the odd one out - and it was reassuring for my Sue and the other humans too. We came across a huge hole in a steep rocky hillside which the humans called a cave. Dolly, the explorer-dog had just come out, so I ventured inside. It was rather dark so my Sue protectively warned me,

"Dave D, please beware of bats".

However, in my excitement, I had thought she said "*cats*" so, in eager anticipation, I had raced in, tail fully up and very excited, searching for these four-legged furry creatures! This had made Sue laugh and I could hear her telling Maria that all she could see from outside the dark cave was my white furry bottom and neck stripe, the pale fur on the backs of my rear legs and the underside of my tail, being illuminated in the darkness! There were definitely no bats in there, but I was wary in case one came in search of food, as some species of bat eat three thousand insects in one night and there were also plenty of dark-coloured spiders ready to catch insects in that English cave! Up in Scotland the spider's web is famous for inspiring a weary soldier by its determination to complete its web.

My Sue was still smiling when I re-appeared at the wide entrance to that cave, my eyes blinking in the bright sunlight, and she told me how I had reminded her of Sam the loveable collie when his mum and dad had taken him on a holiday to Cornwall - a place where I have yet to visit to see our friend, Cynthia. While Sam's mum, Diane, was in the shop he stayed outside with his dad. As they waited, a little girl had gone past and, seeing Sam, she had remarked on what a fluffy bottom he had! This made his humans laugh lots as he was indeed verrrrrrrry fluffy all over!

One of Sue's friends once texted her to say how 'wonderful' it is that I, Dave D, always seems to have 'so much fun'. As you will recognise, from reading my Dave D's Diary, this is *so* true. I love how our friends like to see interesting and amusing photographs of my adventures, how they giggle at my own furry rear end, how they say that they hope to meet me in person, wishing for the opportunity to kiss my face, scratch my little chin or rub my soft Dave D tummy.

Whilst in that cave, and indeed, as the humans had been admiring my rear end, I felt a light tickle on the fur at the top of my head as I had curiously pushed on further into the cave. Turning slightly to the side, I had noticed how a tiny spider had been busy spinning an intricate web, that web now all but covering a small hole in the rock. Water drops were now dripping onto it making a shimmering light, despite the darkness of the cave hole.

I hoped that no delicate spider would spin a web behind me across the cave entrance, as several had done in olden times to keep a couple and their special baby safe from unfriendly people one cold winter. At that historic time, those spiders had persevered with determination, being fully aware of the hugely important task, spinning and spinning, again and again, until they eventually managed to spin their giant web across the entire cave entrance. As a result of that and the frost glistening from each tiny web thread, nobody had guessed that the precious little family were safely hidden inside. I knew that I would be safe outside with my Sue and did not want to hide anyway, just to explore for a few minutes more. After I had once tried to chase a spider across our floor, one Christmas, I had been amazed when Sue stopped me and explained the significance of spiders and how their web was the reason that tinsel had first come about, to represent the frost on that special cave's web, and how even now it adorns trees at Christmas time to remind us how the spiders kept that important family safe. I remembered the cold, dark cave but most of all, the glistening web, so enjoying the feeling of the soft, sparking, silver tinsel which Sue had carefully draped around my neck - representing that protective frost-covered web as it shimmered across that historic cave's entrance.

In contrast, Ms Molly collie had once pulled her family's Christmas tree down onto herself by mistake, tinsel included! Luckily Ms Molly was not hurt and she would still have had wrapped-up surprises to enjoy - which may have been delivered down her chimney ready for Christmas Day. I have learnt that a chimney is narrower hole which usually goes up through a brick house and onto the top of a roof in order to let smoke out from a fireplace log or coal fire below. A giant of a man, whose job is a chimney sweep, comes to clean our Wales house chimney to make sure that soot is not able to catch fire if we make a log or coal fire there to keep us warm. He appears in a white van with a little model chimney brush sticking out from the top on a stick, which always causes me to stare more than once with true collie fascination!

Last visit, the chimney-sweep man was very friendly and made a fuss of me. I sat up and stretched over, giving him both my white paws against his blue overalls. Sue had explained that he was coming to help us, so that made him a sort of friend, and therefore, I was not to bark when he arrived. To me, he was a very tall stranger and even towered above Sue at our house entrance but, although curious, I was an obedient Dave D and kept my bark inside! After covering our red, semi-circular rug in a large piece of strange, coarse off-white material, to stop it being dirtied with soot, he had brought long sticks in - which I felt like pinching and running off with, before he could add his brush and use them to clean the open-fire chimney. Instead, I refrained and watched him with further collie curiosity. We were grateful when he had put the sticks together and cleaned our chimney, making it safe for us to use. Next, he told us to go outside and look up at the roof in order to see his bristly, black cleaning brush peeping out of the top of the chimney, proving that it had been cleaned, which we did, although it looked very silly up there!

On a more serious note, I still do not like to sit too close to the open fire and big flames anyway, so my Sue has stopped putting paper on when I am lying there. However, as the chimney sweep man was fussing me, he was also mentioning how it is important that humans do not put plastic wrappers in the open fire in case they go up and block the house's chimney, causing silent, invisible fumes to enter the room. He also suggested that my humans have a carbon monoxide tester on top of their cupboard, as it can be hard to detect the fumes without one. My Sue once felt poorly and discovered that her previous car was leaking such fumes into her car from the exhaust, through a hole in the boot bodywork. I wish I had been there to give her my paw, but she said she was glad I was not as I might have also got headaches and felt light-headed on long journeys, as I would have been on my back seat cushion and nearer to the hole.

Although a carbon monoxide detector is recommended for every home, a smoke detector is vital, so my Sue frequently changes the batteries in ours, but never forgetting to replace them. Although, being an older collie, and already aware of the dangers, she still makes sure the old batteries are disposed of correctly as some collie pups have been known to become very poorly after chewing such.

Chapter Fourteen

Collie Travel on the Buses and at Sea

Sometimes, as I am sitting quietly in the well-travelled car, when we are on a long drive, my Sue reaches round and holds my soft paw gently for a few seconds, to show she knows I am there and that, though she is busy driving, she loves me. Other times, as you may have seen, I choose to stretch out my leg and gently tap the back of her driver's seat or her shoulder or arm, with my paw to reassure her that I am there, too, and I am enjoying our adventure. This especially helps her on long journeys although she does take regular breaks, so is sensible, and I enjoy my stops, too.

If we arrive at a service station and there are too many dogs near the main area we find a quieter part for a walk and drink. As we prepare to park, I am constantly alert and searching for other dogs already outside, resulting in my mum often becoming sad when she sees me searching obsessively and freezing, the involuntary fear clear in my eyes, as I spot one. On an August adventure, my mum had known that I would not wish to share the available service station dog water bowls, as there were far too many other dogs travelling, all heading to different destinations of their own around the British Isles and maybe even further afield - whose humans had also allowed them to jump out in order to stretch their legs. I was actually heading to our Newport walk and dog-friendly hotel. As a result, I had my own bowl in the car, although the water in my travel bag bottle was by now warm. We explained this to a kind food-kiosk gentleman who made a fuss of me, and who reassured us that his dog, a Labrador, was also fearful of lots of other dogs, before handing us a free cup of refreshing cold water from his tap, to take back and put in my own clean bowl.

However, as our car isn't the most reliable, my Sue often decides to take us on alternative forms of transport. That way she can't lose the registration plate or knock the end off our bumper or even pull half the exhaust off by mistake! I quite like other transport types anyway, as it means that I can sit closer to Sue.

Collie on the Buses

As I have mentioned, people sometimes ask my mum if I am actually an Assistance, Therapy, or Working dog, due to the fact that I wear a luminous, green harness - but, it is just that fleecy material one, which has reflective parts like those on workmen's jackets and road cones. As you know, this trademark harness came with me from the rescue centre, so mum explains that it is just to stop me pulling on our walks. It can also be seen clearly as the strap material reflects when we walk on the darker evenings to keep Mum and me safe near the roads. I love to travel on buses and I watch intently for our bus, my precious travel bag by my side - often early in the morning from the now familiar bus stop in Swinton, Manchester - feeling and looking like an accomplished collie adventurer!

When we are in Manchester, my Sue says how proud she is of me, what a good boy I am, how patiently I wait at bus stops with my red bag and also how sensibly I lie down and behave on the bus. I have so much enthusiasm for travelling, and as the time for our timetabled bus to arrive approaches, I keep calm, although I am full of excitement inside, anticipating our next adventure. Consequently, I see the bus appearing round the distant corner, but continue sitting as my Sue has trained me to. If it is extremely cold on the pavement she will, of course, not give that 'sit' command to me and I will be allowed to just stand and wait or cheekily even jump up to join her on the bus shelter seat.

As the bus pulls in, I frequently stand up and wag my tail. I have always loved our bus journeys and, although I pretend to be modest, I also love the admiring glances I receive from fellow passengers. My Sue has to pay for me on each Manchester bus ride but she does not mind as we love such times together. Once the folding bus doors have opened, we have jumped on, and my Sue has paid, I often sit next to where the wheelchair passengers are, keeping them company. I sit looking out of the front window, but if I see a human passenger looking at me I sometimes give them paw loves and make them smile. However, if they have a dog, my Sue usually moves me to a different place so that I cannot see it anymore, although I do try, and it sometimes catches me peeping round the corner of the seat at it!

One day, whilst in East Yorkshire, I was lying on the floor at the back of the double-decker bus, correctly, with Sue and her mum sitting on their seats. A collie with his humans joined the bus several stops later, but much to my horror, he had been allowed to lie right across the bus's aisle. In comparison, I have manners and am always considerate so I do not block the aisle. Therefore, although still enjoying my adventure, I was staring, trembling slightly and worrying how I would get past that young black and white collie dog without making contact by paw or tail as I passed. I knew I would panic if it jumped up and banged into my back legs or face. Thinking ahead, Sue stroked me and spoke calmly, reassuring me that she had a solution. I was relieved when Sue put my muzzle on me as we stood up to leave, so conveying a silent message to the other collie's owner, who thankfully noticed, heeded, and placed her own collie up on to her knee, next to the window. Upon hearing the 'bus stopping bell' and seeing the green light, I was now able to relax somewhat and trotted proudly down the now clear bus aisle, totally ignoring the other dog, ready to leap off, with my handsome collie head held high, much to the delight of fellow passengers!

In hearing Sue speaking to other travellers who have left their dogs at home, it has brought me happiness - indeed to both of us - when they have commented honestly on how they feel inspired by my own adventures, so much so that they may take their dogs on a bus next time, many for the first time ever. Some will have already done so since they met me on my travels. I hope so much that the others do, but that they also teach them to lie sensibly under the seat or at the side of the bus, and that they and their dogs go on to enjoy as many bus or train adventures as my Sue and I do. Nan is even going to take her Tia collie on a ferry, which makes us even happier, as Tia is nervous like me and it will build her confidence up to go on such travel adventures. She may even write her own diary, one day, with her mum Nan's help!

Last year, my adventures took me upstairs on a big open top bus, at the seaside in Scarborough. It did not have any windows or a roof. On that particular bus adventure, I had been constantly looking for other dogs as we passed them walking on the pavement below our bus with their humans; I got some strange looks, but even managed to allow them to stare back at me without growling at them; at the same time, I had also been so very careful not to nudge the passengers' red *Stop* button which was near to where I was resting my nose - as I so wanted to ride on that unusually breezy bus all day!

I recently sat curled up on Sue's knee as we travelled on the top deck at the front of a bus all the way from dog-friendly Whitby to Scarborough. I had enjoyed a busy day so rested my chin on the front shelf and went to sleep dreaming of more adventures. I knew that I looked cute because as I drifted off to sleep I heard a little girl comment on how the 'clever collie dog' was 'sleeping on the shelf'!

Other times, when I am wide awake, I may suddenly decide to tap a stranger with my cute paw, especially if I feel that my Sue is texting her friends and not paying me quite enough attention! She does look up then, to see what I am up to and usually has to answer questions about me from admiring fellow travellers. I did this tapping at the Oban ferry terminal while Sue was next to me buying their tickets. Sometimes they look at me in surprise but choose to ignore me, like at that ferry terminal, but other lovely people are delighted and full of smiles with my Dave D cuteness.

My friend Toby collie whom we visit in Seaham is funny as he is not keen on noisy trains, so when we arrived by train after our long journey from the Midlands, he and his mum had to hide and wait behind a fence to meet us. Therefore, his Mum decided to take him on the bus instead, to try and help him become used to travelling, but he had never been on a bus before. Toby did sit nicely next to his mum and she was very proud of him... until there was a "Ringgggggg" as a passenger rang the bell to let the driver know that they wanted to get off the bus. Suddenly,

"Woooooooof" Toby went, in response to the bell ringing. This continued for the rest of their journey. Each time a passenger rang the bell, Toby would respond with his "Woooooooooooooof".

Thankfully, the caring driver smiled with understanding. He must have known what some of us collies are like!

Collie at sea

Another time I had my red bag packed as we drove away from the big green table hotel, towards that busy place called the ferry terminal. As we lined our car up there, an official looking man asked Sue and her mum to write their names on separate boarding passes. My Sue asked if she needed one for me, but he said that dogs did not need them! She was surprised, as she thought that all humans and dogs needed to be accounted for on any boat journey. I later found that there were three other dogs on board so they would not have been issued with boarding passes either. I would have liked my own boarding pass, as my Sue could have added it to our travel album.

On this photograph, our car is fifth in the line to board the ferry, but I am taking in some fresh air as I had just jumped out of our car for a drink of water, also making the most of this unexpected opportunity to scrutinize all of the occupied cars for any signs of fellow dogs! It suited me well as it was rather a warm day for me and my humans to sit for too long in our car in the vehicle queuing section, ready to board that huge metal thing called a ferry. It towered over us with a huge opening like a giant's greedy mouth. Little did I know that the camper-van arriving in the distance would contain our dear new human friends, together with Alfie the Bassett hound. Lots of workers travel to the same distant Outer Hebridean island of Barra as us to do manual work, on the islanders' houses, and to deliver goods for their local shops to sell. I was glad that my Sue would be able to buy my dog food when we arrived, because, although I had my huge bag of biscuits with me, I was down to my last supply of meat.

Having returned to my cosy car seat, I was curious when a small man in dark overalls appeared at our window and instructed Sue to 'follow the car in front' - so driving inside the ferry, to a section called a hold. It was very noisy as the car wheels drove over a metal ramp part into the floating ship. I did not like the noise but tolerated it as I knew it would lead us on a wonderful new part of our summer adventure. Dogs and humans were not allowed to stay in their cars when the ferry set sail, so Sue put my lead on me and remembered to take out my red travel bag containing my blue and silver bowls and enough water for the five-hour ferry trip to the Outer Hebrides. I was reluctant to leave the warmth and safety of the car, but I knew that we had to do so. Nevertheless, my nails clicked annoyingly and echoed on that green metal floor surface as we walked away towards the steep steps, so I looked up at our car and imagined my soft dog bed inside, longingly. When the rest of the cars, lorries and vans had boarded, that large heavy ramp lifted, sealing the entrance where we had slowly driven in, ready to set sail. My little, but strong, collie heart beat quickly with excitement and eager anticipation.

As I stood between those stationary lines of cars and other vehicles - even including a huge orange bulldozer digging machine on one, Sue explained that a similar ramp at the other end of the ship would be lowered to let passengers off at ferry ports along the way, and finally at Castlebay, all those hours later. This was all so new to me and I instinctively wagged my tail, loving her gentle, yet enthusiastic, voice and eager for our exciting, knowledge-enhancing adventure to continue.

Lining up with the other passengers, but no dogs in sight, and with Sue holding me on my short red lead, we started to climb the many, many metal steps to the upper part of our ship. Reaching the first deck, Sue pointed out a sign saying dogs are only permitted in the entrance settee area and top deck outside. She wondered how she and her mum would go into the restaurant to eat their usual meal because the entire journey would be a long time without a meal. Being creative and persuasive, I knew that she would find a solution without leaving me alone!

With Sue and my red bag beside me and Sue's mum in her red jacket too, I stared intently, watching with interest as some strong men in red hats hauled the huge ropes which had been securing our now moving ferry to the land, and imagined having a tuggy ball so big that it needed a rope like that! It was something doggy dreams were made of! At this early stage of our journey, I was still unaware that Sue would later make this Dave D dream come true!

With fascination, I watched as the previously calm sea became but a churning white trail made by the ferry as we left Oban, with its large buildings, far behind and we headed across the Atlantic Ocean. I took long sniffs as I focused; my black, brown and white collie fur was ruffled by the fresh sea breeze, and earflaps blowing, which brought me such a wonderful sense of contentment, my spirit of adventure now being in full flow on our exciting sea voyage.

During the journey on that huge ferry, a strange man started shouting. As I have an aversion to the raising of voices, for any reason, mum and I gave him a glare! We soon realised that he meant no harm and was simply alerting us to a dark fin in the deep water below us! Apparently, it was a Minke whale which had a dorsal fin breaking the surface as it came near to feed and must having been swimming at about twenty four miles an hour. These bulky creatures can weigh up to nine tonnes and are dark grey in colour. They have white bands on the pointed tips of their long flippers - as I have a white tail tip - and two openings called blow-holes on the top of their head, (which I definitely do not have on my own collie head!), although the low spout makes it look more like steam. This particular whale caused great excitement amongst fellow passengers, as it was nearly ten metres long. I saw it arch then dive before rising again after nearly twenty minutes. It made a loud noise that reached a hundred and fifty two decibels, which did not impress me, as I had been happy up until then, just admiring the view quietly.

People ran forward to see what all the fuss was about. However, I do not like crowds and my mum knows this, so, despite her interest, and without tightening my lead too much, she praised me for being a good boy, as a way of distracting me, and we watched from a considerably quieter area. Even so, I still gave a slight shudder as I now saw a husky dog on the opposite side of the deck, but ever alert, my Sue had noticed it too, so I was quickly directed away!

It was after going inside the ferry because of this, that I saw the long hound with short legs - who we later discovered was called Alfie. I had actually first caught sight of him as I peered round the corner in the dog-friendly section of the big ferry. He had even shorter legs than I first realised and a verrrrrrrrrrrry long brown and white body with huge, brown ears. My own ears are not exactly short, and, admittedly, they do flap in the breeze of a ship at sea, but his must have been three times as long! I am sorry to say that my Sue did not measure them with her plastic ruler though, so we shall never know their true measurement!

I did not shake or feel nervous as he was on a lead with his humans, attached to his lady owner's hand. On the other hand, I did not go over the top and share my water with him either, as he had his own bowl of water. He, in turn, peered at me round the corner again as he sat with his owners. I had been lying down next to my red bag and water-bowl so stared back. I was so glad that he could not reach me.

Sue chatted to his friendly humans and they asked about me, the little 'tri-collie' who was keeping his distance, but continually staring at their boy. They were understanding about my fears and genuinely interested and concerned, thankfully being not at all judgemental either. Alfie stayed inside the ferry with these human parents for the whole trip, but I was allowed to enjoy adventures on board - both inside and outside. I waited while Sue and her mum took turns to buy food and to hold me on my lead then watching them sit at a table next to the restaurant door. I sat at the entrance to the restaurant on my long lead which was securely attached to Sue's hand, as they ate. The deck attendant gentleman was aware but Sue had convinced him to allow this strange arrangement by explaining that she would not leave me alone anywhere! Long leads are handy especially so Sue never needs to leave me tied up outside any chosen shop. She can reach the counter with me still waiting at the entrance, connected to my long lead, although she responsibly warns other customers not to trip over that lead! Foster's mum lent me his very long training lead on our last Newport collie walk, but, understandably, I had to give it back to him when he went swimming in case he went too far out. I loved the freedom it gave me to run further afield, so enabling me to try and herd an agile whippet, but still with the security of my link to my Mum.

Later on, Sue let me sit on the red plastic seat on the ferry's deck, as she warned me that it was a long journey to the Isle of Barra off that West Coast of Scotland. We watched the Merchant Navy flag flying the Red Ensign, and Sue's mum proudly spoke of her much loved and missed dad, my Sue's grandpa, who had been a Chief Petty Officer in the Royal Navy over seventy years ago and previously, a medic in the trenches, a hundred years ago. He helped so many wounded servicemen and I would like to have met him because of this and as he looked so smart in his uniform on the photograph in Wales. I think he would have liked me, too, and that, with him being a medical expert, he would also have understood my anxieties, even though to many people I am just a reactive or nervous dog.

As we neared land, and being careful not to bang into the orange human life-belt, I walked towards those shiny, white railings in order to see the view from a different angle. The strong sea wind blew my pale, furry cheeks out as I peered through the metal railings, still safely attached to my lead in Mum's hand. It felt quite strange but I liked it, as it was part of the new experience of sailing for me. In fact, I was absolutely loving it!

Although I do love the ferry-boats too, I was always glad to see a shore coming into view in the distance, and to have my paws on dry land again. We approached land at Castlebay and I was amazed to see a real stone castle in the middle of the picturesque bay, temptingly awaiting our exploration. After we disembarked, it was this view in reverse that I would later see from our hotel window, as, smiling, I raised myself up on my back legs, carefully placing one paw on that white-painted window ledge. As I looked out, I could see such a wonderful scene and was glad to realise that the ferry would be returning to Oban soon and leaving us here on this quiet, beautiful, Scottish island.

On other ferries as we island-hopped by car ferry northwards through those bewitching and historical islands of the Outer Hebrides, I frequently made people laugh by being my naturally inquisitive self. One such time was when I waited patiently on deck for the large, green, metal ramp with distinctive yellow sides, (which we had again driven over to board a ferry), to move upwards and seal the entrance - before trying my best to check for any dogs in the cars waiting down below on this smaller car ferry deck, by going under a fold up seat.

Unexpectedly, I had a shock as I went further underneath my chosen seat, because the seat's white flap came down on top of me! As I moved further forwards, it was then half-covering my back and eventually tapped me on the bottom! As you would expect, I had turned my head exceedingly quickly to check that it was not a dog which had touched me... then continued to gaze over the side, leaving just my back-end sticking out along with my two mostly brown muscular legs and pale collie feet, making other passengers laugh, despite the rainy day!

As I had half-anticipated, I caught Sue looking with concern, but also amusement, taking my furry bottom's photograph as I peered down. Nevertheless, I gave her a half-smile, half-collie stare to let her know that I was fine, even though half-covered in the plastic chair seat - also realising how comical I must have looked, judging by the laughter I continued to hear from fellow passengers!

After a while and despite the damp upper deck, I lay down underneath the long row of seats, because that one pesky plastic seat felt rather strange continually tapping my back and causing me to keep thinking that there really was a dog behind me. I was then able to relax and keep a look out across the whole lower deck. The large, metal ramp which would lower to allow us to drive out onto the next island, loomed to our right, like a giant drawbridge on a castle.

As we headed up the islands we arrived at Benbecula which is in the middle of North and South Uist. On the northern side, people and animals used to cross by foot at low tide, and by boat at high tide. The tide was coming in and I did not fancy wading through the channel with all our bags and leaving my dog bed and the car behind. Thankfully, as we approached, still in our car, we saw a causeway - which is that long road across water. As we neared the road, it was there that I saw the sign for the creature which mum had called an otter. She said that otters could often be seen at lower tide, hunting amongst the seaweed for crabs, fish and eels which they use their sensitive whiskers and paws to help them find. She explained that they are said to have poor sight so probably would not notice me. Therefore, I asked if I could leave the car, and waited at their sign for a while with my little red travel bag.

Much as I would love to have seen one, and given it my collie stare, I was aware that many of these otters do get injured crossing that road, so in a way I was hoping that they would sensibly, keep out of sight. We also walked to the left of the lengthy causeway between the sea and a fresh-water stream where the otters had made tracks - which actually looked much like sheep tracks - but I did not see any sheep either! I stopped to lap the fresh water, knowing that later otters would be bathing in that same water to enable them to keep their sleek fur coats in good condition, by grooming and washing the salt out of them to ensure that these precious coats still kept their insulating properties. I was interested to learn from our friend, Valorie, and her dear collies that some otters actually hold onto each other as they sleep in the water, so that they do not drift apart. In addition to that I learnt how the otters can close their nostrils and ear-holes when swimming underwater. I wish that I had been able to do that when I was swimming as some salty seawater had gone up my long nose and even more filled my fur-lined collie ears!

As I continued to search for the mysterious otters, near the salt-water channel, I saw a crab disguised as a rock, but ran and kept my distance when it moved suddenly and made me jump! In addition to crabs, I had been made aware that otters eat snails, small mammals and birds, so was mighty glad that I was a bigger mammal - because even if one or more appeared, they would have left me alone. My Sue still always makes me leave snails alone when I see them in the garden as she says that, as with slugs, she will not risk them making me poorly. The crab that looked like a rock and scared me, caused me to reflect on how Amber collie also came across a disguised creature in her garden, which she had mistakenly thought was a stone... but was actually a toad! Toads tend to walk rather than hop. I used to like to play with pebbles and stones in the garden, but being a collie, and having a high chase drive, if I see any being thrown into the sea I still, instinctively become very excited, strain on my lead and try my best to join the humans who are throwing them - with the aim of chasing after these natural objects. As I have mentioned, my Sue always stops me and distracts me - with a toy if she has one, as a fellow collie actually broke its tooth by catching a pebble, but he is fine now.

Two days later, after leaving North Uist, as we journeyed through the Isle of Harris to Lewis, we had not needed a boat as I have revealed that the two are actually joined together physically - but separated by just two road signs. Both signs were in Gaelic and

English. One said Failte do dh Eilean Leodhais which means Welcome to the Isle of Lewis and the other, facing the opposite way, reads Failte gu Na Heradh, translated as Welcome to Harris.

Just before this, we found ourselves driving over a high bridge to another island called Scalpay, admittedly by mistake, whilst actually thinking we were on the right road - after Sue read the worn map incorrectly! In the past, we could not have made this mistake with the roadway from our first Outer Hebridean Island of Barra to Honey collie's neighbouring island home of Vatersay, as it used to be reached only by boat whereas now there is that causeway joining these two islands.

Likewise, on this stretch of water leading to Scalpay, the previous way across had been a tiny car ferry with even police, buses and ambulances all needing to cross on that small ferry. I enjoyed it when Sue drove us across the impressive bridge and admiring the breath-taking views. I could just imagine the joyful sight, many years previously, when this Scalpay bridge gateway was opened in 1998, by the Prime Minister and an organised procession of vehicles crossed this very same bridge, led by their oldest resident, who was 103 years old, with the emergency service vehicles following behind her. I just wish with all my doggy heart that I had been there too, so that I could have given the wise old birthday lady one or two of my Dave D paw loves.

The reward for us at the far end of Scalpay was a wonderful lighthouse called Eileen Glas - which means green island. I gave my Sue a grateful look as, being a collie mum, she appreciates how much her collie boy loves flashing lights. Sue read that there are three white flashes every three seconds. I watched them intently until Sue distracted me. It was also a famous place to add to my Diary because it was the first lighthouse ever to be built in the Outer Hebrides of Scotland to give a guide to seafarers. The lighthouse was started in 1787 and first lit in 1789. There was a lighthouse keeper up until just under forty years ago, but it is now automated, so at least I knew that no dog would live there with its master any more......so I would be safe if I approached the tall structure.

The red painted stripes of this lighthouse were the same colour as my red lead that was keeping me safely attached to my Sue because of the steep cliffs nearby, just like when we walked the cliff path route from Filey to Topaz's hometown of Scarborough, again with Sue's mum. As on that East Yorkshire adventure and whilst in Scalpay too, although always alert and expecting them, I was relieved, not to have seen any dogs, so had thankfully not needed my muzzle on either of the days.

Dave D's Photo Album!

I dreamt of a perfect life where I no longer needed to stay on my lead or wear my muzzle and where I was never again just a bystander missing out on collie beach games.

They had noticed my twinking Dave D eyes as I walked confidently with my head and tail held so high.

Although pretending to smile, this smile did not last or reach quite as far across my collie face as it usually did, because the sheep had gone!

After lowering my head and lapping up the deliciously fresh water, I pulled such a funny, satisfied face that it made my Sue smile.

Although previously ignoring my intense stares, one of the black sheep creatures eventually acknowledged that I was there, so I returned its stare, now feeling content as my mission had been accomplished.

Mum called me back into the car, but she had needed to ask me twice as my head had been turned the other way - towards the causeway... due to me sensing the presence of sheep on a hillside across the water.

All of a sudden I stared in amazement as we drove past cattle high up on the cliff-top, walking and grazing on plants in the unfenced fields.

Full of curiosity, I looked out at the huge creatures with muddy legs from where they sheltered from the wind and the rain on those hillside ledges next to the sea.

Despite looking all round, turning my collie head this way and that, all I could find were the cattle's hoof prints on that muddy brown ledge.

I approached the little calf enquiringly, before sitting down and staring intently… which caused him to stare at me too. So I stared back - but moved no closer…

As we drove along, we saw signs for deer and even stopped to jump out of the car and look for them, but no deer crossed the road in front of us.

After my first night ever inside one of these tent things, I heard a familiar sound… but stayed looking out from this tent flap, discreetly… unnoticed by the nearby sheep.

Despite the marvellous beach view, I was trembling slightly, so I decided to lie down and look out through the open tent door cautiously - just in case any other dogs were nearby.

I could just imagine myself sitting up proudly in that strange wheelbarrow thing and also admiring the views as Mum pushed me.

Although not being allowed to herd the sheep, I did catch the eye of a solitary creature with huge, curling horns as we drove by. I gave it my firm collie eye as we passed.

I obeyed Sue's command and sat next to my red travel bag, but still focusing on those woolly sheep… and fixing a definite border-collie eye stare in that direction.

I settled down to watch that busy collie working the sheep, but was still prepared to jump back into our car quickly if it came too close to me!

Seeing eleven pairs of beady sheep eyes staring down at me was quite unexpected, so I lay down, mouth slightly open, staring upwards, with my red bag beside me.

I do think that orange lawnmower machines are rather too noisy, and admit trying to chase and herd this big machine to stop it… lifting a front paw and giving it my most intense collie stare.

If only those dogs and humans had looked up they would have seen the distinctive nose and arched eyebrowed face of a collie boy peering down at them as they walked below my castle hideout!

Coming out of the sea and seeing my stance, Honey collie had eventually realised that I was not the most friendly of collie boys and wanted to chase her - but not to play. It served me right when she ran off and stole my food tray!

I felt no threat and, wagging my white-tipped tail, I gave the soft toy rabbit a good sniff, by now also feeling relaxed and confident.

Totally focused and scooping enthusiastically - my nose pointing down, I dug deeper and deeper, scooping pawful after pawful of the soft sand – my long legs turning a sandy colour.

I sat relaxing in the heather more than once on our Scottish holiday with one ear, or both, stuck up… pretending to be a collie-type of hare or rabbit hiding.

To be honest, I was feeling rather pleased with myself and was having such fun as the sand flew backwards, scattering along the beach behind me.

Even though I had a tight grip with my old but sharp collie teeth, much to my dismay, this tough rope was stuck fast in the sand.

I had raced into the dark cave… but all that my Sue could see from outside was my furry white bottom being illuminated in the darkness.

It has brought me such happiness to hear humans comment on how they feel inspired by my own adventures, and may soon take their own dog on public transport for the first time ever - with Koda collie recently taking that initial step on her hour long train journey.

Leaving the warmth of my cushion, I looked up at our car longingly
to say goodbye. My nails clicked on the green metal floor as we
walked away towards the steep steps.

I saw a hound with short legs and a very long brown and white body,
including huge ears, as I peered round a corner in the dog-friendly part
of the ferry.

Smiling, I raised myself up onto my back legs, carefully placing one paw on that white-painted hotel window ledge. Seeing such a stunning view of this Scottish island retreat was totally awe-inspiring.

As I sat proudly on deck, the large metal ramp - which would lower to allow us to drive out on the next island - loomed to our right, like a giant drawbridge.

We saw a causeway between the islands, which was where I also spotted a road sign for that harmless creature which mum called an otter. I inquisitively waited at the sign with my little red travel bag.

We often travel by train, like here on this scenic Cambrian Coastline adventure, and I feel such a happy and fortunate collie boy as I admire the impressive views.

Wherever I am, I try to keep one paw on my red travel bag and an eye on my blue bowl, especially when I see other collie paws nearby… although admittedly, my Sue does share my water with other thirsty dogs on some U.K. border collie group meet up walks.

I enjoy unusual adventures, including one where I even posed in the front window of a mobile phone shop in Edinburgh centre while Mum cheekily charged her telephone - followed by a train journey north across the Forth bridge. I had an amazing view of the estuary.

On one occasion, we went to a dog-friendly bar in Perth, where I was given a red ring birthday gift from a friend. I didn't let go of it all night!

Whilst sitting on the train, if my Sue is busy with her paperwork, I feel that it is my duty to put a protective paw on our bags, so keeping our precious treasures safe.

My seatbelt and clip keep me safe when my Sue is driving us in the car.

The man lay down next to where I sat and looked under the damaged car. I watched him, still wearing my black raincoat along with a very serious and concerned expression on my face.

I peered over the edge, and suddenly I heard the sound of a roaring engine on the road below!

I glared back at Alfie the Bassett hound. He kept appearing at the window and staring down at me, his long floppy ears dangling disturbingly.

It was early evening when we returned to the tent pitches so I was on lookout duty. Surprisingly, but thankfully. there were no midges in sight…

I frequently search for, hear, and chase squirrels in our local forest. I look up, mouth gaping, as I see them scrambling and leaping high above.

As the plane prepared to land, I saw bright lights coming towards me like giant torches. I felt like closing my eyes and putting my paws over my sensitive collie ears.

The following day, I sat confidently in the sand dunes with Sue, hearing that familiar whirring of the plane overhead.

Legs and paws moving determinedly, I ran away from the noisy bell!

I spotted a sheep from the car . "WOOOOOF!" I shouted, my soft
right ear flicking up as I barked.

Chapter Fifteen

Train and Mountain Adventures

Fortunately, in the British Isles we dogs are allowed on trains at any time of the day or night, including on the sleeper trains from the far south of England to the far north of Scotland. However in certain other countries their dogs have to be muzzled and not travel in rush hours. I am a lucky boy because, travelling in the British Isles, I do not need to wear my muzzle on trains unless a dog is in the same carriage and approaches me. Even so, my Sue will take it off again as soon as the dog has passed.

As you know, I love to be out and about and am totally in my element on such journeys, however long or short they may be. When my mum Sue starts to pack up my bright, red drawstring bag I know, intuitively, that she will soon be putting that familiar harness on my furry body, and this means a new adventure for Dave D, the exploring collie! I love the anticipation of not knowing where we will go next. Sometimes a river, other times the sea and other times a mountain. My life is full of excitement and I now live it to the full, despite those unfortunate behavioural road bumps.

As we often travel by train, like on the scenic Cambrian Coastline, which takes us from mid to north Wales, I like to put my protective paws on our precious bags to protect and guard them at the station and on the train, also making sure that my Sue doesn't lose any - and looking intently at passers-by! Fellow travellers smile at me and say that I am a cute boy, but I am just being thoughtful in looking after our belongings. Sometimes Sue takes care of her own bags, so I just have my red travel bag for me to look after. I am always glad of my shiny, well-conditioned, fur coat as the train can be somewhat chilly, even in summer, if the train's air-conditioning is turned on.

Oh dear! I remember the time when Sue and I both weren't concentrating enough and we left my soft, blue collapsible water bowl under our train seat in busy Birmingham. We had been returning from Milton Keynes after visiting Mike, Shirley and baby Natalie. It had been the last train of that particular day, so when Sue remembered and we hastened back down the steps to collect it, the previously packed train was now in darkness! Sue found a kind, but bemused, train worker who let us go back on the train to collect my collapsible bowl. I was glad as I need it on my collie walks when we have a rest break. It did feel strange to be on a dark train near to midnight, but it was a new experience to add to my diary! In addition, at least I didn't have to look around in case there were any other dogs on board to worry about - as I often see them peeping back at me on train trips, like on some of the buses and walks! Wherever I am, I now try to keep one paw on my red travel bag and an eye on my blue bowl, especially when I see other collie paws nearby!

One day Sue even lost her own black handbag, causing her to be very upset as her only car key was inside and the money to buy my low-fat dog biscuits. Luckily, a very caring and honest boy called Benjy found it and took it to the Stafford Police station. Next, a kind police person traced and rang Sue telling her that her handbag had been handed in, with everything still inside. Gratefully, Sue asked for Benjy's telephone number so that she could ring him and his mum to say thank you. I am glad that she usually takes more care of my Mr. Muzzle and has not yet lost that.....for more than a few moments!

We have to board each train in good time, as the doors shut and lock a few seconds before each train is scheduled to leave. The person working on the platform blows their whistle or waves, to signal to the train driver to leave. Once the train guard was carrying a torch so I watched the light intently and tried to chase his torch light and shadow up and down the platform. My head was moving backwards and forwards following it, much to the amusement of the guard. Collies love to watch such lights and shadows but the man thought it was him I liked, which made my mum smile as she knows the real Dave D! However, my wary Sue told me to stop chasing the torchlight, as it is dangerous for humans or dogs, even dogs on leads, to play on train platforms. Next, grasping my harness and with the now familiar command, "Up, up now Dave D", I jumped and she half-lifted me onto the safe haven of the train, ready to continue on our current adventure.

As can be expected, I am always glad of my red travel bag and mum ensures that I keep it close to me. Inside this bag is Mr. Muzzle, my water bottle and essential bowls, along with my food. Sue makes sure that I am always given my food at the usual time, even if we are still on the train. To the delight of fellow passengers I tuck into my meat and biscuits from one of my bowls, then lick my whiskers before wiping my mouth on the train carpet, as is usual practice! Although not endorsing it, Sue had got used to my habit, but was not at all impressed when I tried to do this after my meaty meal at the supposedly dog-friendly hotel near Dundee, so she chased me round the bedroom, frantically trying to wipe my gravy-stained mouth with a tissue, to stop me from wiping it on the pure white carpet!

On actual journeys, I usually sit on the floor of the air-conditioned carriage, with a paw on my red bag, and my nose resting on Sue's leg. Sue makes sure that my exquisite tail is always tucked under me when I lie on the train, or bus, to keep it safe. It is nearly forty centimetres long from its base to its white tip and very precious to me. She is very careful not to touch the base of my tail as she knows that this is uncomfortable for me. During longer train journeys, a kind ticket officer sometimes allows me to actually sit on the human passenger seat... (After it has first been covered with my rug or my Sue's jacket of course!), in order to see out of the train window. Being such an inquisitive boy, I love to watch the people on the platform as we pass through the stations! As you will realise, I do look out for dogs, too, and sometimes prick my velvety ears up, as from a quick glance, I almost mistake bags on wheels for these living creatures! Sue is usually quick to discreetly reassure me, whilst hiding her laughter at my funny Dave D ways!

We go on such fun adventures, including on a long train across the impressive Forth Bridge in Scotland over the Forth Estuary, where there was an amazing view. As I looked out over the water during that journey, my Dave D heart felt so happy and my body so alive, this being such a huge contrast to my weeks in that rescue centre kennel longing for someone to take me to a new home and love me.

Upon arriving into Perth station, and even while we were still moving, my nose was pointing up at the window, tail wagging noticeably, and I was raring to go, so I prepared to exit the train through the yellow and black striped door. I was waiting expectantly for the now familiar green light next to that door to light up and a 'beep' so signifying to humans when to press it and let themselves, (and me), out. Straining on my lead, I was so eager for the door to slide open although I did not need a wee, as I'd already had a long one against an information stand on the walk from Glasgow Central Station to Glasgow Queen Street!

At the large station we were delighted to be met by our kindly friends and enjoyed a walk to their local park, where I had the opportunity to stretch my legs and play with my ball. We went on a big bus to our dog-friendly hotel. As my Sue opened our hotel door, I was surprised but happy to see a dog bowl and paw-print rug just for me. It was on this occasion that we went to the dog-friendly bar, where I opened my birthday cards and gifts, being delighted to find inside them that new red ring from my friend, Ann, and my wasp-coloured yellow and black tuggy from Kathryn in West Lothian, both of which I still treasure. It was this red toy which I had played with in a corner of the bar with Ann, and had later proudly taken into that hotel's lift, then through the maze of corridors back to my hotel room, where Sue had put all my cards up on the window-sill. I had then contentedly fallen asleep with my new, already cherished, red ring still held lovingly in my paws! Prior to meeting my Sue, I had never received a birthday card or gift, in all my years, so I love ripping the paper off these to discover what is inside each precious package.

Over a year later, we caught an early train from Manchester and headed to Dundee for our Carnoustie collie walk, to meet all our friends including Avril, Nan, Kathryn, Kes, Stevie and their collies including the adorable and brave Mist. Sue had made us a picnic lunch for on the five-hour train journey, but she started to eat it as soon as the train started moving, at breakfast time! I have to admit that I enjoyed some of this unexpectedly early picnic, too......although we were both very hungry by lunchtime and had no food left!

It was during this summer adventure that Rosie collie in Dundee travelled by train for the first time ever, along with her caring dad, Steve, me and my Sue. (She behaved admirably and is now a regular little collie adventurer like I am.) After a wonderful few days enjoying park and beach collie walks in that area with our friends we set off for home. Unfortunately, we had not taken any food to enjoy on the return journey, and due to what they called 'staff shortages', a man with a funny robot-type voice announced that there would be no buffet. We were therefore thankful for the bottle of water which we had brought for me and a can of coke that our thoughtful friend, Ann, had given to Sue for on the journey, although my water was somewhat warm!

Therefore, when the very welcome buffet assistant did board the train at Edinburgh, my Sue and I jumped up and eagerly started to walk down the four moving carriages in anticipation of a delicious snack and cold drinks. However, upon approaching carriage four, my alert mum suddenly stopped just before the sliding glass door. I had not seen what she had, yet, but recognised this familiar pattern of suddenly stopping then about-turning if there was another dog around. Inquisitively, but cautiously, I peered through the glass and saw not one, but two large dogs lying across the middle of that next carriage. It reminded me of that collie on the Yorkshire bus and I could not face having to be so close to them in a narrow passageway which my caring Sue knew, so we turned and returned to our seats, the warm water and more wonderful window-seat views!

The day after our Dundee collie walk, we travelled mainly on trains, to the long beach near Sunderland, including on the Newcastle Metro, which has an exceptionally slippery main station area for dogs who attempt to walk here on their way to adventures. Please be cautious as I was and make sure that your human does not rush you as you negotiate that floor on your paw pads. I like to arrive at walks early, as it is understandably daunting for me to walk up to a whole crowd of dogs - but easier if I am there first and Sue keeps me at a distance as they arrive. My mood-revealing tail was down to begin with and I felt as if I wanted to stay at the back, so we let the other collies and humans walk in front of us and followed them slowly. As my tail had been between my legs I knew that Sue was wondering if she had done the right thing in bringing me. I was determined to reassure her and, along with that positive thinking and the sight of an enticing ball being thrown for collies who wanted to chase it into the sea, I threw caution to the wind, barked loudly, focused fully on the collies and pulled on my long lead, indicating how much I wanted to join in. My Sue, perceptively, seemed unsure at first, then unclipped my straining lead and watched with pride as I ran to join Toby and the other collies, chasing that ball up and down the beach and into that inviting blue sea.

I always love to look out of the large window on train journeys because I see so many interesting scenes as the speedy train rushes through the spectacular countryside. I have been told more than once that I look such a funny boy as I calmly sit there, clearly enchanted by the striking scenery and enjoying each part of every journey and current adventure.

We often stop off in Sue's much loved home city of Manchester to meet up with friends. Once, one of our friends had been poorly but he still came to see us and to make a fuss of me, his pal Dave D. As you know, I usually give my paw to my friends whom we meet. Mum and I are always so happy to see them and enjoy meeting them at the dog-friendly bars and cafes. Our human friend, also called Dave, once told me how my Sue had rescued a baby sheep which had fallen down a steep river bank and was trapped on a ledge with the water rising. It had been winter but she had taken her walking boots and socks off to wade in and save it. If I had been there she would probably have asked her human friend to hold my lead - so as not to further frighten the lamb with my presence. As he spoke, I had, coincidently, suddenly felt in need of someone to rescue me, as I had seen a gigantic dog nearby, and had therefore become anxious. Almost instantly, our other friend, Alan, blocked my view with his plastic shopping bag as my expression showed that I could hear the animal in the distance across the road, nails clicking on the pavement and the sound of a chain.

Despite this, I did not feel as scared as when I could actually see any approaching dog. Our friend blocking my view of it meant that the dog couldn't see me either, so I felt safer.

We dogs do feel a range of emotions and we look at those who love us and keep us safe with love and appreciation. This gesture of understanding helped me, as, when I peeped round the side of Alan's large, plastic shopping bag a few minutes later, the other dog had gone. My humans had understood my fear and helped me. I loved them so much for this, though, of course, I do wish - with all my gentle Dave D heart - that I wasn't so scared of other dogs and that my body would not tremble so frequently when I see them.

Another time, our friend, Alan, met us at the Manchester Piccadilly station and we sat in the upstairs dog-friendly bar enjoying a pleasant view through the glass panel. My alert Dave D eyes soon spotted an alluring football below and yearned to join in the game. My furry head moved from side-to-side as I watched two youngish men kicking it backwards and forwards! However, the game didn't last very long as a strict policewoman marched along and told the entertaining men off for playing football in a train station! They pretended to be surprised and disappointed! My Sue got the giggles at their antics and my expressions so she distracted me with my favourite tuggy-ball instead. Understandably, I had to be ever so careful not to fling it too high into the air or it might have gone over the low balcony and landed in the main station area... so the observant policewoman might have told us off too! We then sat on the busy platform together to wait for the train. I had my serious face on as I did not want us to miss our last train, and had to concentrate ready to board quickly but carefully when it arrived.

As you will realise, I consistently wear my usual harness on our journeys, especially when we are travelling on a train and Sue always holds onto the top of it protectively, to help me jump on and off each train to keep me safe from the gap between train and platform. It must be quite entertaining to the station staff and passengers who see us arriving at any station, because, as the doors open, I leap like a flying Dave D collie, with my four paws taking off from the carriage floor, as Sue lifts my harness up too! Indeed, I always spring up high and arrive on the platform in true, unique, Dave D style - with a big enthusiastic grin on my cute, collie face!

On one occasion, Sue had travelled to Manchester without me and she clearly recalls waiting at the door to alight her train, then, as it arrived at the now familiar station, instinctively putting her hand down to Dave D harness level ready to grasp my harness in preparation for helping me to jump off, before remembering that I was not actually with her and still sat on my cushion back home in Staffordshire - probably puzzled and wondering where my Sue was!

Finally, we boarded the southbound train to Stafford and Alan said goodbye to us from the platform. We found our seat and Sue had just motioned for me to lie down.....when .... suddenly, she turned, confused at hearing my long collie tail thumping on the carriage floor! Recognition dawned on Sue … as the reason for my delighted tail-wagging was revealed - it being due to my genuine happiness, for there, in front of me, holding out his hand for a paw love, was a familiar face. Our friend Alan had now secretly decided to board the train and to keep us company! Still sitting in the train aisle, red bag behind me, as Mum had prepared our seats, I gave him my biggggggggggggest Dave D smile as I was already so grateful to him for rescuing me from the passing dog earlier.

I fondly remember our trip to Chester-le-Street near Durham. Sue had pointed it out on well-used a map, (which she had unintentionally ripped by trapping it in our car's boot lid!). We travelled there by train for a collie walk organised by our friend, James and his handsome collie, Jet. We met his lovely family and enjoyed a relaxing walk, before all becoming lost in the middle of a rather posh housing area! Residents were peering out of their windows at us and others staring as they drove by……clearly not at all impressed to see twenty humans and the same number of collies trampling close to their lawns and driveways, up their road - with me following on at the back in my Mr. Muzzle! It made our human collie group friends laugh though and hearing such hearty laughter echoing through that Close, I had a huge collie grin on my face, as did the other collies!

On the news, I once heard that a yellow snake had escaped from its carry-box and was loose on a train in another country. I am glad that I have always felt safe from such on my train journeys throughout the British Isles and that no snake has ever slithered down the comfortable passenger compartment of any of our trains! If I had been there I may have been tempted to put my paw on it, as I like to help humans. However, I am usually kept out of long grass at home, as snakes can hide and bite me, like one bit my friend Spenca collie while he was actually walking on a path near our home in Staffordshire. Some snakes have a zig-zag camouflage which makes them harder to spot, but we do look out for them and avoid overgrown paths. I was glad to hear that the train snake had been caught by brave firemen who had boarded that train. Passengers on another train were not so lucky, because the snake in their train had entered the ventilation shaft, so it would have been harder to catch. Luckily Spenca recovered well, as his mum, Linda, thoughtfully let us know.

Another dog recovering well is the now famous Jasper collie who also enjoys adventures in the British Isles with his owner. When on our journey to Dundee we passed through Penrith train station, in Cumbria, where Oliver lives, this pleasant old town being nearly sixty miles from the Scafell Pike area, where Jasper collie vanished on a Sunday walk and was lost on a mountain-side for over three days and nights in strong winds, ice and low temperatures. This mountain is in the Lake District National Park and exceptionally high, it being 978 metres above sea level. It is actually the highest mountain peak in England! The previous year, I had been walking in a nearby area one Sunday too, with about ten collies and their humans. However, we were only in the valley, first following a river and then continuing up a stony track but, although we walked for seven hours, it was warm and still daylight.

On the fourth night, Jasper was found just before two am, by the torchlight of an exceedingly thoughtful and experienced volunteer, called Geoff, who had ventured into the precarious mountains, just before midnight, heading towards the summit, of Scafell Pike, positively searching for that lost collie with the full moon in a clear sky. I often walk with Sue then we play on the field in the full moonlight as it lights the way. However, the land we are on is usually flat and this was the first time that Geoff had walked this rocky route for some years without his beloved Jack dog who is no longer on this earth physically, but surely was in spirit - alongside his master and in his Geoff's heart - as he had composed himself and kept calm, determined to find Adam's missing collie.

This brave man shone his powerful search torch as he looked for the lost collie, first on Broad Crag mountain, which is a subsidary peak only a short distance north-east of Scafell Pike, and also forming part of the Scafell Chain. Geoff was now in an exceedingly rough area consisting of rocks, blocks and high crags, calling Jasper's name, when his torchlight caught and illuminated Jasper's eyes looking back at him after the tired collie heard and popped his head up from behind a rock higher up on a crag two hundred metres away. As you know, us collies love torchlight, and adore following it with our sharp eyes so I bet that, Jasper loved it too, even though he was probably much too tired to chase the light. Geoff had sat down, but not too near to Jasper, with the torch - which is capable of lighting up sheep, fox and dog eyes even hundreds of metres away - shining on himself, talking gently to Jasper, saying his name, also waving some cheese and ham about - which he could then hear Jasper sniffing. Following this, the determined man moved closer, then climbing up that steep rugged rock, known as a crag, and catching hold of Jasper's collar, at which time the hungry collie grabbed the food from Geoff's other hand! I am sure that I would have done the same as I often sniff food, approvingly and hungrily, especially ham and cheese!

After trying to lift the tired collie to a lower point of the steep mountain under a now strong wind and hazardous conditions, with the rocks underfoot and under paw being icy, Geoff made the decision to stop and rest - keeping himself and Jasper warm in an emergency shelter, which he had sensibly, and thankfully, taken with him in his rucksack. I am so happy that Jasper collie was safe and five hours later, reunited with his master. In addition to search parties and sniffer dogs, a helicopter and police, some of our own concerned collie club friends and their dogs had kindly been out in the same area searching for Jasper by daylight. At dusk, one of our friends and her two Labradors were still searching, with a flask of warm beef stew made with steak chunks, for if she found Jasper. I bet he would have loved this tasty energy food as I know that I would. During those hours when Jasper was still missing we are thankful to Cassie collie's mum, Lisa, who was helping by sharing information about the search and giving updates though our U.K. Border Collie Walk Group page.

Hearing that this collie was safe, his master and so many people throughout the British Isles and indeed, around the world, must have breathed a thankful sigh of relief because after he reached a point where there was a mobile phone signal, wonderful Geoff was able to notify the Police, so enabling assistance to be called for from the fabulous local Wasdale Mountain Rescue Team. This team ascended the mountain and brought Jasper down the steep, icy mountainside packaged in a warm orange sleeping-bag and strapped safely to their make-shift stretcher with black straps. Jasper did try to walk some of the way on a blue lead, (the exact colour of my rescue centre one), helped by a volunteer, but it was now too slippery because of being a scree slope, with sheet ice too, and he was probably very weak.

Although Jasper was used to running and walking there, in daylight, my mum has also climbed in that area with Ray and their Manchester friends, but says how very steep, difficult and isolating it can be for those of us who are not familiar with the area, even more so in the dark. Therefore, I bet Jasper was glad to be back with his master, although also thankful for his long-furred collie coat, which would have protected him somewhat on those cold nights waiting to be found. My own collie coat is shorter so would not have protected me quite as much as his against those elements.

As I sat licking my paws by the radiator that evening, we listened to the news and Sue told me how Jasper's front paws were cut by the rocks and bleeding, he was understandably very tired, but otherwise safe and well. We had also been in that actual valley which he had been recovered to a year previously, this being where he was reunited with his Adam. I am glad that our collie eyes are well-designed for night-time and shine up so brightly when torchlight reaches them. Us dogs do in fact have superior night-vision because our pupils are larger, and we also have a clever eye structure which reflects light back again, explaining why our eyes shine in torchlight, as thankfully Jasper's eyes had - which helped to save him. By reflecting light back through the retina it doubles the light stimulation of parts called rods, which enables light to pass as a signal to our collie brain. Dog's eyes contain two kinds of colour-detecting cells called cones, (much better than those bright traffic cones!), which enable our doggy brains to distinguish blue from yellow but not the colours which you humans can distinguish of red from green. Instead of these we just see various shades of grey. Sheep's eyes light up differently so Geoff had thought that the torchlight would only pick up one eye looking back at him if it had shone on a sheep's face, because of the way their eyes are positioned in their head - and that two eyes would mean it was a fox's or dog's eyes looking back. In addition to when he first clasped Jasper's collar, I bet they both breathed many more sighs of relief as they cuddled to keep warm, waiting for that Mountain Search and Rescue Team.

As one famous collie boy to another, it is Dave D here. I am so glad you are safe and glad you also love adventures in the great outdoors, Jasper. We heard that you and your beloved master, Adam, were running through Kendal in the rain not long after your rescue so are glad your legs and fine and hope your sore paws will be healed soon. Some of my human's family live in Barrow-in-Furness, which is not far from you and I also often go out in the rain with my Sue, but we also sometimes run for shelter when the rain becomes heavier!

We have also heard that you and your Adam travelled to the television studios in Salford to talk about your adventure. My Sue's mum lives near there and I often visit, although I have never been inside those television studios like you have! (Maybe I will, one day!) They saw your local news report but I did not see it as I had returned home to the Midlands. Our friend Ollie the collie and his mum Jean still live in Kendal, so next time we visit, if we are ever running or walking through Kendal maybe you can join us and we can have an adventure together? We will all have to wear long leads, though, like the kind your Adam said he will be using for you next time you both go up on your mountain walks. I already have mine ready in preparation. We will be able to have our photograph taken with you and I promise not to bark, as I am not usually too keen on cameras, having hundreds of pictures taken of me already for my Dave D's Diary book!

Chapter Sixteen

Car Journeys with Drama

As you are already aware, I have a special seatbelt harness and clip for all car journeys. I sit back ready for our trips. I have only ever worn my harness on walks before and been loose in cars prior to this, so being strapped in is new to me. I am familiar with it now, but it used to feel like I was wearing big, bright green braces and I wondered what other dogs thought when they saw me through our car window! These sensible methods keep me safe when Sue drives us to adventures, including collie-walk meet-ups, so I just cross my clean, white paws and relax, enjoying the sun shining through our car window making my nose all warm.

My old harness was black, but I use my green one mostly as it is softer and easier for my Sue to fasten. I heard Sue explaining to her friends how dogs travelling in cars, sometimes to new foster homes, often escape from their owner's or volunteer's vehicle when the car door is opened at their new home, en route, or after a bump or accident as they are in fear and shock. The searches to find some of these dogs, in order to take them home safely, sometimes take days; such times are such a worry for their owners and so frightening for the lost, sometimes injured, dog.

My seatbelt keeps me safe and means that in the unfortunate event of a collision I will not be able to run away and get lost and I will not be thrown forward, risking hurting my mum or her human passenger. There are also seatbelt clips that fasten to our collars, although it is better to fasten them to your harness if you have one. We even put the clip onto my harness for short car trips to our local walk places. En route to one of their daily walk spots - with Sue's old dog, Lucky - they had seen the aftermath of an accident, where a passer-by had helped by climbing into the back of a crashed van, (whose side doors were damaged and would no longer open), to rescue a dog that had been fastened by his harness in the back. The owner was thankful that they were both safe, as he'd sensibly had his seatbelt on too. The pair had just been returning from a trip to the forest and a walk there, so this had taken them by complete surprise, but we always have to be prepared.

I love my special car water bowl as it means that I have a ready supply of water in the back of the car with me on trips. If we are looking for a new place, my Sue often stops to ask for directions. However, as she speaks to the passer-by, she usually winds the window up, leaving just a crack so that I am not able to poke my collie nose out, even if my seatbelt is extended. To be fair, the helpful passer-by, who is giving us directions often has a dog with them, but I am hardly going to leap out of the window to reach that dog, even if it is open!

With having such a curious nature and thirst for adventure, I sit up very proudly when Sue takes me out in her car. Caspar collie, from Perthshire, also used to sit up like me and loved his car journeys with his mum, Fiona. I often stare straight ahead as we go along, like Caspar did, but he was once so tired after his trip to the beach, that he went to sleep like this, still sitting up - but he looked so happy and relaxed, which made his mum happy too. They arrived home safely.

Sand bank collision

I love to sit proudly in the back of our old car, looking out of the little window and eager for a new adventure. I have a black material dog hammock in the back, the four handles of which fit over our car head-rests. It was a gift from our dear friend, Bobbie, and I sit inside this on my soft, grey cushion, (the one with little paw prints on), it also being useful for stopping my fur going on the sides of the seats! Sometimes things go wrong with a little bump, and I am glad of my soft landing! In Scotland, the beach seemed deserted one windy day, so Sue was trying to turn the car in order for me to see the carrot-like thing called a wind-sock, when we heard BANG! - followed by a muffled sound and the car coming to a halt...

I stared out of the dusty window, saw the flapping orange wind-sock she had pointed to, then jumped out and looked at the back of our red car in dismay, for Sue had actually wedged our exhaust into a bank of sandy soil at the side of the road! Consequently, the exhaust was full of sand! Being a caring, helpful boy, I wanted to help my mum to take the sand out, by tapping my paw on the end of the exhaust, but she saw me looking, and warned me that it may be a little too hot and could burn my pads or melt my precious warm raincoat.

Sue carefully removed the unwanted sand and we continued on our way… with the exhaust still attached to the car, albeit it hanging down at a strange sort of angle! When we stopped again, I lay looking, one paw slightly bent in concentration, and feeling like a most concerned boy. Despite this, I trusted that my ever positive and resourceful Sue would find a solution before darkness fell. Her first instinct was to attempt to continue driving us to some kind of civilisation!

Suddenly 'tap, tap, TAPPPPPPPPPPPP. A very different kind of noise… this time came from the front of our car! Mum slowed the car down in a quiet lay-by and knowing that she had unclipped me, I prepared to follow her and to leap out, too - being aware that my red lead was still attached and that Sue could easily grab hold of me. Hesitantly, I sniffed the front and there under our car lay a large, black object, now only half-attached to the vehicle!

"Oh, Sue!" I thought, raising my little pale eyebrows ever so slightly, but without judgement, "What have you done?"

"Don't worry mum or Dave D", my Sue tried to reassure us, although she must have been able to tell from our expressions that we were worrying, big time. Instinctively putting on a brave face, she just calmly turned the music up to try and drown out that scraping noise! We then drove carefully down many miles of deserted roads, even closer towards civilisation with Sue outwardly pretending that all was fine, but surely knowing, that the black item was still noisily and worryingly, dragging along underneath our vehicle. I was thankful when she finally stopped our transport outside a large store.

My Sue ran to find help and came back with a tall, handsome gentleman wearing dark blue overalls, concerned, with kind eyes and with slight stubble. My Sue had found him in the shopping aisle with his trolley and wife and pleaded for help! His lady had given the go-ahead to help us - these English ladies and collie in seeming distress!

304

The man lay down next to where I sat, and looked under the car. I watched him, still wearing my black raincoat, and with a serious Dave D expression on my face. Sue looked somewhat nervous so I nuzzled her leg with my cold nose to comfort her. I did not nuzzle the man's leg or it may have shocked him and caused him to jump and bang his head! The man smiled and said that I looked like an 'intelligent collie-boy'. I would have blushed if I had been human - though as Sue's grandma would have said if she had met me, "He's almost human!" and Sue's mum actually does say how she can almost imagine me speaking!

The obliging blue overall man reassured us that it was only the engine cover hanging down because two screws must have come out. Sue kept quiet, and her knowing look appealed to her mum to do the same, but, being an intelligent boy, I had already realised that we probably lost them due to the impact when we reversed into that sandy soil bank about an hour previously! The man said that he could fix it, easily, if we could find some cable ties! A kind and genuinely concerned lady in the local hardware store listened to my Sue's plight and looked at my handsome Dave D face before rummaging in the back of her shop, returning with six long, white plastic strands - giving them to us, free of charge, with extra… for later emergencies! The accommodating man had by now returned to his shopping, but kindly came out again to fasten our engine cover securely up off the road.

Not long after this episode, we arrived at a new beach camp-site in the dark but as we drove up-hill to the sea-view pitch area for our tents, we heard a terrible crack as the bumper hit a piece of ground sticking up from the main track. Next morning I helped my Sue to find the missing parts of her red bumper and she was able to fix the bumper cover up with one of the spare tags and a piece of washing line wire donated by a fellow camper! Some considerable time later, our equally resourceful friend, Steve, was thankfully willing and able to drill a hole in that front bumper and to secure it for us properly. I knew that this was important, so had been such a good Dave D, choosing to ignore the loud drilling sounds and wait quietly on my cushion in our car as he fixed it. Admittedly, I did keep myself amused by looking out of our triangular car window and fixing my collie eyes firmly on Steve's sensible cat, Lucy, who was inside, next to the blinds, cautiously watching us from the warmth and safe haven of her cosy home!

<u>Drama in the mountains</u>

Having returned to the Scottish mainland, via the ferry from Tarbert on the Isle of Harris, to Uig on the Isle of Skye then over the well-structured bridge, we continued on our memorable adventures. My Sue drove up the twisting, single-track mountain road along a Pass through the high mountains. It looked exceedingly steep, which was confirmed as Sue read out loud the words from a signpost, (in her Geography teacher voice!), warning about it being the greatest ascent of any road climb in the United Kingdom rising from sea level. I could see steep gradients and was glad that I was securely strapped into my harness, because there were also tight hairpin bends turning back and forth up the daunting mountainside. Higher and higher Sue drove, until I felt as if I was at the top of the mountain, but I still could not see the peak. I must have had one of my confused Dave D expressions because Sue's mum explained that although the weather was dry, none of us could see the top of the huge mountains due to mist and low level cloud which was blocking our view. Wow! With amazement and revelation, I realised that we were actually driving into a real cloud! Now I knew how a bird must feel, at 2054 feet high! We drove higher and higher still.

Earlier, on the ferry, Sue had also read out loud from a very useful information sheet, as I lay on the deck and listened, head resting on her knees. I learnt how that Pass's name comes from the Scottish Gaelic meaning the Pass of the Cattle as it used to be a Drovers' Road. I recalled Trudy collie driving sheep and could imagine herds of sheep and cattle being driven up these steep roads by collies in years gone by, from one place to another - either to market or between summer and winter pasture. I felt fortunate that I was not a working collie having to work with sheep in this treacherous area in all weathers.

Nearer the top of the actual Applecross Pass, my Sue decided to stop and park our car so that she could look at the view better and much more safely, when not driving. Having been unclipped from my seatbelt, I stood proudly next to her, taking in that breath-taking view and reflecting on how much my life had changed since I had been left at my collie rescue and re-homing centre just over a year before. I was marvelling at the wonderful year I'd had when suddenly, and without warning, through the mist, a motorbike came into view, its rider heading towards the first sharp bend as it meandered down the Pass. It came to my attention as it had fast spinning wheels and, as you know, I am a typical collie who instinctively likes to follow such moving objects - even though I admit to usually trying my best to resist. In any case, even if I had felt like chasing them, my red lead was firmly held in Sue's protective hand and I doubted that she would fancy or allow a run downhill after them with me! A sharp tug on my taut lead confirmed this, followed by her firm, but fair words,

"Erm… I don't think so Dave D!"

Sue had brought me back to my sensible head mode, as I distanced myself from my typical collie temptation, instead deliberately averting my eyes further down the winding road and away from those wheels! Besides, if the truth be known, I had anticipated the long climb back up afterwards and decided to refrain anyway! So she could steady her hand to take more photographs of me posing at that great height, Sue had trustingly unclipped my lead with a firm, "Stay, Dave D" command. I obediently kept still, standing up tall on a weathered rock, and could still see the motorcycle making its way downwards, then turned my head in the other direction looking out for sheep on the opposite mountain.

All of a sudden, I was shocked to hear my Sue let out a worried gasp. Her own eyes had still been looking out at the motorbike as its rider negotiated those frightening bends of the road far below. Turning my head in the direction which my concerned mum's eyes were looking, I noticed that the bike wheel's tyres were no longer moving it along the grey road, but were spinning in the air as it lay sideways, with its rider lying underneath it. The motorbike had not taken the hairpin bend correctly and so skidded, throwing it's rider off. Worryingly, from higher up behind us a car engine could be heard approaching and appeared round a bend, moving downwards, towards the part of the road where the biker lay still and seemingly trapped. After quickly re-attaching my lead, Sue started to run with me, to the top of a flat rock with a view of the upper road and attempted to signal to the on-coming driver to slow down, indicating that there was a problem ahead. Thankfully, the warning was heeded and that car slowed down as it approached, then reached where the accident had occurred and a small figure leapt out, then rushing over to assist the apparently trapped biker. In the distance we could see how he had helped to lift the bike off its owner, and helped him to its feet. To conclude, they appeared to be talking, then the car left and we saw the motorcyclist remount his bike before moving slowly down to a safer area of the Pass. My Sue bundled me into the car and fastened me in, before we drove exceptionally carefully down that Pass to join the motorcyclist, to ask if he was injured and to offer him some of my spare water. He accepted the fresh water, stroked my fur briefly, accepted a quick paw love, and reassured us that he was unhurt, but just shaken. We stayed with him a short while, before continuing our journey.

Lost number plate

Another time, on a very sunny day in Shropshire, Sue nearly lost her front number plate completely! It happened as she negotiated a roundabout on an A road heading towards a motorway for North Wales, on the way to one of our popular collie meet-up events.

It had been a week of extremely hot weather so Sue had made sure that I had plenty of water to drink in my big, silver, metal bowl at home. She had bought me an even bigger bowl and filled that too, so I wouldn't ever have an empty water bowl. However, the heat had caused our car number plate to fall off on our driveway, as, unusually for a human's car, it had been fastened on with a sticky foam adhesive strip before she had bought it, instead of being screwed on as is the norm. So we could continue our journey, my Sue had placed the unattached front number plate on the dashboard in front of the steering wheel, so it could still be seen - as is required by law.

As it was such a warm, sticky day, Sue opened the passenger side window and small, back triangular windows. I liked the windows being open and feeling the refreshing breeze, as it ruffled the fur on my Dave D neck, also allowing me to point my long nose out, admiring the views... looking forward to my next action-packed adventure.

Suddenly, as we turned onto the roundabout road, I heard a slllllllliding noise. Pricking up my soft triangular ears and looking forward, I was just in time to see the long, plastic registration plate slide the entire length of the car's dashboard! It continued out of the passenger window onto the hard, tarmac road! Ooops! My Sue had actually tried to grab it with one hand whilst steering the car with the other... but it had been too difficult to reach and clattered to the ground anyway! My Dave D lips curled into a half smile and I noticed Sue smile too, though her surprised expression indicated that this was also combined with disbelief. The whole sequence was a somewhat funny event to witness, but the fact was that we still needed to retrieve our number plate... and we were the other side of that roundabout by now! I stretched my long white paw out over the seat to touch my mum's shoulder as my way of telling her that all would be fine. I knew that Sue was reassured as she told me,

"I know, Dave Dog, we will turn round at the end of this road and go back to look for our number plate."

I was secretly concerned, and hoped that a big lorry had not driven over our number plate and smashed it, when mum voiced the same fears. She whispered,

"I hope it's not broken in half"... her hands shaking but lips still seemingly smiling at the latest silly thing which had happened, this being much sooner than we had anticipated on this latest adventure!

After turning round and returning to the roundabout Sue parked on a grass verge and told me to "Wait in the car and look after it" as this was a busy main road. I obeyed and sat upright peering forwards out of the window, mouth slightly open.

"Be careful then my Sue", I willed, after having spotted our number plate, still intact, in the middle of the busy roundabout road where it had landed. Picking it up, Sue noticed that its numbers and letters were intact and all legally readable. However, I imagined that it would have been very appropriate to have my own special Dave D registration number and letters - DD12 HAH on this occasion! Returning from my daydream, I saw that Sue was inspecting the back of her number plate, and realised that all actually remaining were four useless white stripes where the adhesive strips had once been to fasten it to the car. I was ever so relieved when she returned to me and the car so that we could continue on our journey, obviously not setting off again until my ever-resourceful mum had sticky-taped our retrieved registration plate securely to the dashboard....without too many customary pieces of my dark collie fur being stuck to the clear tape!

Our next but one journey took us to the west coast town of Blackpool, where I enjoyed a much safer - and totally drama-free ride - on a number-plate-free car, cuddled up to my friend Lauren. It helped us to shelter from the rain but the music was not quite as good as that in my Sue's car! This vehicle did not have room for me to take my dog cushion either, or anywhere for my harness to clip on to, and did not even seem to take me beyond the place where we had started out from - which is also very different to what I am familiar with. Nevertheless, I enjoyed it and Lauren kept her arm gently around me, which made me feel safe.

"Thank you Lauren," I tried to tell her, before alighting with a quick Dave D smile.

Puncture

On another adventure by road I had again eagerly leapt into my place behind Sue's well-used car seat in anticipation. She had clipped me in and I was sitting up proudly, secure in my fleece harness, looking straight ahead as she drove. We had driven sixty miles up the motorway with no problems. As some dogs with sore legs may find car rides painful because there is pressure on their joints as the car turns or goes over bumps, I am aware that Sue's old dog had a special non-toxic memory foam gel cushion for in the car. Lucky melted into it and her ageing joints were cushioned from any jolts. My mum will buy me one if I ever need it in the future, to offer extra support, comfort and to prevent any unnecessary pressure on my joints during our journeys. Unfortunately, my actual behavioural road-bumps are taking longer to overcome as they are not as easy to cushion. However, I am exceedingly proud to admit that I am making excellent progress and have come on in leaps and bounds in my own, personal collie journey - gaining such true confidence, trust and self-discovery.

Last time we drove to Manchester, for a collie walk organised by Rachael and Sir Leo collie, we had a puncture, but Sue had been oblivious and was becoming increasingly puzzled by frequently seeing fellow drivers attempting to communicate with us from their own passing vehicles. Reflecting this, she had kept looking in her mirrors, then saying to me,

"Why is she flashing her lights at us Dave D?" or "What do they keep signalling to me for?"

I had looked out at fellow drivers but could not lip-read or interpret their signals either. We only discovered the flat tyre when Sue parked on the hard shoulder at the side of the motorway nearer to the end of our journey. The breakdown van man said that the other three wide tyres had compensated for the flat one and kept the car running smoothly. We continued on our journey.

All of a sudden, as we drove towards the slip road, at Eccles, we heard the sound of a different engine from our diesel one... as a familiar car passed us. Ever alert, I poked my nose out of the back window to my right - with my usual Dave D curiosity and protective instinct towards my Sue, before moving back into the middle of the car. Much to my own amazement and my Mum's happiness, there looking back at us were our two dear collie club friends, Rosie and Craig. I gave my biggest Dave D grin through the window.

I was so happy to see them. I had enjoyed them fussing me on the last collie walk in Heaton Park with their own obedient and much-loved collies. It was in fact, only a few hours since my Sue had sent a message to Rosie for Craig: "Good Luck in your Driving Test". He had clearly passed that Test as our dear friend Laura in Middleborough also has recently, making us so very proud of them both. I gave my best Dave D smile to our friends again. Craig winked at me. Rosie was smiling at me, too. As we stopped at the traffic lights and their car continued into the distance, I could see Feebie and Barricade collies in the back. Although more cautious of their collies, I loved my human friends so much and followed them with my adoring eyes as they continued up the road and out of sight.

The next day, on our way back from the local park, I determinedly and expectedly pulled on my lead, towards the big house on Manchester Road where our friend Tommy lives with his friends. As you know, they all make me and my Sue so welcome; I give them all paw loves and make them smile. I still do not bark when I am visiting them in case I frighten the gentlemen.

On car adventures, if my Sue and her mum are hungry, we stop in a car park off a main road near a place called Flint not far from where my similarly nervous fellow collie, Dyson, lives with his mum,

Wendy, and also the Thomas family's lovely grandparents. As my Sue once took us through the drive-through food take-away and we reached the food collection window, (although keeping an eye out for dogs, but no longer feeling restricted) I let off my very best, "Woooooooooooooof", much to the amusement of two members of staff behind the window counter! If I could talk I would have happily explained to these ladies how I had sniffed and could smell their freshly-cooked chips and that my collie mouth was hungrily watering. Being totally honest, as is often the best policy in life generally, I was also expressing my delight at the opportunity of an alternative to my usual low-fat chews and low-fat biscuits!

Biscuits

Another time we were at a meeting for humans and I had been allowed to go into the hall, on the strict condition that I sat quietly, which I did. When the humans started to have their hot cups of tea and coffee with appetising human biscuits towards the end, although grateful for my fresh bowl of water, I was not the least bit happy when the lady handed my Sue a biscuit, saw me staring up at her, and simply said,

"None for the dog".

I was not just 'the' dog! I was 'Dave-Dog', and, I willed a biscuit to come my way. As if by magic, as the tea lady moved away, one single, round biscuit accidentally slid from her china plate onto the wooden floor....right next to my front paws!

As soon as she turned away, I looked to my Sue for permission, received the signal, and ate it all up! As you can imagine, I much preferred this to my low-fat chew and Sue had not wanted to appear mean by refusing me the treat, but I could tell from her frown that she was not really happy about the unexpected situation. She is very aware that to a twenty plus kilogram dog such as me, one small human oatmeal cookie is the equivalent to one whole hamburger in human calories.

Some time ago, my collie friend Bobbi Bob was walking along the pavement, on his way home from the shops in Munlochy, on the Black Isle, near Inverness - after his human had purchased him some special dog-biscuits - when suddenly he had a big shock. There, high up in a stationary lorry cab and giving him a hard stare, was an eight foot high spaniel! Its spaniel eyes followed Bobbi Bob, moving round his lorry cab windows from front to side, staring as he passed by! Bobbi Bob was not going to be frightened by a little dog in a big vehicle. I am afraid I would have glared back like I did when Alfie the Bassett hound kept appearing and peering down at me from the window of his van, those long, brown ears dangling, as I was next to our car eating my biscuits at camp-sites and in lay-bys on my Scottish island adventure holiday. Even so, Bobbi Bob was ever so polite and walked briskly home, keen to share his experience with his collie club friends and to others who were in the area!

Chapter Seventeen

Insect Experiences and Protectors.

After seeing my Sue's mum wearing one, and knowing that even deer on the Outer Hebrides move higher up hills to escape biting insects, I did not hesitate when Sue placed a strange - but comforting - green net, on my head whilst camping. As you can see, I look such a handsome boy relaxing on the brown waterproof mat in my very own collie midge hood. I felt proud and treasured to realise that my caring humans were looking after me as well as themselves. Despite this, we all must have looked mighty strange, had we been seen by anyone other than the camp-site midge creatures themselves!

Midges are various types of 'gnat-like' flies and some do bite, so we had to be extra careful. I am exceptionally grateful to Sue for my annual vaccinations and regular trips to our experienced vet for a check-up; we also collect that tube of protective treatment – administered through my carefully parted fur to the skin at the back of my neck each month. I am glad that my mum has placed me on what they call a Pet Plan as I do like my familiar vet and caring nurse, always being keen to independently jump onto their scales for my regular weigh-ins!

To be honest, here on my holidays, I liked the attention and I did feel rather pampered as Sue put some human skin cream onto her hand, then onto my Dave D fur - oh so carefully, avoiding my red collar and silver-coloured metal name tag. My Sue reassured me that this soft cream has been found to be very effective in preventing midges from landing on us dogs and biting us. She called it a midge-repellent, even used by hardy local fishermen, also giving some to her mum, to put on her own skin. Humans need to remember the importance of putting sun-cream on us dogs too, and also that pale-coloured dogs especially need this on their ears and noses, as realistically, they are more likely to be burnt by the sun.

Due to the weather being somewhat windy, a helpful local shop-keeper had informed us that this should mean the midge population would be down that day. It had been warm and sunny with stronger winds and little rain as night fell, by which time we were tucked up all warm and cosy in our blue tents. Midges like cool, damp and still conditions, hating direct, strong sunlight and anything more than a gentle breeze. Unfortunately for us, damp conditions provide perfect breeding grounds. A single midge is a nuisance, yet almost invisible to the human eye, but I, Dave D, could spot them and had been leaping around on my back legs, snapping the air and trying, unsuccessfully, to catch them with my mum smiling at the amusing scene, yet still telling me to "Stop it Dave D!" Unlike me, my northern muzzle brother, Ekko Collie, is afraid of any winged insect, but these creatures measure just one millimetre in length and have a wingspan of less than two millimetres, so it was rather difficult to catch one anyway. The male is happy to feed off plants and nectar, not animals like me, but it is the female of the species which is vicious, so I was hoping not to be bitten if I actually captured one of those lady midges!

Earlier, we had relaxed in front of our pitched tents, after feeling lucky that the usually intrusive midges were not bothering us and that

317

we could still enjoy cooking our meals on the two little stoves. I was thankful that there were no other dogs on our site and talking to other campers, we learnt the historic tale of how the 'Highland midge' spoilt many day trips and camping holidays. It is even said that in 1872, over a hundred years ago, even Queen Victoria decided to abandon a Highland picnic after being bothered by the midges.

That evening as we went for a refreshing walk, unusually - and surprisingly - my Sue kept hurrying me up and refusing to let me stop and sniff like I usually enjoyed to, as part of my routine. As my expression must have been one of confusion, she explained to me that this was because the displeasing midges cannot keep up with a normal dog and human walking pace so, if we are out and about, walking or doing something else active, we won't be bothered by them until we stop. I did understand and deliberately lifted my furry Dave D head high, making an effort to resist temptation to explore the interesting smells along the way. Sue had to amend her usual routine too and to change out of her dark clothes! The local humans had advised her to try not to wear dark clothing, as for some reason, midges prefer dark-coloured clothing to light garments. Therefore, she also had to put on her long-sleeved, paler, but not as comfortable, blouse and longer trousers.

It was early evening when we returned to the tent pitches, so I was on unofficial look-out duty at the entrance to, and inside, our tent itself, but, surprisingly, there were no midges in sight. We had been warned that midges are at their worst in the early mornings and late evenings, so these are the times to avoid being outside if you can. With us camping this was not ideal information, so the midge-hoods came in handy, just in case. We were still able to sit outside looking out over the sea and beach, to enjoy watching the sun going down in those beautiful evenings without being bitten, then tuck up warm in our tents as darkness fell.

Wasp encounter

Home is our cottage in Staffordshire, with a long garden which I love to explore. My Sue bought this for herself and her old dog, as Lucky had weak back legs and could not manage stairs very well in a house. Sue had anticipated it being safer for her, but still had to put a scarf gently under Lucky's tummy and hold it above her dog, to take the weight off her back legs - so assisting Lucky when she tried go up and down the one steep garden step in her later years without falling - as she may indeed have to do for me when I am older. My Sue has a doggy rear leg harness for use in such times, too. Despite that step, it is a perfect home for us and there are so many interesting sights and smells around our residence. I love to watch bees and wasps visiting the familiar flowers or a solitary pigeon or seagull sitting on the chimney pot, both here and at my friend Marilyn's house. Sue loves the look of total focus and solemn concentration on my Dave D face, as I gaze at the beaked intruders. Apparently, many of my fellow collies, including Hemp, also study birds with interest, so I am not unusual. Sue remembers how her Grandma May used to have a much-loved beagle dog called Kim - who was not in the slightest fazed by any seagulls which he spied near to his seaside home. In contrast, Georgie beagle only met them for the first time recently, and they caused her great concern. Georgie's Mum had to laugh as her little dog tilted its cute head on one side, listening and wondering where the noisy squawking noises were coming from.....before linking this commotion to the large white feathered seabirds nearby! They did not touch Georgie, so she was safe. Unfortunately, the noises I was soon to hear in my lovely home were less harmless!

On our walks near to where we live, I also look for what I know as muppets, which are actually animals with long tails, also known to humans as squirrels. My Scottish pal, Style collie, knows them as 'tree beasties' and, like with me and the word 'muppets', she leaps up when her human says the magic words! We search and chase them from the forest floor, then stand silently looking up high in the trees, as we hear them scrambling, I watching with my mouth slightly open, as they dart above us in those tree top canopies. This is when Sue always notices my missing tooth the most and my funny expressions make her laugh so much on our forest walks.

Although immensely grateful to my Sue for keeping me safe with the cream and midge headgear, I must say how I feel that it is my duty to protect her too. This opportunity arose late one evening after I had stayed up late with her as she was planning lessons and marking work in her students' books. I had been such a patient boy, resting with my head on their books again, as I seem to spend many hours doing, looking sideways at her from time to time, waiting and longing for, my 'walkies' signal.

Sometimes, I gently tapped her hand as she wrote, to remind her I was still there, that it was late and I had still not had my afternoon or evening walk. I knew how my mum felt guilty about not walking me earlier, so I always gave her a loving look at the same time to reassure her that I still understood. I knew that she would always walk me, no matter what time, and I was quite used to chasing my ball by the light of the moon or our car headlights anyway! We knew that people living nearby may have found this a strange sight, but I am happy playing by this form of light which I have become accustomed to! I was relieved when she had written the last comment on her final student's Geography exercise book and completed her final lesson plan, as I knew it would soon be that much treasured walk time!

We ran to the grassy area in the middle of our horseshoe-shaped road and I chased my ball. It was the luminous one to match my harness, which was just as well because the moon was out of sight! When Sue gave the signal to return, I ran towards my precious home and waited at our new front door, looking forward to sleeping on my white cushion besides Sue's bed.

Just one thing still concerned me and was worrying my Dave D head. For days I had been hearing a variety of very strange noises in the ceiling of Sue's bedroom. I had padded down the hallway several times in search of the culprit but had not seen any evidence of what was making the scraping and popping sounds. It reminded me of the sound the strange yellow gorse bush plants in Scotland made as they popped and their seedpods burst, so causing the seeds to fall out - but this one was much louder. Though usually floppy-earred, I was listening intently as my ears are almost like miniature satellite dishes with strong facial muscles connected to each ear. I can raise and lower just one ear, at a time, too which makes my Sue smile as she thinks that I look like a very funny boy!

When I lift my ear up like an antenna, it is like opening the door to my inner ear canal, and I can place it in the direction of the sound I am listening for. I can also hear a wider range of sounds than humans, so I didn't blame Sue for not realizing that there could be a form of danger. Dogs can hear noises up to four times further away than humans, even with the television on! To be honest, much as it understandably delights Jim, Mary and Christopher, I am not as into tilting my head and watching television as my fellow collie, Lass, is - especially the Wild West films which she loves, because I find them much too noisy! When I do look up suddenly, it is usually because a dog has barked on the television, even though Sue is quick to reassure me that it is not actually inside the television box, so I will be fine and I need not worry.

That particular evening, Sue yawned widely and I could tell she would soon be retreating to her bed. I yawned too. It appears that I can catch human yawns! It is said that if the yawning voice belongs to a dog's owner, that actually makes their dog five times more likely to yawn too! We were both tired. Others say that it shows a particular bond when we yawn after our master or mistress does. Even if I just hear Sue yawning in the next room, this sets me off yawning too. As you will have recognised, Sue and I do have an unmistakable bond regardless of this.

That particular night, as I lay down to sleep in the bedroom and my Sue sat up in bed, reading her magazine, she looked up at the ceiling above her bed briefly, with a puzzled expression on her face. I sat upright and knew that she could hear the noise above her head, which was concerning me too. It was a flat roof, as our bedroom is a single storey extension, so I thought that it may have been one of those 'tree beasties' scampering across it. The noise seemed louder than the previous morning, a scraping, crackling and also that popping noise. Sue saw me looking up at one area of the ceiling, tipping my concerned head and she finally realised that I was not actually looking at shadows round the room like I often did. She appeared to be hearing the same sound as me. The 'creature' was so close that disturbingly, it seemed like it could almost have been in our room - or may even have actually been about to fall through the ceiling into our room! She told me to 'lie down' again, which I did, but I had my ears on full alert and licked my nose and lips - which is what us dogs sometimes do if we are nervous, as a way of trying to calm ourselves down - in my case because of the intruding noise situation and my concern for Sue and our home. I sat up straight and pointed my nose upwards, my eyes focused on our ceiling.

Eventually, Sue prepared to settle down to sleep, so told me to 'lie down' once more, but I was most concerned and put my paw on her bed as if to say,

"No, please stay awake, there is danger!"

Worryingly, Sue just patted my furry head and put her magazine on the floor next to me. I tried again, with an increasingly anxious paw movement - but was dismayed when she proceeded to turn off her bedroom lamp, next putting her head under the soft duvet and covers. Sue had tried to hide her concern that something would fall through our ceiling as we slept, and had pretended to ignore the sounds we had both heard during the past few days. I know my Sue well, so I could tell from the look on her face that she was frightened, and this greatly upset me too. It was one-thirty in the morning. I could sense *real* danger. I was not happy. My Sue was at risk. I had to protect her. I sat upright and let out a low pitched, "Woof!" - barking again and again, which to those who are able to decode dog language would be interpreted as me showing my concern that something was wrong. Humans would be wise to always answer a canine alert call such as mine and indeed, barking dogs have, over the years, been recorded as actually having saved many lives throughout the British Isles and around the world.

"Dave Dog, what is it?" my Sue asked nervously, as she turned the lamp back on. As she did so, the noise directly above her head intensified resulting in her looking even more scared. I could tell that the sounds from above were louder, which signified imminent danger. This time it was my turn to try and hide my own fear because, as I looked up, the ceiling paper above her bed seemed to be moving, as if something really was about to come right through! I rested my head on her bed, giving her my gentle paw, to let her know I loved her and was there for her, so we could investigate together.

As a dog I can make a hundred different facial expressions and the one I made then was of unmistakable dismay. With trepidation, Sue anxiously stood on the bed and, although not usually allowed, I nervously jumped up too and put my paw on her bare foot as she put her own hand on the ceiling paper gently. As she did so, a huge wasp or bee-like creature made a hole and flew out into the bedroom, followed by another and another. Straining my collie neck, I looked up once more and, to my horror, I saw a large hole forming, in the bedroom ceiling as more and more of the evil-looking dark brown or black and yellow-coloured insects flew into the bedroom.

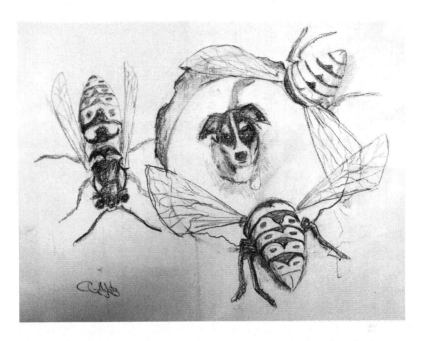

I knew this was verrrrrrrrrrrrrrry bad news. My Sue has a severe allergy to some insect stings and was at immediate risk of anaphylactic shock, where her airway could start to close up, if stung by even one bee. It means that her heart may be unable to pump enough blood through her body due to the allergic reaction. I nudged her leg with my nose and she leapt off the bed, grabbing me by my collar, pulling me into the hallway and slamming the door behind us. I ran to tell my human dad, making whining noises until he heard Sue's jumbled shaky words shouting for 'help' and to 'seal the hole up', as there were 'creatures pouring through the ceiling into our bedroom'. Throwing caution to the wind, my dad looked surprised but raced in, opened the window and tried to seal the ceiling hole with tape - a roll of which Sue had pressed into his hand as he ran by. By now, dozens of those winged creatures were flying round her bedroom. In the safety of one of our other rooms, I let Sue hug my soft, fur-covered body to help us both to calm down. My brave dad appeared from the bedroom, having been stung twice on his head and we made him sweet tea to help him but thankfully, his body did not have a bad reaction. That night I slept on the sofa with my Sue, snuggling up to her close, as there were still so many insects in our bedroom and it was not safe to return until the man who takes away insect nests arrived and treated them before attempting to remove them.

However, next day, the pest control person made it clear that they were not willing to come and remove the remaining insects until my Sue had her new Epi-Pen in case she got stung as he disturbed the creatures still in their ceiling nest. People and dogs who are allergic to such as stings need to be given a shot of adrenalin from a special syringe-type pen in order to delay the effects of any sting by causing an increase of blood flow throughout the body, so that there is time to call for a doctor or vet to come immediately as a matter of urgency. The next day Sue ensured that she asked for a prescription for a new Epi-Pen, from her doctor, as her other was out of date - then I went with her in our car to collect it from the chemist's shop. She will now be more prepared and therefore safer if a bee stings her in the garden or on our walks.

Many dogs, like Kizz and Kai collies, are allergic to jellyfish stings but others are allergic to bee or wasp stings, so it is important that we are not allowed or encouraged to snap and try to catch them like we do flies. As with a human being stung, it can cause our tongue to swell up and block our airways no matter where we have been stung. If it does happen, and a dog seems to be having a bad reaction, he or she must be given CPR and a vet called or taken directly to a vet for urgent treatment. You will need to ask your vet about an Epi-Pen for future emergencies. Humans can take part in a basic Pet First Aid Course to help them feel more competent and confident in case of any emergency relating to us pets. For animals that have already had an allergic reaction to insect bites or stings from such as bees, or contact with jellyfish, ask your vet about obtaining a prescription for an Epi-Pen and be sure to take this with you on any trips or walks. If your pet has an anaphylactic reaction, inject the epinephrine - adrenaline - where you have been directed, using the 'Epi-Pen', to delay the effects and seek emergency veterinary assistance immediately. Humans are directed to use the Epi-Pen in their own thigh. My Sue now always keeps hers in her handbag, and if I required one I would keep it in my red travel bag with my muzzle, which I also need with me at all times.

That next day, I stared curiously, as a tall man in a white overall-type suit came to my home ready to take away the cause of that crackling and scratching noise, which we could still hear underneath the thin tape - it once again reminding me of the black seedpods on those gorse plants that crackled and popped. By coincidence, these plants also had the scent of coconut like my Sue's shampoo. Considering my own Dave D health, I have learnt that coconuts can help me as a natural remedy, making my own collie hair coat even shinier and glossier. The healing properties of both liquid and solid forms of coconut oil are said to help any of our dog skin wounds to heal quickly, also soothing our skin and even stimulating fur re-growth, should I ever need this. Indeed, collies Amber and Blade are no longer itching since their mums gave this natural medicine to them. Clever Amber even takes her two spoonfuls a day of the pure solid coconut oil straight from a spoon! In addition, the oil of this coconut seed has been known to improve our gums, also acting as a winter moisturiser for our paws, nose and ears.

As I again looked up at the man's strange outfit, being thankful that my Sue was safe from the winged insects, I realised how the suit was necessary protection to prevent him from being stung as he helped us. I listened as he told my dad how this scratching, crackling noise was not in fact caused by bees, but by young wasps moving about in the nest and how they were confined to their cells like convicts, but can move and wriggle about to some degree. I was glad that I was not stuck in that ceiling cavity.

Listening to the man talking to dad, I learnt that as the nest is being made from the plasterboard and paper ceiling material, it is flexible and will move. As this happens, it makes that crackling and popping noise which we had heard. He explained that when a nest starts to make a noise you can be sure that it is becoming reasonably large with a good number of young wasps contained within that nest! It was scary as he said that the louder the noise is the larger the nest will be, so I realised that there must have been an extremely big nest above my Sue's bed, and that she would have been in much more danger if I had not barked, causing her to turn the light on and investigate. Those wasps could have entered the room as she was asleep, and most probably stung her like the gorse plants had hurt me when I brushed against them on holiday, pricking my skin, as the wasps had stung my own dad.

The huge man continued to explain that most often when this noise can be heard from indoors, the nest is usually either touching the ceiling plasterboard or behind the plasterboard of a wall! Indeed it must have been, before wasps from it started to come through that hole into the bedroom. My Sue was happy to return home from work, then followed me as I padded down the hallway in order to show her that the wasps had all been removed. We rung for a decorator man also called Dave, to come and repair the hole so that Sue would not need to worry any more. It was funny because each time Sue called my name, or said "Good boy Dave!" the confused decorator would turn round, causing her to blush more than once!

Lucky escape.

That evening as we sat cuddling up together, Sue showed me a photograph of her old dog, gentle Lucky, and told me what had happened one day as she was busy gardening at her old house after work. Lucky had been in their front garden with Sue when a wasp or bees' nest had been disturbed in the garden hedge. The insects had risen up and attacked Sue, stinging her several times on her arms. The last time she had been stung on her foot, her tongue had swollen up and she had found it hard to breathe. Sue's doctor had recommended medical treatment if it happened again and she was meant to have been having tests to check for a possible allergy to bee or wasp stings. She had been busy the past few months and not made time for this important test, so therefore was now panicking. That time, as when she pulled me to safety, Sue had pulled Lucky inside and shut the door, then called for the emergency services and hoped that she would not stop breathing before they came. Lucky lay down next to her, comforting her by resting her head on Sue's leg. I would have sat up, given her my paw and nuzzled her sore arms with my cold nose to ease the pain and keep her awake in case she lost consciousness.

When the ambulance arrived, with its blue flashing light, two men in green overalls had rushed up the path and into her house with their medical bag. As I would have done, Lucky had barked in astonishment but, in the drama, she had been shut outside by mistake. I would have stayed at the closed front door and tried to get back in by barking and standing on my back legs to look in through the window to check on Sue, now alone with the two strangers. However, in this case, Lucky was not used to being off her lead outside and wandered off, so this was not good. The men were treating my Sue and she had not realised that her precious old dog was shut outside and had strayed down the cul-de-sac.

After tests on Sue, including having her blood pressure taken, the main paramedic had explained that they must have been wasp stings, as bees leave part of their body behind, as their stinging part is attached to their digestive system, but wasps have different acidity in their stings and can sting several times. The paramedic showed her the swelling and red dots from the wasp stings on her skin as evidence. As she was still breathing normally, he explained that Sue must have an allergy to just bee stings. It is unusual to be allergic to wasps and bees, but not unknown.

As the paramedic gave Sue a glass of water from their kitchen tap, she saw Lucky's water bowl and called for her faithful dog. She did not come and comfort her. The other ambulance man realised that he must have shut her out and ran off down the street, still in his green uniform, looking for her and calling her name, much to the bewilderment of several neighbours, who had been twitching their curtains. Thankfully, by the time Sue had made her way to the front door, still somewhat shaken, the ambulance man was returning up the street, guiding friendly but puzzled Lucky with his hand on her collar! She was safe too. I would have been seven years old when this happened but I did not know my Sue then – although she worked in the same area where I lived with my previous owner.

Upon visiting Scotland and The Isle of Harris, we came across the Great Yellow Bumble Bee drinking nectar with its long tongue from the deep flowers on the land near to the higher sand dunes. This bee was large, striking, and distinctive. Its body seemed too heavy for the size of its wings, but it still flew past us so quickly, reaching speeds of ten miles per hour. We did not stay too close to the buzzing bee – just in case, and need not have worried the following time we visited, because on this occasion there was no sight or sound of this rare creature. It is also known to be sighted in the purple heather-covered hills, feeding from their purple flowers, which enhance poems and songs and are now also forming part of my diary. I was interested to learn that these particular bees hibernate underground, but was hoping that they would not also gather in ceilings, like the wasps had done.

I am glad that I was a good friend to my Sue and kept her safe. Likewise, Peter's perceptive collie called Bessie was a good friend to Rocky-cat and she stepped in to save the day when Rocky was being

329

chased by a big, black dog, (but that dog was not me!), so warning it off and therefore keeping the family cat safe. As you have read, I am usually a good boy when I see a cat. I know that Erin in Staffordshire will like me when she meets me, even though I am a mostly black dog too, because I am a gentle collie boy who loves all children, especially when they stroke my soft fur and throw toys for me to play with.

Chapter Eighteen

Plane Spotter, Cockles and Socks!

I knew what to expect, as I had seen the road sign of an aeroplane as I poked my collie nose out of Sue's car window, straining on my harness and causing Sue to indicate with her hand that I should put my peering nose back in the car immediately! These road signs gave us various pieces of information throughout our travels, including when otters, cattle or deer may appear in front of our red car. We had even seen that one warning us of tractors! I had never taken much notice of the road signs meant for humans until this latest adventure. I was noticing other things too, such as the small purple flower on the grass beneath one of these airport road signs. It reminded me of that purple dog-plant I had seen on the island of Vatersay but this one did not have heart-shaped petals - although it did have a delightful fragrance. These plants are in fact the food of butterflies. I do chase butterflies, but never hurt any, or Sue would have something to say! Next, I warily looked round for aeroplanes and listened out for them because my Sue had mentioned that they would be landing on the beach!

I had seen planes high up in the sky before and had walked on beaches, but I had never seen a plane on the beach!

Day One

This particular morning, one minute I was fast asleep on my familiar rug in my hotel basket, dreaming of chasing an assortment of coloured balls down long, sandy beaches, and the next I could hear my Sue's voice calling me from her nearby single bed.

"Wake up Dave D. We are going to have to hurry to see the plane land on the beach."

This sounded odd. I belonged on that beach, not an aeroplane machine! I thought how much I would rather my ball be flying through the air and landing on the beach for me to chase, but, being an obliging boy, if it made my Sue happy then I would try to be happy too.

Very soon, we had made our way along the circular island road, then turned left along a bumpy lane and arrived at the small airport car park. There were certainly many different types of interesting characters there. After she had seen me and made a fuss of me, a local lady informatively told us all about their airport in that wide, shallow bay at the far northern tip of Barra island, continuing to proudly comment on how the most amazing and impressive part of this is that their runway is actually on the beach!

Whilst still keeping a look out for other dogs, I only half-listened as we were told that the famous airport is unique because it is the only one in the British Isles, and even in the whole of Europe, where scheduled commercial flights land on a tidal beach and use it as the actual runway. At high tide the runway would actually disappear underwater, but it was low tide now and I could see miles of sands like in my dream.

I listened with interest but was still hesitant and concerned for my Sue, too. Although on my secure lead, I was curious, but somewhat unsure, about putting my precious collie paws on the unfamiliar Cocklestrand beach, even though I learnt that layers of shells had built up over time to make it firm enough for a small aircraft to land on, so there would be no problem for my Dave D weight - (especially with me having lost nearly three kilograms by cutting out snacks and keeping to my low-fat chews!)

When I heard the word 'walk', I was already fully aware that this may have just meant a 'sit' initially, as the trip to the Outer Hebrides saw us frequenting the sand dune area near to the Traigh Mhor airport runway so that mum could take close-up photographs. As you will realise, I much preferred to be on the beach myself and wasn't so sure I wanted to be close-up to those bird-like flying machines. In fact, the only birds I like are quieter, they being those familiar pigeons or seagulls which I stare at on chimney tops! I was a good boy and waited with paws crossed, guarding my red travel bag and keeping her company until mum had done what she had set her heart on.

I could always work out each time we were on our way to see the small planes, as I would see one of the familiar aeroplane road signs! On this occasion, I listened with interest, to the friendly security man called John as he told mum how, in the past, due to a very high tide, the little plane had to be expertly winched to safety, overnight, in a separate area near the café! Even while we were there, that day's plane was late arriving from Glasgow, maybe due to the wind, and as a result the tide was too high for the runway to be used for the scheduled return flight. Consequently, the delayed plane was moved higher up the beach next to the sand dunes and the pilot waited for the tide to go out again before it could take off with his new passengers!

I was fit and healthy as were my humans during our holiday, but we were still reassured to hear that emergency flights occasionally operate at night from the airport, with vehicle lights being used to illuminate the runway and reflective strips laid onto the beach. Being a helpful Dave D, I considered how my harness has reflective strips but I was sure that the safety conscious airport staff would not have let me stand there to help guide any plane down as it would have been dangerous - and the pilot would most likely have been distracted by a collie like me on the beach runway!

We had gone to the welcoming cafe briefly, so were still on the soft grass next to that car park when I climbed up onto a narrow, blue fence to see what all the eager humans were straining to search for. Feeling uncertainty, I turned to Sue behind me and gave her an ever so strange look as I heard a sudden clear, whirring noise overhead. Poking my Dave D nose in that same direction, I saw a large, white object - like the dot of a white sheep on a hillside, but in the sky, approaching the wet beach next to where we were usually lying low in the sand dunes.

"It's there!" shouted my Sue, excitedly, pointing to the sky. I looked towards her and gave that cartoon dog expression again from my wooden fence perch - with one ear sticking up comically and the other firmly at the side of my head, my mouth wide open as if to say,

"Yes, I can see it, Mum"!

I had presumed that Sue would now lift me down from my collie post, so that we could run towards our sand-dune vantage point, but she let me stay where I was for a better view. The plane had landed before we knew it! A very efficient man in a yellow jacket appeared to assist as the powerful propellers continued to spin. It was not too loud, but loud enough, although I did not mind as next time Sue said that we would definitely be hiding in the sand-dunes, which would muffle the plane sound somewhat.

Day Two

The following time, when the plane arrived, it was somewhat less deafening to my usually sensitive ears, and I was determined to be a good boy instead of pulling on my lead and preventing my mum from taking a much-wanted photograph for my Diary of it landing with me in the foreground. We could see it better from a short distance away.

"It really is going to land on the beach again!" Sue observed and declared with obvious delight. I loved to see my Sue happy once more so it had been worth the very long wait for that day's flying machine to arrive.

'I saw bright lights coming towards me like giant torches. My ears pricked up for a second. As the whirling came closer and closer, I felt like closing my eyes and putting my paws over my delicate collie ears, but knew that I would be safe with Sue and the other spectators. With an expression of puzzlement, I watched from our sand-dune hiding place, then turned to look back at my smiling Sue, who was taking *more* photographs and once again, my doggy heart felt so happy for her.

I could still see bright lights on the front at either side, and all of a sudden, white wheels, the colour of the sheep I had seen earlier, appeared from the plane as it was landing. It circled like a huge bird, before gliding for a few seconds then landing with a thud. I froze on the spot, staring straight at the marvellous machine and breathing a sigh of relief as its wheels touched down on the wet sand further up the beach.

I must have still looked bemused because my Sue instinctively placed her arm half round me, gently, so making me feel much safer. It really was like the most gigantic bird ever! I also felt proud and such a lucky boy, as not many town or city collies see a real plane landing on a real beach runway, and my life is full of such adventures!

I watched in amazement as eighteen passengers and a smartly dressed pilot descended from the plane, also being thankful that there was no dog arriving on that particular flight, or indeed anywhere to be seen. In addition, I heard someone tell Sue that if there had been a delivery of newspapers from the mainland on-board, there would have had to be less passengers due to weight and space restrictions.

These arriving passengers had to walk in a roped walkway held in place by a yellow machine on wheels, to keep them safe away from the plane's propellers, which were still rotating. I was glad that my paws were nowhere near those propellers and that I was safely watching from the sand dunes in my little red collar with my matching travel bag! Sue normally carries lots of bags on our journeys and the people did not have many. I realised why when a little door opened in the plane's nose and their other bags were taken out and loaded onto a van to be taken to those waiting passengers.

Sue asked a lady if dogs are allowed in the little planes. She was told that they were, but had to stay in the hold not inside the plane where the seats are. However, she explained that some kind pilots may let the dog sit with their owners at the back of the plane. I would want to sit on Sue's knee on my blanket and look out of the window!

On Barra island, I loved to run on the far-reaching beach with my ball when the plane had just left, because the wait for it to take off was sometimes long - so it needed me to be a patient Dave D, again. Even so, it was worth it to see my Mum happy, seeing the new passengers boarding their plane with their small bags and seeing the pilot wave to us as his plane began to move along the beach ready for take-off. The beach is just a beach to me, but to humans it is apparently, set out with three runways in a triangle, marked by permanent wooden poles at their end and the tide washes it twice a day. At high tide these runways or landing strands are covered by the powerful sea, so vanish completely, and my humans seem fascinated by viewing this famous area of sea at high tide, too. I peeped through a closed gate to look at the beach-landing plane close up as the men moved that yellow machine which had marked the passengers' safe walkway.

Sometimes we heard the whirring of the propellers on either side as the twin-engine aeroplane turned in front of us, then heading out towards the deep sea. I watched in fascination as sea water sprayed up into the air off the plane's small but strong wheels as it raced along its rare beach runway and into the open sky again.

I also loved the fact that there was a field full of sheep just over the road opposite this unique airport. I sat with my back slightly hunched, and gazed round the worn fence post with wonder, always giving these sheep some of my usual Dave D stares as they looked back with concern. Therefore, as they ran I felt almost like a real working sheepdog! I was quite impressed with myself for moving all but one of the four woolly sheep from one side of the field to the other, whilst still on my lead! Maybe I could be some kind of part-time working collie sheepdog after all?

Day Three

On the third day, my mum walked me closer to one of the two strange, orange, carrot-shaped objects, which blew in the breeze and which I had only seen in the distance before. As it towered above me, I kept turning my head to stare at it, not particularly appreciating the loud, flapping sound which it was making!

In fact, it reminded me of a giant copy of the carrots that Elwood Blues spaniel loves to eat back home in Staffordshire. As if she had read my thoughts, my Sue said that it was called a wind-sock! Again, my thoughts turned to mischievous dogs and Elwood. We usually find our spaniel's hoard of dad's socks in the garden under the bushes. He pinches them from the washing rack, before ripping holes in them, so Sue is forever retrieving these socks and having to wash the undamaged ones again. Trixie's much-loved old dog used to cause her mum to blush by pinching other more embarrassing items and running out through the side gate to do her usual 'meet and greet' of a visitor to their Surrey home, whilst still holding that unbecoming item in her mouth! Following on, this meant that their visitor would also be met by Trixie chasing after her dog, requesting that she return the item as it was needed! Dougal collie once pinched and chewed up his dad's new prescription glasses and a week later, his mobile telephone. As for Lass, she did not get as far as eating her mum's actual glasses, and just chewed Mary's glasses case... but also ripped pages out of her diary, including some with important birthdays written on them, and chewed these! I do hope that Lass will not rip out or chew even one single page of my Dave D's Diary when her mum and dad read it. It is no wonder that the gentleman who recently won the lottery hid his ticket well away from his auntie's dog, who also liked to chew things!

What Blue collie once took was his dad's precious mobile phone ear-piece, and then proceeded to chew it up into little pieces. His dad was not happy, but Blue thought that he had done well and his loving mum, Carol, noticed how he just wagged his tail, even when being told off! Felix collie chewed up an expensive new pair of his mum, Lorna's boots, so she hid them under the bed until it was bin collection day, so that his dad would not know, but Felix kept pulling the damaged boots out again! Much to his mum's surprise, fun-loving Buster collie had even ripped a cushion open and covered the living room in stuffing, before rolling all over in it. However, it was probably only because each of these dogs had been missing their human mums or dads - and liked the smell from any of their skin cells which had been on those objects or items from when their much-loved human had last touched them.

Returning to the beach airport and to foot socks and wind-socks, a wind-sock is found at airports to help the experienced pilots to work out which way the wind is blowing, as this helps them to decide which is the safest path to take when landing - or taking off - in the aeroplane. Importantly, it also tells human visitors and their dogs when the airport is in operation. My Sue read a weathered red and white sign which I had been sitting by, warning people not to go on the beach when it is flying, as this means that a plane is due.

The plane was expected to take off soon, so Sue prepared the camera, but I suddenly heard footsteps behind us, so started to become tense in case a dog was approaching. As if she had read my thoughts, Sue turned to look, too. To our relief, it was just two cyclists and no vexatious dog! I thought I had seen an outward-looking dog or sheep in a parked car earlier but my Sue had pointed out that it was just a cuddly white toy on the car's dashboard! I did feel silly, but Sue and her mum had given me loving cuddles, which almost stopped me from worrying. I still hoped that the toy would not slide out of that window and hit me when the car started up. It reminded me of when our car number plate had been on our dashboard and had comically slid off through the open passenger window onto the Shropshire road. My Sue tried to distract me by pointing out a special reddish Fire and Rescue boat which was always kept at this airport in case a plane ever landed in the sea and passengers needed to be taken to safety by that boat. The previous day I had found a little wooden boat nearby and thought of the people with their dog who had got into trouble at sea, and how happy they must have been when rescued by the lifeboat in Wales. Therefore, I decided that I would keep my paws safely on dry land, so just cheekily boarded and sat in the beached yellow and white wooden boat to acquire a feel for a small craft.

Cockle Pickers

As we hid in the sand dunes in the permitted area near to Barra island's airport (low so we could not be seen too easily), I also noticed that the beach was popular with what my Sue called cockle pickers at low tide. They would also have been asked to observe the wind-sock to see when the airport was in operation. Cockles are hidden inside a shell and are a food eaten by humans. John had mentioned a tasty sauce which locals made from cockles. The first time I really knew about these cockles, I had thought that my usually reliable Dave D eyes were deceiving me when I heard an unmistakable engine sound, only to see a large, white van driving out to sea from the shore over the dry, sandy beach onto wetter sand! "Be careful", I had felt like barking, "You are too heavy for that sand". Suddenly, people emerged, jumping out of that van. Others approached them from parts of the beach and started touching the sand. It was like something from one of those weird movies my human dad watches! My mum laughed at my shocked expression and reached over to tickle under my chin, to stroke my ears and neck in order to reassure me that all was fine.

Sue saw me watching inquisitively and explained that cockles stay in shallow water to feed and when the tide goes out, they burrow a few inches under the sand. In a more muddy area, the cockles which in this case are under a few inches of mud, must be dug out using special tools or your hand. In this instance, I would not have liked to use one of my valuable paws for that particular digging purpose. One tool is called a craam, and the workers use this to actually scoop cockles from under this sand. It is like a three pronged fork, not the five-pronged type that I see my humans eat with.

We watched as one man had a special bucket to hold the cockles and the craam in his hand to dig them up to the surface. Some people use a 'jumbo', which is a plank of wood with handles on either side, this being used to disturb the sand. This movement encourages the cockles to come to the surface. A 'rake' is used to gather all cockles that come to the surface and to sort cockles by size. Small cockles are left in the sea to grow. As I had waited in the doorway, that kind lady at the post office had revealed that, in days gone by, many of the local humans became frustrated by how the strong wind picked up and knocked over their buckets, so tipping their precious harvests of cockles onto the beach. It was still an extremely windy beach and my ears were frequently blown up and down!

There is also a type of seafood found in the Outer Hebrides called dog whelks, which are additionally known as dog winkles or rock snails. These dog whelks are a kind of meat-eating sea snail. I had kept well away from these, only noticing their pointed spiral shell shapes in a variety of colours including blue, green, brown, yellow, orange and even pink, like the different ice-cream colours. Although I love ice-cream, I had not tried any dog whelks, preferring to stick to my usual food. We learnt that dog whelks have a single muscular foot to attach themselves to rocks, whereas I have four paws and do not attach myself to rocks, although I do walk over them. These creatures also use their own tongue like a drill to bore through the shell of limpets for three days, then make their tongue into a straw shape to suck the liquid insides up! I am glad that I am an ordinary collie dog and just use my pink tongue for drinking water and washing my fur and paws. Apparently, they have a strong shell and even teeth at the entrance, but it is crabs and birds who like to eat these dog whelks - even though another sea-food called mussels can be eaten in various forms by dogs as a kind of medicine, to help us with joint pain and to reduce inflammation and discomfort. If I need this I may therefore consider taking mussel medicine when I am older - if my Sue wants me to.

On the third day, shortly before that morning's plane took off, and after the white van had left the beach, a car engine could be heard from the beach and a vehicle sped along the sands towards the cockle pickers. We eavesdropped on two cyclists in conversation and learnt that it was the airport security staff warning the cockle pickers to move as the wind-sock was flying and a plane was shortly due to take off from the beach near where they were. Maybe the cockle-pickers had forgotten the wind-sock rule. "Woooooooooooooof" I exclaimed, my expression clearly one of both dismay and concern, willing them to move quickly from near the flight path, before the plane took off.

They scuttled off the beach, holding tightly to their half-filled buckets. We breathed a sigh of relief, then another when the security vehicle had passed our sand dune hiding spot on its return. We and the cockle pickers and their cockle treasures were all safe. Seconds later, as I crouched down next to my red bag and my Sue for safety, I clearly saw the whirring white machine take off, flying high above us and heading for the Scottish Mainland and Glasgow airport. It had taken us just over five hours by ferry but would be just an hour to the big city in that little plane. I was glad that we still had plenty more time to enjoy our holiday before returning to that mainland ourselves.

After the plane had flown past, the airport men then took the orange wind-sock down, so indicating to people and dogs like us, and the white van man and cockle pickers that we were all allowed back on to that beach. I gleefully ran onto that beach after my ball which mum had thrown for me. I was no longer wary of the sandy runway. I don't think many other collies have played on a real airport runway before! I don't suppose many pilots have gone from piloting the small plane which we saw to huge jumbo jets, as we were told that one impressive pilot had either! I know it is important to start with smaller steps in life and build my way up. I am much braver when meeting other dogs now and can even look away from them more frequently when Sue distracts me, rather than stare at them obsessively.

I love to holiday in Wales where my Sue tells me that cockles have been raked up since before the Roman times. There, the cockles were put into a sieve to riddle out the smaller ones. They were then put into sacks and transported on the back of a donkey. I have only seen a donkey once and that was on a beach, in Filey - which is on the east side of England - but I was not allowed to venture onto it, yet... due to a seasonal dog ban! These donkeys seemed to have bigger ears than rabbits and even hares. In fact whilst out for a walk in Cannock Chase forest I recently pretended to be a hare hiding and camouflaged in my ground level hole, but Sue and our friends Elaine and Avril still spotted me!

Women like my Sue used to be the ones to rake for cockles and bring in some money for their families, but this has changed and teams of fishermen are often the ones doing this now. Sometimes tractors will be used by fishermen who have a licence for large harvesting, but we did not see any tractors doing this in Scotland, or else I would have remembered and possibly had a ride on one of them.

The idea of sacks of cockles reminded me of the prized seaweed which a silver-haired café owner on Harris had told us she used to collect at low tide, even in the strong winds, then hauled up and carried on her back in a sack. She would take the seaweed home to her small, white cottage on the croft, which is an area of farming and grazing land, in order to add to the soil as a fertiliser, and help her family's precious crops to grow.

Days later we were near another area where non-living, but flying, objects land. This time it was just a small zone called a helicopter launch and landing pad, where the huge machine would land for the purpose of such as bringing goods for inhabitants and taking islanders to work - as well as for hospital treatment. After noticing some words on a distant signpost as I was approaching it, Sue took a photograph before reading it more thoroughly, and letting out an astonished gasp - then looking extremely worried and quickly ushering me protectively back into the safety of our car. I was not amused at the sign, which may have likened me to an 'obstruction', or my walk being cut short, although I was glad it stopped her taking too many more photographs!

Chapter Nineteen

At One with Nature and Myself

Collies are naturally outdoor active dogs, so I am happiest outdoors with natural surroundings. Returning from the beach at North Harris through those very impressive castle grounds, we saw other natural resources that people used. To begin with, I was puzzled to see humans digging in the land amidst the rocks as we drove past, because I had gained the impression that it is usually dogs like me who dig holes in the earth! They appeared to be collecting large, brown squares of soil, which I learned was called peat, and were marking these with a tool called a marking iron. Following this, they were cutting the peat with a peat-cutter then lifting it with a turf spade, not the ordinary type of spade which I have in my garden. One person would cut, and one would pick the peat up and throw it onto the pile, or into a peat basket for smaller amounts. Over a thousand squares of peat a day were often cut. We admired the fact that there was a real team-spirit, like in our collie group and on our collie walk meet-ups.

I watched with interest how the peat squares were left to dry on top of the hag, (which is a name given to the area they have been cut from), to allow the wind and sun to work on them. This is in order for any moisture to evaporate, like the water in puddles which I sometimes drink out of does, then they will shrink and go hard and dry ready to burn. The peat will be transported to the roadside in wheelbarrows like the one I sat in at the camp-site on the Isle of Harris - an unusual experience which I still fondly recall. Sacks from the fishing industry are often used to bag and collect the peat in, before it is taken away in lorries or on a tractor trailer. It was a steep road for a tractor to travel up and I did not see any there. Over a hundred years ago, the peat squares were collected on a tall, steep-sided horse-drawn wooden cart with huge, wooden wheels. This sounded interesting. I think that I would have liked to have hitched a ride in this cart as it would have been an excellent look-out post from which to spot and observe other four-legged creatures like me!

My Sue was reading about this peat-cutting from an information sheet and mentioned how the peat-cutter tool had a large, wooden handle. I was curious to see if it looked like a smooth-handled stick which would be considered safe for a collie boy to play with! As with the chimney sweep's rods, if I had seen that stick, I would have been tempted to run and grab it, then indicate how I was waiting for it to be thrown for me! Peat is still harvested as another source of fuel by humans extensively in the Outer Hebrides, and to some extent, in Mid Wales, too. The fragrance of a peat fire, within a home, is said to be amazing. In Scotland, in years gone by, the crofters would make open fires to heat water to wash clothes in on their crofts. People still live on crofts there today. To explain more fully, a croft is a usually fenced area of land suitable for growing crops and with grazing rights shared with others who live on nearby crofts. The croft has a small building on this land, too, which is usually rented, but may be owned. I have not yet been inside a croft, but I did see them on the remote hillsides during my adventures and they looked somewhat intriguing.

Banks of peat are also built up like ridges to form two metre strips with a drainage channel between each. These are known as lazy-beds, and crops such as potatoes and turnips are grown here for human and sheep consumption. I do like to eat potatoes myself, and Sue loves potatoes with salt, flour and butter added, then cooked on a griddle. These are known as potato-cakes and she eats them spread with butter. They were firm favourites of her Grandma May in North Wales, too and they would enjoy making these savoury cakes, browning them on the griddle, then eating them together. I love really sweet cakes, but am not allowed them anymore. Wren collie, in Saltburn-by the-Sea, likes pieces of butter on top of her food but they have to be placed a certain way and her dish also needs to be positioned in exactly the right place before she will eat her meal!

Sue shared with us how she had read that the turnips grown there are also known as 'neep'. Hearing her say this, my ears pricked up as it sounded like 'sheep'! Realising, I imagined us actually going to dig fresh turnips and potatoes from a lazy-bed to assist the workers - me with my Dave D paws - as I was now familiar with the digging motion! Seaweed washed up on beaches retains water and is nutritious for plants as well as humans, so is often spread on the soil to fertilise crops and helps them to grow even better. I already had experience in carrying seaweed on my head, during my red ring beach drama, so no doubt I could have helped the workers, in however small a way! Sometimes, that seaweed called kelp is dried off and burned to form ash which is also used on the soil as a productive fertiliser. I hope that I do not find seaweed wrapped round my dinner potatoes though! When the hard-working people had gone, we went to their field as, not surprisingly, my Sue wanted a photograph of me next to the stacks of drying peat.

Despite the cool air and dusk light, and although night-time was fast approaching, we jumped out of our warm car, and walked over the surface grass, to examine those peat piles which were resting on the hag and also on the pale blue wooden crates. Hesitantly, I placed a single paw onto one of them. The peat felt strangely soft and warm to my paws, which did take me by surprise. Without thinking, I turned, sat down behind my red bag and held one of my white Dave D paws in front of me to let Sue know that this peat had felt warm to my soft pads. She quickly reassured me that this warmth must have just been due to the sun shining on the peat all day and said that there was no danger to my collie paws like there can be on very hot pavements - when our pads may actually become burnt or blistered or change from their normal colour, so causing us to lick or chew them.

I learned how the peatland areas such as this are also a place for breeding birds and interesting plants, but if anyone had passed by at that exact moment, they would most likely have wondered why there was a small tri-coloured collie sitting in that field holding his little paw in the air. In Sue's defence, if I could talk I would have explained that I had not hurt my peaty paw but had just been temporarily a little confused by the warm ground, as I sometimes am by pavements and beach pebbles on hot days. This 'blanket bog' is a type of peatland found in the uplands which we were travelling through. I had been glad of a dry day, with no rain and no wet fur, except for my paws from when I paddled in the sea earlier.

We had previously read that there are often brown hares hiding amongst the peat stacks or in the densest heather, which grows well in this deep soil base, but which has to be moved in some areas before the peat is cut. Indeed, the mountain hare actually eats heather as one of its food sources, whereas the hare itself is eaten by foxes as well as those eagles! I would not fancy eating heather myself, although, as you will have realised, those low-fat biscuits which mum gives me are still not high on my menu choice either!

My friends Megan, who lives near Bolton, and Rachel, in Whitburn, both like foxes but I did not see any of these creatures, as the wet nature of peat deters the foxes from taking up residence there. Despite this, I believe that bushy-tailed foxes can sometimes be found along the edges of some peatland areas, where they will be searching for food. I have never seen a fox at home either, but have heard they can bark, whimper, pant, squeak or yap. In Scottish folklore there are tales of the fox and the wolf, which usually end with the fox tricking the wolf out of its dinner. Strangely enough, when I went on my own more recent adventures to Scotland, it was actually that younger fellow collie who tricked me out of my own dinner!

Whilst on the islands, my collie eyes saw a variety of unfamiliar birds and I watched them eating their own particular food. At the airport beach, the long-legged oyster catcher turned or flipped pebbles with its long bill then snapped at the food underneath, such as a crab or pretty starfish with its central disc, five arms and tube feet. I kept my distance as I did not wish this bird to snap my long furry legs or feet with that huge beak! Most gulls have white-tipped wings but I noted that, in flight, the kittiwake gull looked as if it had dipped the tips of its wings in black ink. I have sometimes looked like I have been dipped in white paint myself when I have brushed against one of my Sue's freshly painted doors! Even worse was when I knocked the whole can of lime green paint over and made green paw prints up and down the kitchen floor and on Sue's duvet cover! Midnight Labrador got his muddy paw prints all over his own human's duvet cover, but at least that washed off, unlike my Dave D paint-prints!

Regarding bird-watching, I still prefer pigeons and watch for them on a daily basis as they sit high up on chimney and roof tops, but I have learnt to be a good boy and not chase any birds I see. They do, no doubt, sometimes need chasing away, but I know that Sue would not be happy if I gave chase. I also understand that some birds migrate for the winter and I do wish that the pigeons would, too, even if it was just for a few months! However, I do, in certain circumstances, believe that it is fair to chase cats out of my garden if I feel that they may hurt the birds. Having been brought up to respect cats, and stare, but not to touch, I have never hurt any - but I have glared at many!

I love going to visit our friend, Michelle, after a long drive to Manchester, as she makes us so welcome. Once, as I was stretched out, lying on the floor in her cosy flat, (simply relaxing, beneath a high, open window and almost asleep), I pricked my collie ears up when I heard Michelle tell Sue that her cats, Tiggie and Felix, had been 'hopping in and out of that nearby window all day'! Felix was the same colour as me and I imagined that both those cats would have done more than 'hop' to reach that window if I had been around giving them my Dave D stare! Although curious, I hoped that they would not appear through that lounge window again whilst I was there. I was meant to be on my best behaviour and would not have been too happy if either a striped or black and white cat had landed on my head! I was also still secretly disappointed not to have seen the famous cupboard-opening Beethoven cat looking at me out of his window, when my Sue was having our car tyre changed at the garage opposite his, and Welsh master, Edmond's, home in Porthmadog, Gwynedd, North Wales. However, I do like this place's name though, because it has the word *dog* at the end of it and I am a clever collie dog who often visits that old harbour town on my holiday adventures.

In Scotland, I also saw what my Sue said could have been a long, thin-necked whooper swan with a distinctive yellow bill. Swans are one of the largest flying birds on the planet and Sue's Grandma May adored seeing them swimming so elegantly in the River Thames, when visiting the Reading area - where I have been on my recent travels. They stop off in Scotland, having made a long, overseas flight of five hundred miles from Iceland, with no opportunity to rest on the way. I would be very tired if I walked five hundred miles, but I know I would be encouraged to take plenty of rests and water stops on my journey. Next year I may be travelling to see the seaweed-eating sheep on North Ronaldsay, but we will not be stopping off at Fair Isle, one of the habitats of skua birds, on our way north east from the Orkney Islands to the Shetland Islands afterwards; the reason for us refraining is because of these often vicious birds. The skua birds are about fifty-six centimetres long and their wing span is nearly as long! They have grey or brown plumage and white markings on their wings, and they also have longish bills with a hooked tip and webbed feet, with sharp claws.

After hearing about her mum's experience, Sue has decided that Fair Isle is not a suitable place for any collie to venture. These birds' nests are actually on the ground, and Barbara had needed to protect herself from the skua birds by continually putting her small, blue rucksack on her head because the adult birds kept swooping down at her from behind, repeatedly dive-bombing her as she walked along one of those Fair Isle cliff paths. If I had been there and any of the birds had tried to do this to my Sue, she could have put my red travel bag on her head, like the grouse's red comb, and I would have tried to snap at them, as I snap at flies.

I kept seeing birds high above us as we walked on the rarely used paths and hillsides of the Outer Hebridean islands or drove along their winding roads. I frequently poked my nose out of the small car window, as if to say,

"Yes, here I am, that handsome, charismatic collie from England", and they often seemed to look, unappreciatively, then take cover in those bushy heather plants. Although I saw some small, furry squirrels whilst in Scotland, there did not seem to be as many as there were back home in the West Midlands. As has been disclosed, I do occasionally chase the lively squirrels, especially after they reveal that they are there, high up above me, by cheekily dropping husks from freshly stripped pine cones onto my head or at my paws. Even if I see them on the forest floor, they must know that I am a dog hurtling towards them, as they quickly scamper up and into the very tall trees. Just as I pick up full speed, I usually hear Sue calling,

"Stop Dave D!" anyway, and skid to a halt on the dry forest floor - resigning myself to just staring at them with one of my serious, yet somewhat laughable, collie expressions!

Back to the Outer Hebrides and the peatland. Although it was dry the day we visited that particular peatland, it is due to the frequent wet conditions there on the Isle of Harris that bog mosses and other plants break down very slowly, gradually forming these layers of peat. In Scotland, much of the human drinking water comes from peatland areas, and this water is a key ingredient that adds to the flavour of their famous malt whisky. I much prefer water and it is better for dogs. In fact, that day I was starting to feel thirsty as Sue also recognised from my expression. Although I always have my bowl and bottle of water in the warm car, I love the feel of fresh, cold water trickling down my sensitive throat. Hearing the sound of water, I instinctively lowered my head and prepared my pink Dave D tongue, in anticipation. As if she could read my mind, Sue stopped me, as I attempted to drink water from a stream at the side of the field, and re-directed me to my bowl of clear, clean water.

I was glad, as the field water had looked a somewhat peculiar colour. Sue explained that peat often stains the water yellow or brown due to the tannin which is found in plants. Humans even drink water when it is this brown colour from their taps, in some parts of Scotland, including at camp-sites we have visited. Although it is not harmful to dogs who sniff it, peat can give them poorly tummies if they actually eat any. This peatland is also the reason that Loch Ness water is a dark colour in parts. Many plants can actually be poisonous to dogs. Flowers can also cause reactions in us which vary from an itch to loss, so it is clearly best for humans to teach their dog not to eat plants and flowers, whether indoor or outdoor types. Being aware that humans do child-proof their home and garden, you must also make your home and garden pet-proof especially for us dogs, your four-legged children. I am aware of a partial list of the most dangerous common plants and flowers which can cause rashes to us dogs. These include the cactus, chrysanthemums and ivy. In addition, flowers and plants that cause upset stomachs to us dogs are carnations, holly, daffodil, tulip clematis and chrysanthemums. Furthermore, some plants can cause organ damage if we eat them, examples being such as even a small amount of azalea, a crocus, foxglove and juniper, mistletoe and rhododendron. Please keep such plants out of our reach. The striking red berries of the holly bush are also poisonous to humans, too, especially children.

Due to the peat on my paws and to be on the safe side, Sue gently brushed any of the peat off me with her tissues and only let me jump back onto my cushion when my paws were perfectly free of any of the soft substance. As we drove away, I looked back at that somewhat familiar object with a moving wheel on top lying in a field near to some peat squares. My Sue explained that it was only one of those wheelbarrows, now upturned, its single wheel being blown by the wind, awaiting another day of use carrying newly-cut peat squares to the roadside in their sacks, for transportation the next day. I think that the people of this island will use their wheelbarrows for the collecting of peat much more frequently than camp-site visitors will to take their belongings down to their tent pitch, as at our last camp-site where I enjoyed my wheelbarrow ride!

In olden times, the Scottish folk used to drag heavy wooden carts with collected peat on, from the hags, before they used wheelbarrows - rather like the sledges that we use in snow. This sledge-type object was used to pull the peat squares to the crofts, where they were used for the fires or crops. After my previous transportation by wheelbarrow experience, my Sue told me of a strange, competitive wheelbarrow game that humans play, where they pretend to be wheelbarrows and race along on their hands with someone holding their legs acting as driver. It sounded very strange to me. I would not like anyone to hold my two precious back legs while I try to walk on my two front paws! I am not even keen on mum lifting my back legs to put the elastics of my raincoat round them, and anyway, would much rather sit in a real wheelbarrow and let my Sue push me! However, one winter after Sue gave me a home, I was given the opportunity to lie down on a sledge briefly. My inner fleece jacket was fastened comfortably around my tummy and neck which does make me feel warm and secure in all weathers, even snow. The unfamiliar sledge was a little bumpy at first but I soon felt relaxed enough to lie and enjoy the ride as our friends pulled me and Sue on the field. We all kept a look-out for any approaching dogs - even then with my muzzle at the ready - but thankfully, none appeared.

Handsome Jack collie from Lancashire used to love being outside when snowflakes had fallen and would then lie happily in the snow watched by his admiring mum. I love snow, too, and am totally captivated by it, so my heart is always lifted as I see it start to flutter down outside my window. Like charming and much-loved Bailey collie with Kieran, Connor and Cameron, and their mum, Laura, I also adore jumping up, up, up, on my strong back legs, tail wagging, catching the snowflakes in my mouth, running along leaving paw prints in the snow, digging and walking in drifts up to the top of my long legs.

My tough, thick collie paws help greatly in this chilly weather. Snow often sticks to my fur and my already pale eyebrows, which must make me look rather funny because I see Sue smiling. She also smiled with Sarah and Steve when their handsome Max the spaniel used to run in our Staffordshire forest snow, before emerging with a huge doggy grin and funny 'snowball legs', where the snow had stuck to his long fur, needing removing by his loving mum! I must admit that my caring Sue also rushes to remove any snow when it has unintentionally become packed into the end of my muzzle as I have played, because she realises how it makes my nose very cold indeed - much colder than usual! Merlin collie also has a muzzle and he recently managed to cover his neck fur in sticky-bud balls from plants as he tried to take his own muzzle off. As a result, his devoted mum,

Angie, had to remove them to help him. In addition, she had to cut some long fur off his poor tail in order to remove the thistle blobs, so Merlin's collie tail is now a fan shape in parts - but will soon grow back.

It was on our adventure in North Harris where I first saw rocks which formed part of a moorland, because in the heather moorland area near to where I live in Staffordshire there is just moorland and lots of trees. These rocks were in the peatland and I recognised that much of that peat must be covering natural rock, as this rock was appearing from under the peat at certain points, most noticeably in dips and hollows. I had noted that it was a strange, magical kind of lunar landscape, a moonscape, and hearing Sue read all about it, I learned that the rock was called anorthosite and was the oldest rock, not just in the British Isles - where I we were travelling and writing my diary about - but in the whole world! I looked at the long word as my Sue does and encourages her hard-working students to do, when she teaches them spelling and reading strategies.

"Look Dave D, you can find the word 'north' inside the name of this rock, which is the direction that we have been heading from the last ferry port, and the word 'site', like in the camp-sites which we have visited: 'a' – 'north' – 'site' nearly spells anorthosite! We just need to add an extra letter o after the word north."

Hearing this, I conjured up an image of our camp-site in the north and found it to be a very useful way of remembering how to read and spell this particular word. I wondered if little Summer had shown Polo collie how to sound out and read the more difficult words, as she read that book to her on the patio. I can imagine that gentle Polo would have given Summer one of her funny howls as her way of saying "Oooo, well done!"

I also discovered that the rocks there on Harris are very similar in composition to those found on the paler areas of mountains on the moon's surface. I have never been to the moon myself, but on my travels in Scotland I often saw it clearly as I played with my ball at camp-sites in the warm, summer evenings. I was fascinated by its bright, yellow light and how low it frequently seemed to be. Sometimes, as I lay, relaxing, turning my head in order to face that moon, one white paw tucked under me and the other, protectively touching my beloved football, I felt as if I could almost put up an enquiring paw and touch the moon, or even run, then jump to catch it!

Jess collie has been nearer to the moon than I have, as she has actually climbed Ben Nevis which is 1344 metres high and located at the west end of the Grampian Mountains in Scotland. On one of my holidays, I stayed in Fort William at the foot of Ben Nevis with my Sue and we admired it, knowing how this is the highest mountain in the British Isles, but did not climb it. We were told that it is lovely in sunshine but scary in a storm, so I am glad that Jess and her humans made it back safely. Next year I am going to the Snowdonian National Park, in North Wales, where many of its ancient mountains were formed by volcanic forces 450 million years ago. All being well, I will be climbing Snowdon which is one of the mountains 1085 metres above sea level, and the highest point in our British Isles, outside of the Scottish Highlands. We will reach the summit and café at that mountain-top then stop to drink, relax and admire the view including such spectacular countryside - if it is not too cloudy, before making our descent in a little train on the Snowdon Mountain Railway, which will be fun! I heard Sue mentioning how many years ago, when I was still a puppy and with my previous owner, her Grandma May and some of her family had travelled half-way up Snowdon and back on this impressive narrow-gauge railway for her ninety-fourth birthday. May had been so funny and actually thrown her walking-stick behind her as she stepped out of the carriage, so that it would not be on the photograph which Sue was taking! If I had been there I may have chased after that smooth stick instinctively, but would also have returned it to her and given this charming old lady some of my special birthday paw loves too! I do now admire and protect that old walking-stick which my sentimental Sue still keeps safely in our home.

It is traditional for walkers to carry a stone from the foot of a mountain to add to a pile of stones called a cairn on top of the mountain. Lola terrier in Staffordshire keeps a treasured smooth stone in her red fleece-lined basket, which she suddenly flicks out with her little paws or nose, causing that stone to be propelled across her mum's hard wooden floor, before landing with an ever-so-loud clatter and making her humans (and my Sue) jump! It is a special stone because Lola brought it over a hundred miles back from her own holiday, where she found it on a Welsh beach. Before meeting my Sue I have sometimes carried a stone a short way but would not fancy carrying one all the way up a mountain in my mouth, so perhaps mum would keep it in my red travel bag for me to add to the cairn when we reached the summit? I knew that across the sea on our next island, Skye, which we were heading for, there would be bare, black, jagged rock on top of high mountains called The Cuillins. Despite them hiding some magical pools encircled by quartz-encrusted rocks and linked with an underwater arch, there is a lack of water on the ridges, but Sue always carries my water bottles for me, anyway. Sometimes they leak and she has a wet back and legs - which she often tries in vain to hide! I did not think that these mountains would be good for me to tackle, despite my tough paws and the fact that I would be even closer to the moon. Jasper collie's owner announced that he was 'over the moon' with the safe return of his best friend Jasper, after his adventure being lost for days on that high Cumbrian mountain, this term meaning that he was delighted to have his dog home in his arms and by their fire again.

The real moon is very important as it pulls the sea in and out with its gravitational force. When Sue says, "We will wait for the tide to go out before going to the little beach", I know this is to do with the rise and fall of that sea level. There are two high tides and two low tides every twenty-four hours, as I previously discovered at that Scottish beach airport. At two coastal locations on my travels round the British Isles, I came across two tall, impressive-looking structures, each holding what I now know to be called a Time and Tide bell. I have learnt that the human's idea of these unusual bells is to create, celebrate and reinforce connections between different parts of the

British Isles including between the land, sea, community and environment.

The bells are actually designed to be rung by the sea at every high tide, the water moving a clapper which is suspended inside and will then strike this bell. We had last seen one of these bells when we had driven just under six hundred miles further north, just off Bosta beach, on the Isle of Lewis - but had not stayed there long enough to photograph that particular one, as there had been too many other dogs for me to cope with comfortably. To be honest, I did not mind posing next to one of these Time and Tide bells on the less busy beach at low tide when there was no sound echoing from it, during my visit to Cemaes Bay, which is on the rugged north coast of the island of Anglesey in North Wales. Although my tail was still up, my facial expression suggested a yearning to move and was a clue to my Dave D desire for Sue to hurry up with her photograph of me!

However, I was far from happy when my Sue fully expected me to return to that same beach and venture near to this huge structure twelve hours later when part of it was under water! To explain, even though the scenic beach area was nearly covered as the small waves had been rolling in gently, that large metal bell was now tolling and extremely loud to my sensitive collie ears! Ding, ding, ding, dinggggggggggggggggg! I was *not* happy! I certainly did not intend to paddle nearer to the bell for a photograph either! The dark green bell was playing, its pitch seeming to create a varying musical pattern, as the bell became more submerged! Grrrrrrrrrrrrrrrr!

As you will realise, I did not stay near to this bell at that twelfth hour for very long, as the sea continued to ring it, indicating high tide. Legs and paws moving, determinely, on the wet sand, I had decided to rebel and run pell mell past Sue with her much too familiar camera, up the steps - continuing along the promenade to my Sue's mum, who was sensibly sitting on a bench, quietly enjoying the pretty harbour view! I became but a furry blur as I escaped from the noisy bell's sound, causing Sue to be far from impressed!

These tides are connected to gravity, which also pulls us down so that we can stand and this means that things which Sue accidentally drops, such as my muzzle and lead, do actually land on the floor. Humans cannot tell when I am embarrassed but my Sue always blushes when people run after us with one of our belongings in their hand and the words,

"Excuse me, but you have dropped this!"

"Oh my Sue", I think to myself, fully knowing how she makes these mistakes with often trying to do too much - but also wishing that she would attach my muzzle to the end of the lead handle more frequently instead of carrying it loose! We have had to retrace our steps so many times searching for this muzzle - although thankfully always finding it! An even better strategy would be for her to consistently put it into my red travel bag, because at least that would make more of a noticeable sound if she dropped it!

Low tide means a bigger area of beach to run on and I also prefer to swim from the Criccieth beach at low tide when the water does not become deep as quickly. As I am swimming there, I look out for common seals. I was curious after hearing that they have dog-shaped heads and noses with v-shaped nostrils. As for the fact that the male seal roars underwater, maybe I should have made my Sue's mum jump by roaring when she had thought I was a tiger that time in our Ayr hotel!

The first time I saw one of these dog-shaped seals was from the top of Criccieth castle, where I had actually been looking out for dogs through one of those arrow holes. In Scotland, I saw them again, and could tell that their coats were dappled. There, I watched, with fascination how one seal was hiding in the seaweed at low tide, quite close to the road, and as the tide came in how another seal seemed to have made itself into a banana shape by bending its supple body, in order to be clear of the water as the tide came in higher. I would not like to live half in and half out of the sea all the time like they do. I prefer dry land and my cosy bed, no matter which part of the British Isles I may have travelled to with it!

As we headed back towards the Scottish mainland, via the islands, we prepared to see the famous canal and loch network at Fort Augustus, where beautiful Loch Ness is also to be found, and where I was to admire the vast stretch of water. I recalled beaches I had visited throughout the British Isles over the past two and a half years since my Sue found me. I remembered how I was so afraid of water in the form of waves crashing on beaches and the sudden noise as they hit the sand. They made me jump and run away up the beach, but Sue has always been quick to comfort me and to reassure me at such times, although still encouraging me to confront my certain fears. To help me to feel more secure, Sue still sometimes goes into the water waist deep when I venture into the sea, whether I am paddling or swimming with my strong legs. We have even been swimming in the Irish sea together!

When I swim, my Sue says that I actually look like a little seal from a distance. I have learnt not to drink the seawater as it is salty, although I was amazed to see the spectacular fresh waterfall flowing over the cliff and into the sea on the beautiful north-eastern coast of the Isle of Skye. I realised that this water would not have been salty if I had caught it and lapped some of it before it had entered that clear, blue sea. In reality, I stayed on my lead, well behind a metal fence, and knew that I was not allowed anywhere near grassy cliff edges, plus I had a fresh bowl of water waiting for me in my red travel bag safely back in the car. On our journey we recognised that Scotland has countless waterfalls and there is plenty of rain to feed them. The highest one has a sheer drop of two hundred metres!

The sound was very loud as the water hurtled down and entered the plunge pool area of the sea, below. It looked a long way down and I imagined becoming very wet if I stood underneath that particular waterfall. It is not being wet that bothers me, even when it rains, but it is the sound of water hitting the pavements, trees and buildings that can be very intense and amplifies because, like so many dogs, I have such sensitive ears.

When we go to the seaside, and walk down to the beach, whether at high or low tide, as soon as I glimpse the water I look directly at Sue, silently asking her for permission to go off my lead. I am often looking which toy she has brought for me with expectancy, and willing her to throw it along the shore, initially in the most shallow water. Sue always admires how I emerge from the sea as if I am in a movie, water glistening on my fine, black coat fur, which is clinging tightly to my legs. As my expression reveals, I am not so sure how I feel about Sue placing her beach towel on to my head afterwards, in order to dry off my fur, as this always raises eruptions of laughter from all who see me standing there! I just look at them with my bright, brown collie eyes, give half a Dave D smile, and let them laugh, because, luckily, since meeting my Sue, I have developed a very good sense of humour!

Many of my fellow collies love water, especially young Blaze, who is confident in water even now as a puppy. He adores going out in his garden, even if it is pouring down. In fact, he did this recently, then went inside and shook himself right next to his human parent! The rainwater from his fur went all over his mum and the furniture .... and also the wall! Consequently, his understanding mum put Blaze's special red towelling robe on her little collie to help him dry off. The very next minute, she turned around and he was outside in the rain again, still in his towelling robe, splashing and becoming even wetter! "Oh Blaze! You are funny!" she must have thought, lovingly.

Emma labrador loves water, too, and on a recent walk with her mum, Jan, she found a wonderful tractor track full of black, muddy water, which she wallowed in! Emma did enjoy her wash and towel-down after, though. I love it when I am being rubbed dry, too. I am not sure how my Sue would react if I had a mud bath like that, although she did seem to think that I looked cute when I once paddled in mud by mistake and had four muddy off-white legs!

Although I hesitate when walking near or approaching any water, in case it is too deep, Coco-dog in Bristol is fearless and adores water. She recently took her dad, Nigel, by surprise on one of their local golf course walks. Having spied a huge water-butt full of water, Coco suddenly leapt straight in, with her collar and lead still attached, then started swimming around the water-butt with just her head showing and a big happy smile. It was like her own huge, deep, tough-sided paddling pool. As for Raasay collie and his big doggy pal, they once refused to come out of a pond for two hours, as they were having so much fun, therefore both looking like wet rags when they eventually did come out! I am sure that I look much the same when I emerge from the sea after playing. Garden ponds are smaller and may be deep. It is for this reason that my Sue has wisely put a strong wire cover over our own pond to prevent me or any other animals from falling in and becoming stuck in there.

Sammie collie also loved water and was obsessed by it when her mum, Louise, took her and her toy to the seaside. Louise once threw her ball down the beach, so Sammie chased it at full speed into what she thought was the sea. Unknown to her, it was, in fact, a dip and a deep pool just before the actual sea, so not as shallow as anticipated. Therefore, Sammie grabbed her precious ball and ran back to her mum as fast as she could, but her face said it all, and she had not been at all impressed! As you are aware, I love being by the sea, although I have admitted to having been a little afraid of the larger waves initially. Likewise, lucky Georgie beagle went on her first ever holiday recently - to a dog-friendly hotel by the sea with her own mum; understandably, she was also wary of those sea waves.......and my Sue told me how Georgie looked so comical as she kept running up to them again and again, warily touching those waves with her black beagle nose curiously, before retreating off up the beach each time! She did become more confident of the waves towards the end of her holiday, so her mum was exceedingly proud of Georgie for facing and overcoming some of her own fears. Being a sensitive and caring collie boy, I always admire fellow dogs who succeed in conquering some of their worries, as I can identify with them so well.

Heading up from Uig ferry port when we reached the Isle of Skye, Sue had pointed out various other interesting features, also telling me about our friend, Pamela, who loves this island so much, her collies being named after Scottish islands. Rona was a true sheepdog in her movements and concentration, but at home, so gentle. Once, whilst her mum was entertaining visitors, when it was time for them to leave, one guest could not find their coat. The mystery was solved when it was discovered that Rona had removed her coat from the chair and wrapped it round herself in her basket! She also liked to focus on and herd Raasay collie, demonstrating her collie-inherited crawl, and was able to ignore distractions when playing with a ball, which was like her prey. I still find it hard to ignore distractions when playing, but I have improved significantly and I will keep trying. I like my Sue's motto which is to persevere, to be determined and not to give up easily.

After our hour-long ferry crossing from Tarbert on the Isle of Harris, and before driving clockwise round the eastern coast of the island to Portree, then heading for the Skye Bridge, we stopped and alighted to admire the view from high above the quiet ferry port. It was extremely windy and my collie ears were blown up into the air, temporarily forming two pointed, upright ears, very much like the more permanent ear styles of Red and Wren collies. Nearby, I could see the leaves on some tree branches moving in the wind and the branches themselves starting to wave, too.

I learnt that this powerful wind is harvested by a type of windmill that Sue told me was called a wind-turbine. As we drove along the winding island roads, Sue suddenly pointed to our left and I could see these large turbines overlooking us from the tall hills. Seeing a much sought after photograph opportunity, my Sue told me to look out for a lay-by or passing-place. She usually preferred a lay-by... but I was, understandably, more attracted to the passing-place idea, as I had spotted a sheep running past one, which I indicated with a firm "Woooooooooooof", my soft-furred right ear flicking up as I barked. However, Sue is well aware of my tricks and my desire to herd, but there is a time and a place, and she was having none of my nonsense, as I realised when she continued driving! To tell the truth, she knows me extremely well and knew that, if given the chance, when we were away from any roads, I would probably have just run away from the sheep, like Dyson collie back in North Wales did, when those family chickens chased him!

To be precise, the site we could see consisted of twelve turbines and each of the turbine machines looked quite scary. As we pulled into a real lay-by, and had established that it was a safe place, in every way, mum reassured me that I would be fine and put my short lead on, so I felt more secure right next to her. High above us, the blades of these white wind-turbines moved powerfully in the sky, now actually looking so subline and mighty. I heard Sue reading about how they were helping to capture the energy from the wind and change it into electrical energy for use in twenty-one thousand homes and businesses, which I found impressive and much more productive than the wind just momentarily blowing such as my collie ears up and down!

Approaching the fence separating us from the turbines' field, I half sat, to steady myself, in case I went dizzy with looking up at them, before turning my head fully. I looked curiously as the whirring sound seemed to echo mysteriously around us. Following my eyes, and also looking out at the green hills all around, my Sue said how she was glad to learn that the electricity produced by this wind-farm flows through inconspicuous underground cables. I agreed as I much prefer to see the natural green hills than to see bulky cables snaking across them! It was very clever, but it takes more than that to impress me and besides this, I do not think that I would like to see these big, white wind-machines high up on the hills where I live. They also continued to make that strange, buzzing noise which caused some discomfort to my collie ears. Not realising this initially, Sue had laughed and said that my ears looked like those turbines' outward pointing blades!

Reflectively, I thought about other sources of power besides the wind, and about that of the torches with their electricity which comes from batteries. As we neared the end of this latest holiday, I reflected on the past few weeks of enjoyable and treasured adventures together and fondly remembered all the lights and shadows which I had seen from the various sized tents at our many unforgettable camp-sites.

I continued to think gleefully about the campers' torches and lamps which these lights had come from. I recalled how, in our own tent and round the site, like at home, my Sue always tried to distract me with a toy when I became fascinated by shadows. Despite this, I remembered how I *was* allowed to chase torchlight patterns when we were walking in the forest at dusk, or even round and round Sue's parents' kitchen when her dad, Brian, shone his big, orange spotlight or the light he strapped to his head! I had also been permitted to stare intensely at Joshua's trainers which he was wearing when visiting me after his return from Peru with his mum, Kay, his Dad - my Uncle David, and his sister, Emily. Even though I was standing still, my eyes were following these amazing trainers' flashing red lights, and I was almost transfixed, much to the delight of everyone who saw my amusing Dave D expression!

The enchanting bright torches and lamps in our tent did not need such mighty machines as wind turbines to power them, but I could see how the use of onshore wind turbines to generate energy was an excellent method of harvesting wind power. However, I suddenly became somewhat distracted by the view on the opposite side of the road, which was much more to my collie liking. I had spotted a whole field full of fluffy white-fleeced sheep!

It was here that I had eagerly pulled on my lead towards those unexpected sheep, glad of my soft, fleecy harness so that the strain was not on my neck. I had stared and stared. They must have seen me because the front five and the back four of these sheep had suddenly started moving away up the sloping green hill - followed by more sheep and nearly in a straight line! Wow! Although not having realised at the time that my Sue had been impressed, I had still displayed a modest little grinning expression, but deep down my heart was pounding with excitement and I was proud of myself, too! Indeed, I have generally started to feel more at one with nature and with myself. Before meeting my Sue, I had only ever travelled short distances in any car and walked on pavements or in parks, so I am soooooooooo loving my adventures and new experiences.

I feel as if I have achieved so much throughout the past years of my new life. As I enjoyed a forest walk recently, I was even like a guest of honour after we came across a picnicking couple and the gentleman, who was with his new fiancée, Tanya - having only just proposed to her - called out, and asked us to take their photograph. With understanding, I had happily put my ball down and waited, being so good and not even barking at their camera, afterwards being rewarded when he played with me and my toy.

In contrast to my life at the beginning of this Diary written nearly three years ago, after a recent walk, where I thoroughly enjoyed paddling in the sea and being on this sunlit beach, as we walked back up the slope, another couple noticed me and stopped their conversation, both smiling and saying simultaneously,

"Happy dog".

They had indeed noticed my twinkling Dave D eyes and my own smile as I walked confidently with my head and tail held so high. Hopefully, this will be echoed by all readers of my Dave D's Diary across the British Isles and beyond, and I will have put a smile on your face, too. I hope that you have enjoyed sharing my adventures.

About the Author

Sue Morgan is currently an English, History and Geography teacher, also co-ordinating a literacy programme in two Staffordshire Academies. Sue specialises in the support of children and adults with difficulties in literacy, including dyslexia. She very much enjoys teaching and has taught in primary and secondary schools in England for over twenty years.